This Is Our Music

SCC Library

3 3065 00353 0718

Santiago Canyon College
Library

D0219692

THE ARTS AND INTELLECTUAL LIFE IN
MODERN AMERICA
Casey Nelson Blake, Series Editor

Volumes in the series explore questions at the intersection of the history
of expressive culture and the history of ideas in modern America. The
series is meant as a bold intervention in two fields of cultural inquiry. It
challenges scholars in American studies and cultural studies to move
beyond sociological categories of analysis to consider the ideas that have
informed and given form to artistic expression—whether architecture
and the visual arts or music, dance, theater, and literature. The series
also expands the domain of intellectual history by examining how
artistic works, and aesthetic experience more generally, participate in
the discussion of truth and value, civic purpose and personal meaning
that have engaged scholars since the late nineteenth century.

Advisory Board: Steven Conn, Lynn Garafola, Charles McGovern,
Angela L. Miller, Penny M. Von Eschen, David M. Scobey, and Richard
Cándida Smith.

ML
3508
. A53
2007

This Is Our Music

Free Jazz, the Sixties, and American Culture

IAIN ANDERSON

PENN

University of Pennsylvania Press
OCM 70259065
Philadelphia

Santiago Canyon College
Library

Copyright © 2007 University of Pennsylvania Press
All rights reserved
Printed in the United States of America on acid-free paper

10   9   8   7   6   5   4   3   2   1

Published by
University of Pennsylvania Press
Philadelphia, Pennsylvania 19104-4112

Library of Congress Cataloging-in-Publication Data

Anderson, Iain, 1967–
    This is our music : free jazz, the sixties, and American culture / Iain Anderson
        p.   cm.—(The Arts and intellectual life in modern America)
    ISBN-13: 978-0-8122-3980-5 (cloth : alk. paper)
    ISBN-10: 0-8122-3980-6 (cloth : alk. paper)
(Contents: The resurgence of jazz in the 1950s—Free improvisation challenges—the jazz canon—Free jazz and black nationalism—The musicians and their audience—Jazz outside the marketplace.)
    Includes bibliographical references and index.
    1. Free jazz—United States—History and criticism.   2. Jazz—Social aspects—United States.   3. African American jazz musicians.   4. Black Arts movement.
I. Title.   II. Series
ML3508.A53   2006
781.65′5—dc22   2006048961

Contents

Introduction

In the summer of 1960, jazz composer and alto saxophonist Ornette Coleman, trumpeter Don Cherry, bassist Charlie Haden, and drummer Ed Blackwell recorded *This Is Our Music* for Atlantic records. The album captured an original musical vision that had polarized performers, critics, and fans since the quartet's New York City debut the previous year. Coleman reordered structural principles to afford the members of his group maximum melodic and rhythmic freedom. By allowing each musician to play inside or outside conventional chord, bar, pitch, and tempo guidelines, he pursued an expressive and collective approach to improvisation. On the session's one standard tune, "Embraceable You," Coleman's motivic development quickly departed from Gershwin's melody line, the chord sequence that anchored it, and the four-bar constraints on each phrase. By placing these innovations at the center of his musical conception, rather than referring to them as passing embellishments, he changed the entire sound of jazz.

Individually, Coleman's temporary allegiance to tonal centers, and high-pitched bent notes, allowed him to approximate a wider range of human sounds on his horn than previous instrumentalists. Collectively, the absence of orthodox musical reference points forced other band members to contribute to the performance in new ways. Following the saxophone into—or propelling it toward—uncharted territory, the group sacrificed some of its cohesion for improvisational daring and range. Thus the unison introduction by Coleman and Cherry to "Embraceable You" sounded ragged or sloppy to some listeners, the perception of harmonic dissonance between the instruments occurred frequently, and the rhythm section rarely propelled the other players with any urgency. At the same time, the Quartet's spontaneity radically altered the emotional appeal of Gershwin's song, replacing the relaxed ballad interpretation favored by Nat Cole or Charlie Parker with a plaintive dirge-like quality. Later in the year, Coleman recorded an album that gave his music a name: *Free Jazz*.[1]

The trade press quickly employed this title to describe the work of performers exploring similar musical territory, including Cecil Taylor, John Coltrane, Sun Ra, and later Albert Ayler, Archie Shepp, Bill Dixon,

Pharoah Sanders, Marion Brown, Muhal Richard Abrams, Roscoe Mitchell, Joseph Jarman, and many others. Yet a musical analysis of Coleman's innovations cannot adequately define the movement to which he contributed so much. For a start, these instrumentalists used free approaches to improvisation in numerous contrasting ways, drawing upon some but not all of Coleman's practices and combining them with distinctive personal approaches to tone, melodic construction, rhythmic pulse, and just about every other stylistic trait. No wonder jazz writers used so many terms besides free jazz to try to encapsulate the music's essence: free form, abstract jazz, atonal jazz, anti-jazz, avant-garde, space music, and "the new thing," to name a few. I define the movement also by its cultural identity, by the meanings that listeners attached to it. Free improvisation included stylists as diverse as John Coltrane, Cecil Taylor, and Ornette Coleman not only because they shared a commitment to experimental music but because they dominated a controversy over the ownership of jazz implicit in the title *This Is Our Music*. Whose music was it? At various times during the 1960s, musicians, critics, fans, politicians, and entrepreneurs claimed jazz as a national art form, an Afrocentric race music, an extension of modernist experimentation in other genres, a music of mass consciousness, and the preserve of a cultural elite. The debate over its meaning framed the reception of free improvisation and greatly influenced the standing of jazz in American culture.

Jazz music has traveled a long way toward respectability in a short period of time. Its access to the universities and arts foundations, after initial confinement to bordellos, speakeasies, and other disreputable spaces, confirms Lawrence Levine's premise that "the perimeters of our cultural divisions have been permeable and shifting rather than fixed and immutable."[2] This book explores the question of who makes decisions about the value of a cultural form and on what basis, taking as its example the impact of 1960s free improvisation on the changing status of jazz. By examining a key transitional moment in the realignment of hierarchical categories, I synthesize issues of race, economics, politics, and aesthetics in an investigation of the competing definitions of American identity.

In order to account for the music's shifting fortunes, I draw upon and seek to extend recent literature on canon formation in jazz. The notion that jazz has a tradition, a history of styles linked by a common set of values that scholars can trace to its earliest days, has proved both a useful and a troubling concept for the music's champions. Critics, academics, disk jockeys, magazine poll participants, musicians, government agents, entrepreneurs, recording executives, and others win acceptance for key aesthetic and ideological traits by promoting representative artists, recordings, and performances. Their choices shape the canon, a repository of its founders' tastes that masquerades as a definitive pantheon of great works. In jazz, as in the disciplines of English literature, art history, and film studies, the canon—as the religious antecedents of the word implies—acquires a sacralized aura by embodying supposedly timeless, universal qualities.[3]

Despite the similarities among college texts in each of these fields, the content of artistic canons is far from inevitable. The critical war between "moldy figs" and modernists to define jazz during the 1940s, no less than conservative attacks on multicultural university curricula fifty years later, revealed that the perceived authority of canons can provoke fierce debate over their construction. The controversies demonstrated also that strategies of authenticating the past reflect a discourse of power, and, as Levine has argued passionately, canons are subject to repeated revision.[4] Many theorists have questioned the very idea of a grand tradition, uncovering the subjective basis and exclusionary process of selecting artistic masterpieces. Guardians of the jazz heritage, including Wynton Marsalis and Stanley Crouch at Lincoln Center, continued to battle over the music's identity even as academics and reporters exposed the agendas behind their tactics.[5]

In recent years scholars have drawn attention to the role of canon formation in elevating jazz music's prestige, arguing that critics' ability to isolate and privilege characteristics such as improvisation, swing, and blues has established the basis for a historical honors list of best performers and performances. As Scott DeVeaux has explained, the tradition supports a view of jazz as an autonomous, organic art form that has evolved according to an inherent internal logic. It provides a framework for judging the legitimacy of past, present, and future achievements, a source of integrity that holds jazz accountable to a higher standard than commercial entertainment. Dividing jazz into distinct periods makes sense of growing stylistic fragmentation and offers its boosters a convenient method of explaining the music's past as a story of inevitable progress. In addition, an unambiguous historical narrative provides musicians—and African Americans in general—with a catalogue of achievement and heroes.[6]

Those critics who shaped the intellectual culture of the postwar jazz world and laid the foundation for the emerging canon did not resemble their counterparts in art and literature on the surface. The champions of modern jazz during the 1940s and 1950s drew upon the prevailing standards of journalism—accuracy, objectivity, and efficiency—to separate themselves from the enthusiastic hobbyists who had previously dominated the jazz discourse in America. Writers such as Leonard Feather, Whitney Balliett, Ralph Gleason, John S. Wilson, and Dan Morgenstern supplemented their day jobs, often at mainstream newspapers, with a variety of jazz-related activities. They wrote album liner notes, penned criticism for jazz magazines, produced recording sessions, concerts, and radio shows, and even wrote, arranged, and performed music. Few participants in this unique world of ideas maintained strong academic affiliations. Marshall Stearns taught English at several colleges and universities, none of which allowed him to introduce jazz courses into the curriculum. Indeed Stearns established the Institute of Jazz Studies, the first scholarly archive dedicated to the music, at his Greenwich Village duplex in 1953. Jazz music's failure to make an impression on established thinkers, especially the New York Intellectuals, particularly frustrated a younger generation of writers such as Martin Williams, Nat Hentoff, and Amiri Baraka, who had absorbed the New Criticism and a commitment to modernist complexity from the *Partisan Review* and other journals of cultural and literary criticism. Though the circumstances of jazz music's production tested these critics' commitment to the autonomy of art in the coming years, their engagement with modernist innovations reinforced jazz music's respectability and its nascent pantheon.[7]

In this tale of dissolving cultural boundaries, writers usually assign experimental musicians of the late 1950s and 1960s a spoiling role. The innovations of Ornette Coleman, Cecil Taylor, John Coltrane, and their followers appeared too avant-garde for the emerging jazz aesthetic and too militantly black to represent a national art form. Yet free improvisation had an important impact on the status of jazz besides temporarily stalling the conversation about who or what belonged in the canon. Asserting the limits of critical rhetoric, I argue that the music's unstable identity during the 1960s interacted with evolving aesthetic imperatives, the career choices of leading performers, promotional and technological developments in the music industry, expanding access to education, new directions in arts funding, and changes in the composition of jazz audiences to produce unintended and unanticipated consequences for its institutional standing. My evaluation of jazz music's changing status derives, therefore, not only from debates over the canon and the construction of a historical tradition—a literature that places tremendous emphasis on the role of critics and intellectuals—but also from an attempt to understand the ways in which the context of the music's production and presentation influenced its reception.

My conception of the structural forces that have shaped jazz music's place in American culture has benefited greatly from Lawrence Levine's 1988 book *Highbrow/Lowbrow.* By uncovering a nineteenth-century past in which many classes and social groups shared a common public culture, including Shakespeare and opera, Levine demonstrated that recent paradigms of cultural value have not always prevailed. Drawing upon the work of Paul DiMaggio, Levine attributed the stratification of cultural categories at the turn of the century to a desire among traditional urban elites to insulate themselves as a class, avoid dependence on mass tastes, and maintain the authority of their cultural leadership at a time of declining social and political influence. Levine's premise of a fluid cultural hierarchy informs this project, and his study revealed some of the building blocks of a ranked order: the development of esoteric aesthetic styles, attempts to modify audience behavior through changing venues and standards of deportment, the importance of European sanction, the withdrawal of art from the marketplace into the realm of nonprofit sponsorship, and—yes—the professionalization of criticism and the expanding role of nonperformers as cultural custodians.[8]

This book addresses the ways in which the cultural boundaries described by Levine and DiMaggio evolved in the twentieth century, particularly during the 1960s. It examines changes in form, such as the impact of modernism on the ordering of aesthetic value and the role of avant-garde movements in strengthening elitist sympathies. Above all, the relationship between free improvisation, jazz, and American culture highlights two issues that warrant extensive consideration. How have attitudes toward race—and particularly the efforts of African American artists and intellectuals to define a place for themselves in American life—transformed the cultural hierarchy? And in view of the broadening audience for the arts, brought about by a wider distribution of wealth and education since World War II, do the old distinctions between high and low still carry any significant meaning?

I have drawn upon the work of scholars who have attempted to answer some of these questions: David Hollinger and Matei Calinescu on modernism and the literary canon, Peter Bürger on the avant-garde, Pierre Bourdieu and Andrew Ross on the creation of taste and transmission of values in culture, and Joan Shelley Rubin on the dissemination of literary publications, to name a few.[9] It is tempting to view the blurring of traditional boundaries, such as the simultaneous honoring of Mikhail Baryshnikov, Chuck Berry, Plácido Domingo, Clint Eastwood, and Angela Lansbury in 2000 by the Kennedy Center for the Performing Arts, as a sign that the hierarchical model has little contemporary relevance. Levine himself has proposed that jazz music—by combining classical and vernacular techniques and by bringing the heritage of African Americans to national prominence—has done more than any other genre to revise contemporary definitions of art and culture.[10] While I agree that the active choices of artists, audiences, and entrepreneurs have significantly reconfigured the ranked order of American culture, the fate of free improvisation during the 1960s holds out the possibility that jazz music's champions—and potentially supporters of other rising art forms too—have not only transformed but also accommodated themselves to an enduring process of stratification.

Although its musical components coalesced in New Orleans around the turn of the century, jazz emerged in the 1920s as the harbinger of a new cultural style. Urban, permissive, and spread by the new phonograph and radio technologies, it became a flashpoint in the war between traditional and modern values. Its association with racial and ethnic outsiders confirmed its marginal status, although as the decadent twenties gave way to the Great Depression a widespread celebration of the common man won new respect for the pluralist, collectivist swing orchestras of the day. The big bands were big tents. Their sophisticated blend of section work, virtuoso improvisation, and smooth 4/4 tempo appealed to dancers and listeners of all social backgrounds.

For a decade after 1935 swing served as America's popular music, but few big bands survived wartime economic exigencies and the privatization of leisure endemic to the postwar suburban exodus. Neither urban nightlife nor the big bands disappeared, but they faced stiff competition that fractured the audience for jazz. Former swing vocalists such as Frank Sinatra and Peggy Lee captured the public imagination and launched solo careers in increasing numbers. Pared down orchestras known as jump bands introduced a prototype rhythm and blues style to urban black neighborhoods, where Louis Jordan and His Tympany Five spoke to the experiences of recent arrivals from the rural South. The most inventive experimental performers of the war years developed an abstract, unpredictable music known in the press as bebop. Though its supporters in the critical establishment fought hard to win acceptance for the innovations of Charlie Parker and Dizzy Gillespie as the logical— and ultramodern—extension of more orthodox jazz styles, its reputation in respectable circles remained ambiguous. Much of the public viewed bebop as a complex but confrontational form, on account of its subculture as much as its musical style. This image of modern jazz as hip and transgressive, at odds with the worlds of art and commerce, confirmed it as a music for initiates and adventurers.[11]

Chapter 1 accounts for jazz music's transformation into "America's art form" during the 1950s. Critics, politicians, businessmen, and performers bolstered its reputation by enshrining the principle of freedom as a core artistic and philosophical value. This legitimating construct served both the State Department's use of jazz as a diplomatic tool, to counter Soviet accusations of racism and cultural backwardness, and the desire of jazz promoters to extend the music's popularity within and beyond American borders. I demonstrate that its recognition as a national cultural symbol, at a time of heightened Cold War tension and increased domestic arts consumption, contributed to and benefited from changes in the music's production and presentation. Cool, West Coast, and Third Stream jazz cultivated a growing audience of high school teenagers, college students, and young professionals by reconciling complex and accessible musical devices. Entrepreneurs developed college, concert hall, and festival venues—which required modified behavior from these listeners—as alternatives to nightclubs. New formats such as Long Play recordings and television displayed the music's artistic potential. Yet I conclude that the growing respectability of jazz at home and abroad rested upon a fragile consensus. Although traveling ambassadors such as Louis Armstrong and Dizzy Gillespie helped extricate American foreign policy from an embarrassing dilemma, their tours highlighted issues of domestic discrimination that soon divided the jazz community and threatened the music's newfound status.

During the late 1950s and early 1960s, two major challenges to jazz music's canonical values occurred in the realms of aesthetics and ideology. Chapter 2 examines the emergence of free improvisation in the music of Ornette Coleman, John Coltrane, and Cecil Taylor, and the subsequent controversy over modernism in the arts. Echoing the uproar over abstract expressionism in painting, supporters and detractors identified technical facets of each performer's style that appeared to strengthen or weaken the evolutionary link to jazz music's past. Yet developments in the jazz business soon engulfed this musical analysis in a broader debate over the industry's institutional structures. I show that poor working conditions and shrinking audiences exacerbated the discontent of a second wave of African American experimental musicians, including Archie Shepp, Bill Dixon, Pharoah Sanders, and Albert Ayler, who—more than any previous generation of performers—saw themselves as artists. The critical establishment's insensitivity to flaws in the industry's racial and economic framework led many innovative musicians to question the liberal principles at the core of jazz music's Cold War identity. Even before issues of ownership and membership polarized the civil rights movement, they undermined white commentators' prerogative to define jazz music's basic traits.

By mid-decade, a younger generation of musicians and critics began to forward devastating critiques of the music business that explicitly linked free improvisation to militant politics. In Chapter 3, I explore the writing and activism of cultural nationalists such as Amiri Baraka, Larry Neal, and A. B. Spellman, who interpreted "the new thing" as a reassertion of neglected elements of the African American musical tradition. Dismissing its compatibility with western genres, they drew jazz into the orbit of the Black Arts Movement and placed it at the center of an Afrocentric, separatist black aesthetic. Claiming that the innovations of Coleman, Coltrane, Taylor, and their followers spoke primarily to African

Americans, the music's radical champions hoped to overcome its minority appeal and debt to classical modernism through a powerful combination of musical analysis, myth, and ritual. Their militancy and valorization of black artistic genius, if not their didactic philosophies, attracted many of the most maligned performers in jazz—free improvisers themselves.

The Black Arts Movement embraced experimental musicians as heroes, yet the controversy bitterly divided most fans. These listeners above all dictated the reach and influence of critical rhetoric over the next few years. Chapter 4 investigates the composition of jazz audiences during the 1960s, especially for free improvisation, and reveals a small, predominantly white, middle-class, educated, and often intellectual or bohemian listener profile. After assessing the explanations forwarded by historians and contemporaries, including the music's growing obscurity and the availability of radical and accessible alternatives such as soul and rock, I explore a number of strategies adopted by free improvisers to counter or compensate for the precarious existence of experimental jazz. I pay particular attention to the emergence of musicians' self-help collectives such as the Jazz Composers Guild in New York City, and Chicago's Association for the Advancement of Creative Musicians. I argue that the terms of their existence underscored a growing stratification of the African American public sphere, the marginal position of free jazz in the music industry, and its peripheral relationship to black communities.

In Chapter 5, I propose that the music's difficulties in the marketplace, and simultaneous embrace by young African American intellectuals, had profound consequences for the status of jazz during the late 1960s and 1970s. The absence of a sizeable audience enabled trade writers to frame "the new thing" on the edges of the tradition. By consigning free improvisation to the avant-garde, opponents found a way to solidify the jazz canon by defining this music's place at its margins. Yet radical claims of black ownership combined with formal changes in the music to enhance the appeal of jazz to universities and foundations that faced pressure to recognize African Americans' heritage. At a time of expanding access to the arts and education, academia and philanthropic organizations offered valuable sponsorship and prestige as experimental performers demonstrated that the taint of commerce for one branch of the music had become very slight indeed. In an ironic paradox, the music many claimed as an expression of the black experience survived primarily through white custodianship. At the same time, free improvisers gave credence to a history of black ideas and accomplishments through their participation in college, endowment, and foundation programs. At many of these institutions, "outside" performers represented the first generation of African American musicians to challenge Euro-centric values and to inject a greater degree of plurality into elite-sanctioned culture. That many of the twenty-first century's most visible musicians and critics ignore the pioneering efforts of free improvisers, and continue to theorize them out of the "classic jazz" canon, speaks to more than personal taste. It illustrates the enormous stakes in the battle to define jazz during an era when it depends to a greater degree than ever on funding and status acquired outside the commercial music industry.

Chapter 1

The Resurgence of Jazz in the 1950s

"Jazz Makes It Up the River," declared a *New York Times Magazine* head-line of August 24, 1958. "The long voyage from New Orleans barrel-house to public respectability ends in a triumph." Gilbert Millstein, author of the accompanying article, was not alone in recognizing a dra-matic improvement in the music's fortunes during the middle and late 1950s. "Jazz Achieves Social Prestige," marveled Leonard Feather in a *Down Beat* article of 1955. The same year, *Life* magazine's photo-spread acknowledged a "New Life for U.S. Jazz," and a few years later *Esquire* celebrated "The Golden Age of Jazz" with a twenty-page feature and photo special. Jazz music's glowing reviews shared two common and repetitive elements. First, they characterized the music as an art form, not the folk or dance music of its past but a cultivated creative achieve-ment that shared the spirit, and increasingly the audience of the best modern classical music. Second, reviewers identified jazz as the product of a sociopolitical environment unique to the United States. Thus numerous magazine features employed similar metaphors for jazz: *Esquire*'s editors dubbed it "America's major original art form" or "America's one indigenous art form," *Collier's* recognized it as "a true American art form," and *High Fidelity* as "America's . . . vital art form."[1]

The increasing acceptance of jazz as "America's art form" during the 1950s appeared unlikely at the beginning of the decade. Bebop, the dominant style of the late 1940s, had capitalized upon the complex musical language of wartime jam sessions to exploit a niche market for virtuoso improvisation among urban sophisticates. Musicians such as Charlie Parker, Dizzy Gillespie, Thelonious Monk, and Kenny Clarke struggled to make it pay on the fringes of a collapsing dance band econ-omy yet failed to make the transition from popular to art status willed by their supporters in the jazz press. The difficulty lay not only in their ambivalent engagement with the legacy of western art music, although bebop's belated exploration of chromatic harmony and unsettling rhythmic momentum (signaled by explosive bass drum bombs and double-time passages) underlined the distance between the traditions. More seriously, the music industry's persistent institutional racism dashed expectations of meaningful professional advancement raised by the swing era's business boom, infusing musicians' artistic stance with a militant style that proved difficult for cultural gatekeepers to digest. Owing as much to the urban hipster as the avant-garde modernist, bebop's code of language, behavior, and dress, and recurrent association with illegal drugs, carried the allure and the menace of a racialized nonconformity, its comedic and tragic sides modeled alternately by Gillespie and Parker. White admirers of bebop frequently mistook hip transgression as the only authentic expression of black identity, rather than as one manifestation of a diverse and contested culture. As such, they helped distill public perceptions of the musicians as deviant outsiders through a series of essential symbols such as the beret, horn-rimmed glasses, zoot suit, goatee, and hep talk. These images disturbed greatly those musicians, critics, and businessmen who had pinned their hopes on the potential for modern jazz to shepherd the music to respectability.[2]

Jazz music's ability to overcome these disadvantages and emerge as a national cultural symbol owed a great deal to the convergence of interests between Washington's foreign policy imperatives and the desire of its supporters to extend the audience for jazz in the United States and overseas. During an era in which both superpowers placed tremendous importance on the power of propaganda to win and lose potential allies abroad, State Department officials desperately sought a reply to Soviet accusations that portrayed the United States as "culturally barbarous" and "belied by racial and religious discrimination."[3] Aware of the music's immense popularity abroad, critics such as Marshall Stearns and Ralph Ellison intervened in the Cold War debate over American exceptionalism by equating jazz with democratic individualism and cultural consensus. By subsuming bebop's marginal identity into a vision of jazz as a representation of wider American values, they solidified Washington's interest in the form. Indeed, the capacity of musicians to model progressive race relations precipitated government use of jazz on the Voice of America and through sponsorship of highly successful foreign tours.

The State Department's cultural diplomacy contributed to and benefited from an impressive resurgence of jazz in America, most noticeable for its embrace by a sizeable middle-class audience that read magazines such as *Esquire, Harper's,* the *Saturday Review,* and the *New Yorker*—all of which instituted regular jazz columns in the mid-1950s. During an era in which promoters of highbrow forms popularized classical music and abstract art among a white-collar audience—much as the Book-of-the-Month Club extended the readership for literary "masterpieces" between the wars—musicians, critics, and entrepreneurs mobilized jazz for respectable consumption. Jazz music's success would have been unimaginable without the emergence of new styles that combined sophisticated and accessible devices in a way that, as W. T. Lhamon, Jr., described it, connected "congenially" with a public increasingly alienated by the "heedless autonomy" of high modernism.[4] At a time when Clement Greenberg, Dwight Macdonald, and other defenders of a hierarchical order increased their protests against mass culture to a fever pitch, cool, West Coast, Third Stream, and arguably hard bop provided the vehicles for jazz music's mediation with a new audience.

The success of these "modern vernacular" jazz styles hinged upon the democratic, participatory spirit of consumption that pervaded the affluent society of the 1950s and extended to the field of the arts. The tremendous renown of conductors Leonard Bernstein and Arturo Toscanini, ballet choreographers George Ballanchine and Martha Graham, painters Jackson Pollock and Willem de Kooning, and jazz musicians Dave Brubeck and Miles Davis testified to what Jacques Barzun described in 1954 as "America's Passion for Culture."[5] The Cold War environment of international rivalry heightened an awareness that a great nation ought to produce great art, an expectation confirmed by Van Cliburn's instant popularity after winning the First International Tchaikovsky Piano Competition in the Soviet Union during 1958. New methods of presentation stirred an interest in the arts among many Americans out of touch with the museum, theater, or concert hall. Television provided an alternative exhibition space catering to audiences isolated in the growing suburbs from direct contact with modern art, classical music, jazz, and ballet. In a similar vein, jazz and classical music gained a tremendous boost from the development of Long Play records, with their unprecedented ability to approximate or reproduce live performances. Equally important for jazz, which in many ways raised its profile while established highbrow forms lowered theirs, festivals and campus concerts (with their evolving expectations of audience behavior) provided reassuring alternatives to nightclubs. Through a variety of forums and media, manufacturers and advertisers spread stylish modern images beyond the growing community of museum and concert devotees, translating modernist gestures into saleable fashions. By commodifying culture as a means of self-improvement, these developments tied the arts to a consumer ethic that everyone in the affluent society could hope to fulfill.[6]

Yet jazz music's growing reputation depended upon an unstable concord. Predicated upon concerns with America's international stature, government exploitation of jazz exacerbated—as it attempted to paper over—the dissonance between a projected image of equality and a domestic reality of segregation and discrimination. Television played a less important role in disseminating jazz than other art forms in part because it depended upon visual representation. Potential sponsors frequently balked at showing integrated bands on screen out of concern for the southern market, a recurring reminder that traveling musicians hardly represented the whole nation as Washington claimed. The discontent that rumbled beneath the surface of many State Department tours would eventually disrupt the music's legitimating construct and polarize critics, artists, and audiences. In addition, growth and prosperity in jazz (as in the general population) appeared to many artists unequally distributed on the basis of race. The increasing prominence of white "star" musicians continued to frustrate many African American performers who felt themselves closer to the jazz tradition yet stymied by their comparatively difficult access to financial rewards. Thus while jazz appeared to extricate United States foreign policy from an embarrassing dilemma, and re-establish itself on a viable financial footing, consequent battles over ownership and identity politics within the jazz community soon threatened the music's newfound status. In the early 1960s, free improvisation provided a focus for interrogating the aesthetic and ideological dimensions of "America's art form" established during the previous decade.

Jazz music's evolving identity as "America's art form" was firmly grounded in the Cold War milieu. It remained linked to a popular discourse that attempted to articulate what the country stood for and to demonstrate its principles in action. Neither imposed on the music by aggressive cold warriors nor generated organically among communities of musicians and listeners, the phrase's constant recurrence in popular and trade magazines spoke to the overlapping concerns of performers, promoters, critics, and foreign policy makers. Although stylistic changes by themselves may have inched the music toward broader recognition as an exemplar of artistic modernity, the government's promotion of jazz as a representative American form compressed stylistic and racial divisions and solidified the music's ideological resonance among both domestic audiences and opinion-leaders in nonaligned nations. Thus the government's need to reach beyond its borders and engage the Soviet Union in a battle of ideas critically shaped the music's reception at home as well as abroad.

On April 20, 1950, President Harry S. Truman stood before the American Society of Newspaper Editors and called for a "Campaign of Truth" to counter a Soviet policy of "deceit, distortion, and lies" abroad. In doing so he simultaneously confirmed the premise of United States foreign policy, which divided the world into two opposing ideological camps, and acknowledged the importance of propaganda to maintaining allies and influencing neutral countries in favor of the American way. Ever since the victors failed to agree upon peacetime settlements for Poland and Germany at Yalta, during the last months of World War II, the United States and the Soviet Union had viewed each other's attempts to secure a European sphere of influence with increasing suspicion. Determined to check Russian power in the western continent, Truman framed his military and economic aid package to Europe as a matter of principle rather than a strictly geopolitical issue. In a speech of March 1947, the president outlined the moral dichotomy between freedom and dictatorship, democracy and totalitarianism that justified foreign policy considerations. By dividing the world into polar opposites, the Truman Doctrine supported intervention in favor of unsavory but strategically significant regimes (for example, nominally democratic Greece) and helped overcome American isolationism. By equating any victory for communism with a defeat for freedom, however, it extended America's commitments worldwide and strengthened fears of domestic subversion whenever events turned sour.[7]

America's new role as protector of the free world soon ran into severe problems. During 1949–50 the Soviets successfully tested a nuclear weapon, China fell to Mao, and communist North Korea attacked South Korea. The specter of open—and now potentially nuclear—warfare limited the president's options abroad, yet inaction threatened to encourage Republican allegations that Truman tolerated communist activities.[8] The field of ideas and information offered one of the few arenas in which the United States could act aggressively to counter perceived Soviet insurgency. With the stakes of warfare growing by the month, propaganda provided a weapon the superpowers could use to win friends and influence governments without coming to direct blows with each other. The Smith-Mundt Act of 1948 provided the initial mechanisms for combating the spread of communism by establishing committees on informational and educational exchange to advise the secretary of state. Truman's 1950 call for a "Campaign of Truth" acknowledged that the use of culture to actively refute Soviet overtures and build consensus in Europe peacefully would represent a key weapon in the Cold War.[9]

American agencies used a variety of methods to educate allies, enemies, and neutral countries alike about the advantages a partnership with the United States could bring. Student exchange programs and overseas libraries targeted foreign decision makers, the Voice of America beamed news from an American perspective across the world, and the Central Intelligence Agency (CIA) even launched disposable razor blades by balloon across the Iron Curtain. Believing that the most effective propaganda occurred when its origins in the United States executive branch remained hidden, the CIA frequently concealed its authorship and funding of cultural initiatives. From 1950 to 1967, for example, covert agent Michael Josselson ran the Congress for Cultural Freedom. Its news service and magazines, musical performances and prizes, touring art exhibitions, and prestigious international conferences were designed to elicit the sympathy of West European intellectuals for an American worldview and transform the noncommunist left into a bulwark against Soviet influence.[10]

Each program stressed the virtues of "Americanism," a variety of American exceptionalism that officials contrasted with an unflattering picture of the communist system. Government agencies told the world that the United States represented democracy and human rights, freedom of choice and religion, technological progress, and material abundance. Sometimes the emphasis changed in order to press home an ideological advantage or in response to a Soviet ploy. The Soviets had long ridiculed Americans as "culturally barbarous" and showed off their own artistic successes through traveling productions by the Bolshoi ballet and other performance groups.[11] The U.S. response had proved faltering and sporadic, despite some well-received collaborations between the State Department and the American National Theater and Academy (ANTA). By 1954, President Dwight D. Eisenhower (who shared Truman's two-worlds vision) sought and received from Congress an Emergency Fund of five million dollars annually for musical and dramatic presentations abroad and U.S. participation in international trade fairs. Permanently established two years later, this State Department funding program drew the arts fully onto the Cold War stage. In the next ten years, ANTA—under the auspices of the State Department—sent 206 artistic groups on goodwill tours to 112 different countries. The recipients of government sponsorship included all four of America's permanent ballet companies, two modern dance troupes, at least one symphony orchestra each year, exhibitions of American painting, school choirs, and musical shows such as *My Fair Lady* and *Oklahoma!*[12]

The State Department's deployment of jazz musicians as part of this program hardly resulted from a whim or fancy. Although they faced increasing interference from congressional representatives, American officials vetted carefully those cultural productions they sent abroad. As early as 1945, the Office of Military Government in Germany evaluated potential touring plays according to their moral utility. Henrik Ibsen's *Peer Gynt* and Robert Sherwood's *Abe Lincoln in Illinois* received approval for their lessons in "Liberty and Democracy," while William Shakespeare's *Julius Caesar* and *Coriolanus* were banned for their "glorification of dictatorship."[13] Indeed, the government's use of jazz, especially bebop, in a foreign relations capacity represented a calculated risk. It provides a revealing insight into the multiple and changing meanings ascribed to a cultural artifact and the contest for primacy in interpreting them. Bebop's association with deviance persisted into the mid-1950s. In April 1955, for example, a British member of the United Nations Commission on Narcotics, John H. Walker, reported an undeniable connection between marijuana use and "that form of entertainment known as bebop and rebop." Walker observed that the excitement of a "bebop session" increased a young person's chances of developing a drug addiction.[14] Jazz music's appropriation by American beat writers such as Jack Kerouac and Allen Ginsberg, and its subsequent centrality to the late 1950s beatnik fad, only reinforced this impression. Rather than shy away from such a negative identification of jazz with delinquency, however fanciful, the State Department had every reason to reconstruct the music as a symbol of the best rather than the worst side of American life.

Washington's determination to reinvent the image of jazz, in conjunction with musicians, critics, and businessmen, owed much to its popularity throughout the world among key target audiences of American propaganda. Any attempt to draw an audience profile for jazz abroad, to pinpoint key reasons for the music's popularity, or even to determine which types of jazz enjoyed greatest acceptance risks excessive generalization. Live jazz quickly followed the first recordings abroad during and immediately after World War I and proved extremely popular in England and France, although the music's success extended beyond these countries. Frederick Starr found that between 1919 and 1924, jazz reached every major city in western Europe and as far as Istanbul and Shanghai. The quality and content of this music varied. James Lincoln Collier described much of it as "dance music with raggy inflections" rather than jazz.[15] Its syncopated beat and appearance of improvisation satisfied dancers and other young, cosmopolitan audiences, whose embrace of American jazz set them in opposition to the established hierarchy of European arts cherished by their elders. For them, jazz—like the movies and comics—provided a novelty, a consumable spectacle characterized by its pulse and style as modern. "I recall the shock, the sudden awakening this staggering rhythm, this new sonority brought," composer Darius Milhaud remembered of hearing a jazz band for the first time at the Casino de Paris. "It seemed to represent the spirit of a new era especially for the young."[16] For artists like Milhaud and intellectuals such as Jean Cocteau, jazz offered the potential to revive European music with its new techniques. In the February 1929 edition of *Le Courrier Musical*, Frenchman Jacques Janin described the way many listeners recognized in jazz "the example of a new form of the modern sensibility and advocate its transfusion into the blood of our music, hoping by that operation to increase its vitality."[17]

As in the United States, the foreign audience for jazz during the 1930s increasingly separated between dancers, classical music performers, and Bohemian artists—who saw it largely as a means of invigorating a secondary endeavor—and an expanding listening public, which regarded the music as a self-contained art form. Europeans undertook most of the writing and analysis that established and codified the music's aesthetic basis. Collier has attempted to dispel the long-held assumption that Europeans took jazz seriously before Americans by unearthing many forgotten jazz reviews from the domestic press of the 1920s. Nevertheless, his findings do not change the fact that Hugues Panassié, Robert Goffin, and Charles Delauney—all Europeans—first began systematic scholarship at a time the sporadic American jazz press temporarily dried up. All three pioneers saw their endeavors in the fields of criticism, history and biography, and discography translated into English, exerting a fundamental influence on the theory and practice of jazz writing in the United States and the rest of the world.[18] During the 1930s, their work helped inspire and inform the debates of growing communities of musicians, writers, and fans. Organized in metropolitan or regional Hot Clubs, these enthusiasts gathered and exchanged recordings and discographical information and helped promote concerts. By the mid-1930s, they supported European tours by major artists including Louis Armstrong and Duke Ellington, and extended stays by such notable expatriate musicians as Coleman Hawkins and Benny Carter.

Events surrounding World War II invested jazz with renewed ideological significance in Europe and provided the foundation for its later use as a diplomatic tool. The Nazis helped identify jazz with resistance to oppression throughout much of the continent after they labeled it "degenerate music" and banned its performance in the late 1930s. A few years later, Charles Delauney informed *Down Beat* readers about the "overwhelming burst of enthusiasm by Frenchmen for jazz" during the German occupation, as "the symbol of, or last tie with, the outside, free world."[19] After 1945, jazz music's popularity as a symbol of liberation paved the way for Louis Armstrong's stunning reception at the first European jazz festival in Nice during the summer of 1948. Joe Glaser, Armstrong's manager, capitalized upon his client's international reputation by building a new image for the trumpeter as an ambassador of goodwill.[20] A 1950 European tour, which included an audience with the pope, elicited a thank-you note from the State Department, and during a return visit to the continent in 1955 the American press began to comment upon Armstrong's utility to the American cause. "The world has lately become obsessed with the value of cultural offenses in a cold war," reported *Newsweek* in late 1955. "In such a strategy, the simple emotional impact of jazz cuts through all manner of linguistic and ideological barriers." The most pointed observations came from *New York Times* writer

Felix Belair, whose front page headline in November 1955 announced "United States has Secret Sonic Weapon—Jazz" and urged its use for propaganda purposes. Following Armstrong's Geneva concert, Belair lobbied for federal subsidy of foreign jazz programs to promote interest in American democracy.[21]

Worldwide interest in jazz during the postwar era resulted also from America's new superpower status. This assumption of international leadership precipitated a growing fascination with the country's culture and a new opportunity for the United States to export that culture abroad. Anywhere America stationed its forces, for example, Victory Disks, jukeboxes, and especially armed forces radio disseminated jazz and jazzy pop sounds among foreign listeners.[22] Trade and informational exchange between the United States and its potential allies also brought jazz to the attention of foreign peoples. The *New York Times* reported that in Thailand, an American stronghold on mainland South East Asia, jazz records and native bands achieved extensive popularity and represented one of "the United States' most potent weapons in winning the goodwill of the Asians" before a jazz group ever visited. Thus when Benny Goodman arrived on a 1957 tour, he found to his surprise a monarch who insisted on playing saxophone with the orchestra and audiences adept at American-style jitterbug dancing.[23]

Indeed, the popularity of jazz abroad had not gone unnoticed in Washington. As early as 1950, the Voice of America's Harold Boxer invited Leonard Feather to produce a series of jazz programs for worldwide transmission. Although *Jazz Club USA* received no special promotion and ended after a couple of years, it precipitated positive feedback from government officials in foreign countries, particularly behind the Iron Curtain.[24] During the early 1950s, bebop became the music of choice for the "stiliagi" or "style-hunters," a stratum of upper-class Soviet youth whose dress, language, search for individuality, and rebellion against official mass culture marked them as a kind of Soviet beat generation. The communist youth paper *Komsomolskaya Pravda* caricatured the "stiliagi" in a cartoon as a layabout in a zoot suit, and remarked with distaste:

His stare is vacant . . . his hair is full of brilliantine, his walk is languid, his ideal is the divine Linda [sic] . . . He sits holding one leg over the other, chewing American gum which somehow found its way into his hands. He smiles crookedly, his answers are made in a lazy voice, he is indifferent to everything except the possibility of getting a shirt from abroad.[25]

In late 1954, United States ambassador to Moscow Charles E. Bohlen informed his superiors that a jazz program designed specifically for Soviet youth would attract a large audience. Consequently, the Voice of

America launched the program *Music USA* in January 1955, featuring a 45-minute jazz segment. The Voice of America initially directed the program toward Scandinavia, known to have a large fan base, only to receive a deluge of requests from other parts of the globe to broadcast at a more reasonable hour. As a result of the successful trial, Voice officials moved the program to prime time all over the world. Hosted by the genial Willis Conover, soon known as "the world's favorite American," *Music USA* quickly became one of the agency's banner productions.[26]

Incoming mail and the Voice of America's market research placed *Music USA* among the most popular programs on air. In 1956, *Time* reported that Conover received one thousand letters a week from fans, and by 1962 the rising volume of correspondence confirmed it as the agency's most listened to show, a status that solidified its proximity to the critical evening news transmission every day. By that time, the Voice estimated that *Music USA* reached approximately thirty million fans in eighty countries.[27] Feedback from communist-controlled regions proved difficult for the government to obtain, although western visitors discovered that jazz fans behind the Iron Curtain frequently taped and exchanged recordings of Feather and Conover's programs. Jazz proved equally popular in nonaligned countries. In a 1958 survey of 9,500 Voice listeners in Indonesia, *Music USA* placed third behind two local language broadcasts. The following year, the Voice sponsored a worldwide contest to determine the composition and tastes of its audience, identifying "a very high response" to *Music USA* among more than 65,000 entrants.[28]

The Voice of America's analysis confirmed the agency's success in reaching its intended audience. Radio had the potential to address a diverse cross-section of the public, and the 1959 survey revealed a broad range of listeners from high-ranking officials to businessmen, professionals, farmers, factory workers, and housewives. Students and teachers under forty-five years of age comprised the majority of respondents, however. This profile mirrored important segments of the United States Information Agency (USIA)'s core target groups, which as a result of the "Campaign of Truth" centered on "opinion molders" (educators, authors, and journalists) and "decision makers" (political, industrial, and labor leaders).[29] Teachers clearly fit the first group, while students represented the future of both. Government officials demonstrated similar priorities in planning the second and much more visible prong of America's jazz offensive, public performances across the world by touring ensembles.

The Voice of America's successful jazz broadcasts precipitated the defining moment of the cultural ambassadors program. On March 23, 1956, the State Department dispatched Dizzy Gillespie, flamboyant bebop band leader, on a ten-week concert tour of the Middle East and the Balkans, with scheduled stops in Syria, Lebanon, Pakistan, Turkey, Greece, and Yugoslavia. ANTA organized the program on behalf of the State Department, although the USIA helped book appearances and federal funds guaranteed the group's expenses. ANTA included a jazz band in response to numerous field requests and the prodding of Representative Adam Clayton Powell, Jr., who had admonished the administration to send fewer ballets and symphonies abroad in favor of "real Americana." Accompanied by a twelve-piece orchestra and jazz critic Marshall Stearns, who served as lecturer and musical advisor, Gillespie attempted to educate, entertain, and demonstrate the artistic accomplishments of America's most popular cultural export. His concerts featured an illustrated history of jazz in the first half, followed by the latest experimental modern jazz after the intermission.[30]

Gillespie's tour proved a triumph for international relations, and its propaganda success launched a flood of similar excursions during the 1950s and 1960s by Louis Armstrong, Dave Brubeck, Woody Herman, Duke Ellington, and many others. Jazz groups selected by ANTA traveled to all parts of the globe, including, in 1962, a trip by Benny Goodman to the Soviet Union. "This music makes our job so much easier," reported Donald Heath, U.S. ambassador to Lebanon, after Gillespie passed through. "Maybe we could have built a new tank for the cost of this tour," added another official, "but you can't get as much good-will out of a tank as you can out of Dizzy Gillespie's band."[31] The musicians enamored themselves to their hosts by conducting demonstration clinics, appearing at diplomatic receptions, and familiarizing themselves with local customs, although they sometimes resented restrictions on their access to a broader audience. Dizzy Gillespie famously refused to continue a concert in Ankara until "a horde of ragamuffins" was allowed into the compound, to the consternation, presumably, of the policemen who had been trying to keep them behind the walls. Typically, however, the musicians on this and subsequent tours circulated among students, educators, artists, journalists, foreign dignitaries, and other privileged elites. Knowledgeable and uninitiated audiences alike—the orchestra played for both—found something appealing in the group's synthesis of big band section work, bebop dissonance, rhythmic complexity, and compositional brilliance. Hard driving yet intricate riffs underscored the leader's stratospheric flights, which themselves dissolved back into sophisticated ensemble arrangements.[32]

The group made its diplomatic impact immediately apparent. Upon arriving in Athens, Dizzy Gillespie conducted a concert for students who had stoned the USIA office the previous day in protest at American support for British control of Cyprus. When his group started to play, however, the same students responded with a solid wall of applause,

Figure 1. Dizzy Gillespie, cultural ambassador, during his 1956 tour of the Middle East on behalf of the State Department. Courtesy Institute of Jazz Studies, Rutgers University.

throwing items of clothing in the air, and chanting the bandleader's name. The next day a local English-language newspaper carried the headline, "Greek Students Lay Down Rocks and Roll with Diz."[33] In 1958, the State Department sent Woody Herman's orchestra to South America less than three months after demonstrators—angered by U.S. economic policies and support for regional dictators—stoned, shoved, heckled, and spat upon Vice-President Richard Nixon in Caracas and Lima. Nixon had cut his trip short, and Herman's band retraced his steps in order to alleviate some of the anti-American feeling. State Department memoranda confirmed the band's public relations success among the very students who had led the anti-Nixon protests.[34]

The reception afforded these bands confirmed the expectations of jazz promoters, who had long recognized the music's appeal to young people abroad. They composed such a large proportion of listeners at foreign concerts and jazz clubs that *Time* dubbed the music "a kind of Esperanto to the young generation from 15 to 25 . . . even [in] countries with boiling anti-American prejudices." Government officials noted that jukeboxes playing American jazz, to which visitors frequently danced in the aisles, often proved the most popular aspects of United States trade exhibitions.[35] Jazz music's appeal to young people throughout the world had considerable advantages. By introducing American culture and ideas into foreign countries, the State Department hoped at the very least to win sympathy for the American way of life. As one observer noted at the time, the premise of the Smith-Mundt Act held that "if other people understood us, they would like us, and if they liked us they would do what we wanted them to do."[36]

Yet there was always a danger that jazz music might strike the wrong chord, so to speak, that it might appeal to the wrong instincts or for the wrong reasons. It was one thing to nurture discontented Soviet youth by beaming jazz across the Iron Curtain, but government officials did not wish to associate the music with rebellion among neutral and friendly countries. They wanted American cultural exports to represent universal values, common among all classes and countries and exemplified by the United States. Reflecting a growing American obsession with the causes and effects of juvenile delinquency, social scientists had already begun to theorize that jazz resonated among the young as protest music. Psychiatrist Aaron Esman argued in 1951 that jazz represented "a forbidden impulse in the psychology of American culture" on account of its shady origins in Storyville. As a result, he continued, it appealed primarily to those groups dissatisfied with repressive norms, namely "intellectuals, Negroes, and adolescents . . . who, consciously or unconsciously, regard themselves as outside the accepted cultural framework and as unbounded by many of its conventions." Esman's location of jazz within a paradigm of libidinal and social deviance echoed earlier readings of bebop's subculture, while addressing broader Cold War anxieties about stability, security, and the possibility of sexual containment in the atomic age. Three years later, Norman Margolis, another psychiatrist, compounded the association of jazz with unconventionality by equating each of its stylistic innovations with a movement either toward or away from the dominant musical tradition. He took this vacillation between protest and conformity to mirror the ambivalence of adolescent revolt, a connection that Margolis believed explained the psychological source of jazz and its prevalence among youths.[37]

Esman and Margolis contended that the music experienced weaker resistance in Europe on account of the continent's less Puritanical cultures. Yet the terms on which Europeans sometimes embraced jazz also concerned proponents of its use abroad. Panassié, Goffin, and Delauney cloaked their advocacy in what Ted Gioia has called the Primitivist Myth, "a stereotype which views jazz as a music charged with emotion but largely devoid of intellectual content, and which sees the jazz musician as the inarticulate and unsophisticated practitioner of an art which he himself scarcely understands." This tendency resulted from each of the writers' close association with the primitivist movement in European art, a fascination with exotic, supposedly natural and uncivilized African forms that promised to regenerate the decadent western tradition. Although primitivism had helped win early consideration and acceptance for jazz on the continent, it threatened to stall the government's ability to capitalize upon the music's popularity abroad. By equating jazz with blackness, and blackness with intuition and spontaneity, European critics reinscribed its distance from enlightened musical norms. As a result, the Russian ministry of culture simply claimed that jazz was not "cultured." "The legitimacy of jazz and the literacy and intelligence of its players is the thing that needs to be proved there," wrote bassist Willie Ruff after a 1959 visit to the Soviet Union.[38]

United States officials felt that to export jazz successfully in a diplomatic capacity, they had to continue correcting its image from a folk or protest music to an American contribution to a higher culture. A USIA memorandum from the period made this policy clear:

In view of the wide acceptance of jazz as an art form both in the United States and in many foreign countries, and also in view of the fact that a few less-informed groups in some areas still consider the music to be primitive and undisciplined, the agency suggests that less emphasis should be given in using jazz purely as an attractor for casual entertainment. The agency recommends that programs featuring jazz . . . have as their main objective the projection of jazz as an art form and as a significant aspect of American music.[39]

As a result of this policy, the Voice of America attempted to expose Europeans to the most sophisticated jazz forms. *Music USA* exercised a tremendous influence over the tastes of foreign listeners, especially in communist-controlled countries where access to other sources remained restricted. "Eastern Europe's entire concept of jazz comes from Willis Conover," marveled promoter George Wein after one visit to the continent. While the Voice paid tribute to traditional and swing styles that remained popular abroad, it introduced its listeners also to a great deal of bebop and post-bebop jazz, which at the time enjoyed limited appeal.[40] The State Department's music programming policies raise some important questions about the shifting reception of jazz in the United States. When and how did the domestic view of jazz change enough for the Voice to package it as "an art form" and "a significant aspect of American music?" How did jazz dissociate itself from protest and rebellion and remake itself in the image of the American way? The answers center around changes in the music's production, presentation, and reception at home by performers, critics, audiences, and entrepreneurs.

By the mid-1950s, the United States government had a tremendous incentive to show the world the best side of American culture in order to further its Cold War initiatives. Policy makers were aware that jazz music's global popularity already made it a conduit for goodwill, thanks to the efforts of Louis Armstrong and others. The earnestness and sophistication with which foreign audiences approached the music invariably impressed Americans. "For the most part they find jazz a subject for serious study," reported Belair in 1955. "Theirs is what most Americans would call a 'long-haired approach.' They like to contemplate it, dissect it, take it apart to see what makes it what it is." Unlike traveling ballets and classical orchestras, jazz struck Europeans as uniquely American, not derivative of their own cultures. At the same time, its growing compatibility with the international modernist movement in the arts reinforced jazz music's distinctiveness from traditional Soviet classicism and enhanced American contributions to a transatlantic aesthetic conversation.[41] As U.S. propaganda efforts increasingly shifted toward nonaligned countries and newly independent nations emerging from European colonization, the music's hybrid roots offered seemingly limitless potential to win friends.

The music's Cold War role, and the esteem in which foreign audiences held it, critically influenced the place of jazz in American culture. However, its broad-based acceptance as a sophisticated artistic contribution within the United States and hence by Washington would have been inconceivable without significant changes in the music and its performance environment. Despite its popularity abroad, many of America's leadership elite shared traditional prejudices against jazz as vulgar and lowbrow or deviant and oppositional. As a result, Voice of America officials programmed jazz and popular music only reluctantly, despite immediate and voluminous requests from foreign listeners.[42] The ability of musicians, critics, and promoters to equate jazz with a genuine artistic sensibility derived partly from changes in the music itself that brought one wing—the cool, West Coast, and Third Stream musicians—closer to the appearance of a fashionable and utterly respectable modernism in classical music. While hard bop and soul-jazz stressed very different virtues, all styles benefited from changing performance venues and new technologies that showcased the music's artistic potential. Even as stylistic fragmentation accelerated, cultural critics had already undertaken the first steps toward uniting various jazz forms under the ideological banner of a national American art form.

In the late 1940s, when bebop reached the height of its ridiculous fame and the nadir of its commercial expediency, a number of musicians began to reexamine the fundamental elements of modern jazz. Whereas bebop minimized the need for arranger-composers, owing to the predominance of popular, blues, and theme-and-variation forms, Gil Evans, George Russell, and Gerry Mulligan applied their musical training to the production of sophisticated charts. In contrast to the jagged virtuosity and complex rhythms of bebop, tenor saxophonist Stan Getz harked back to the full, lyrical tone of Lester Young and Lennie Tristano instructed his drummers to keep time with brushes. More than any other recordings, the Miles Davis nonet's landmark *Birth of the Cool* sessions of 1949–50 influenced the style, instrumentation, and conception of much of the following decade's most successful jazz.

Son of a professional middle-class family from East St. Louis, who sent him to the Julliard School of Music in 1945, Miles Davis soon abandoned his studies to play trumpet with bebop's pioneers. Between 1945 and 1948 he worked on New York's 52nd Street with Charlie Parker and Coleman Hawkins, toured with Benny Carter and Billy Eckstine, and appeared on many of the seminal recordings of the period. Davis's fragile, withdrawn solos provided a sharp contrast to the thrust and parry of most bebop horn players. In search of alternative settings for his unique sound, Davis often met for discussions and rehearsals with Gil Evans and several other members of Claude Thornhill's big band. Their collaboration led to the formation of a nine-piece ensemble, which included French horn, tuba, and baritone saxophone, for three studio dates.

The group's unusual size and instrumentation enabled its arrangers to produce a broad range of sonorities, including the dark and mellow sounds of a larger orchestra, without the unwieldy presence of large sections. The band favored fullness and color of tone and impressionistic harmonies over the individual attack and display characteristic of bebop. The slower tempos and relaxed accompaniment (especially evident during the second session in which Kenny Clarke participated) facilitated gracious long melody lines. On "Boplicity" or "Venus De Milo," for example, Miles Davis and Gerry Mulligan's precise and understated execution of these lines allowed for an apparently effortless transition from individual improvisation to orchestral arrangement, always focusing the listener's attention on the intricate design of the total performance rather than the accomplishments of a particular instrumentalist.

With its immediate lyricism and rich harmonic textures, *Birth of the Cool* displayed the potential to attract the most casual of music fans, yet the group made only two brief appearances in public. Neither engagement led to offers of future work, and the musicians soon drifted apart to fulfill existing contracts or locate possible jobs. Gerry Mulligan's search for work took him to Los Angeles, where he sold some arrangements to big band leader Stan Kenton in 1952 and began sitting in with the house band at the Lighthouse, a Hermosa Beach bar where many of Kenton's ex-sidemen played. Mulligan discovered quickly that the nonet's recordings had made a huge impact on California musicians such as Shorty Rogers, Jimmy Giuffre, and Shelly Manne, who had learned from Kenton the value of pursuing new musical sounds, highly arranged compositions, and adoring young audiences. These Kenton alums, together with the Lighthouse All-Stars and Mulligan's piano-less quartet with Chet Baker, helped popularize Davis's cool sound. Although their West Coast style never achieved the critical acclaim belatedly afforded the *Birth of the Cool* recordings, it did much to reconfigure the audience for jazz.[43]

For the most part, independent California labels such as Fantasy, Pacific, and Contemporary recorded the artists who defined the West Coast sound and brought it national exposure after 1952. Indebted to the Miles Davis nonet's tonal and rhythmic enunciation, linear melodies, and elevation of composition, these musicians inflected their improvisations with an academic knowledge of classical structure and form.[44] Many of them had trained with European-educated music instructors or, failing that, mimicked Kenton's tendency to dress up highly arranged music with the pomp and ceremony of the classics.[45] The press reported favorably on their high-minded seriousness. Like several articles on Dave Brubeck, *Time* magazine's 1954 cover story linked the pianist's fascination with counterpoint and polytonality in jazz to his studies at Mills College under Darius Milhaud. Another *Time* feature, on Gerry Mulligan in February 1953, divorced his quartet from negative perceptions of jazz in general and bebop in particular. "Mulligan's

Figure 2. (Left to right) Bob Envoldsen, Bill Perkins, Andre Previn, and Gerry Mulligan recording in 1959. Courtesy Michael Ochs Archives.com.

sound is just about unique in the jazz field" wrote the anonymous reporter. "In comparison with the frantic extremes of bop, his jazz is rich and even orderly, is marked by an almost Bach-like counterpoint. As in Bach, each Mulligan man is busily looking for a pause, a hole in the music which he can fill with an answering phrase." Soon after the article appeared, Mulligan made further headlines by interrupting his performance at The Haig to chastise customers for talking during the set.[46]

Attempts to cross-fertilize elements of jazz and classical music proved equally productive on the east coast, often deriving from those musicians who had recorded with Davis in New York. John Lewis, pianist on the second session, founded the Modern Jazz Quartet (MJQ) in 1952 with drummer Kenny Clarke (later replaced by Connie Kay), vibraphonist Milt Jackson, and bassist Percy Heath. The MJQ remained one of the most popular jazz groups for over twenty years by combining swing-inflected improvisation with classical structures and a serious demeanor entirely appropriate for the concert halls and arts festivals the combo

Figure 3. The Modern Jazz Quartet epitomized respectable and accessible jazz during the 1950s. (Left to right) Percy Heath, Connie Kay, John Lewis, and Milt Jackson. Courtesy Institute of Jazz Studies, Rutgers University.

often headlined. Gunther Schuller, who played French horn on the final *Birth of the Cool* session, frequently invoked the MJQ as the quintessential example of Third Stream music, a concept he spent much of the 1950s and 1960s promoting. A composer, conductor, and teacher for some of the most prestigious music organizations in the country, Schuller envisioned "a possible rapprochement between jazz and classical music" in which jazz contributed "improvisational spontaneity and rhythmic vitality" and classical brought "compositional formal procedures."[47]

Throughout the 1950s, cool and West Coast musicians tended to approximate technical devices from the romantic (and occasionally impressionistic) composers, including fugue and rondo forms, contrapuntal techniques, and rhythmic meter other than 4/4. Their proclivity to imitate pre-modern practices suggests a relative aesthetic conservatism among many classically trained jazz musicians, and the compatibility of these preferences with jazz forms. Schuller's search for new approaches to tonality, rhythm, and composition eventually led him to champion Ornette Coleman's "outside" improvisation. More immediately, his Third Stream experiments encouraged Miles Davis to work within impressionistic symphonic orchestrations that proved more compatible with the expectations of mainstream jazz—and classical—audiences for accessible and respectable modern music. Davis's experience playing flugelhorn on Schuller's *Music for Brass* in 1956 encouraged him to develop the *Birth of the Cool* sounds for a larger aggregation. He hired former collaborator Gil Evans to conduct and arrange a nineteen-piece orchestra on *Miles Ahead,* the first of several immensely popular albums that placed Davis in an expanded symphonic setting.[48]

Miles Davis's tremendous success in the late 1950s owed a great deal to Columbia's concerted marketing campaign. Album covers, liner notes, and interviews focused on Davis's celebrity lifestyle (fast cars, beautiful women, immaculate Italian suits), as his "cool" became the object of others' fantasy.[49] The West Coast image of surf, sand, and sex proved an equally viable sales pitch. William Claxton's sun-drenched photographs became synonymous with Contemporary (and to a lesser extent Pacific) covers of the 1950s, underscoring visually the race-specific appeal of a paradise in which even the occasional African American artists served as props for white leisure consumption.[50] Perhaps most telling, in the wake of national publicity for California-based cool jazz, major record labels began signing some of its biggest names. In the spring of 1953, RCA management invited Shorty Rogers to record a concept album its marketing division had already titled *Crazy and Cool.*[51] Atlantic eventually signed Rogers in 1955, by which time Capitol had secured Jimmy Giuffre's services and Columbia had snared Dave Brubeck from the Fantasy roster. Brubeck's rise to fame suggests not only how profitable jazz became for a few performers, but how the music's audience expanded in conjunction with the ability of entrepreneurs to open new venues.

Jazz music's growing acclaim at home depended upon more than its aesthetic development. The maturation of public forums that underscored its artistic potential proved critical in reshaping the listener profile for jazz. Throughout his career, Dave Brubeck assiduously cultivated an audience among high school and college students. His octet drew only three paying gigs between 1947 and 1949, but their free concerts at colleges such as Stanford, San Francisco State, and University of the Pacific proved much more significant in pioneering the presentation of jazz under the sometimes unwitting sponsorship of academic music departments. As few colleges regarded jazz worthy of concert presentation at this time, the Dave Brubeck Octet played classical pieces during the first half of a show and jazz material after the intermission. When Brubeck reduced his working group to a trio and later a quartet at the beginning of the 1950s, local impresario Jimmy Lyons secured work at San Francisco's Blackhawk nightclub. Lyons hosted radio broadcasts of

Brubeck's band that reached up and down the coast, attracting considerable interest among high school and college students. Despite an uproar in the San Francisco *Chronicle* and city hall over the Blackhawk's suitability for youngsters, its owners instituted an all-ages policy every Sunday to accommodate teens and their parents.[52]

Brubeck's quartet music with altoist Paul Desmond dated from 1951 and epitomized his appealing blend of techniques and devices. On a live recording of "I'll Never Smile Again" from December 1953, for example, Brubeck's single-note piano solo gradually gave way to fistfuls of dissonant block chords played against the beat, before subsiding into playful counterpoint with altoist Paul Desmond. On this early recording, as in later popular numbers such as "Take Five" and "Blue Rondo à la Turk," Desmond's graceful alto served as a fitting foil to Brubeck's structuralism. Whenever the leader's curiosity with classical design or unusual meter threatened to degenerate into stiff formality, Desmond's fluid melodic tone restored a sense of spontaneity and lyricism.

Brubeck's wife Iola took another crucial step in unlocking new venues for jazz. Concerned about her husband's fatigue from long out-of-state road trips, she contacted over one hundred west coast colleges listed in the *World Almanac* to recommend the Dave Brubeck Quartet for campus concerts. By the time drummer Joe Dodge joined in December 1953, the band was beginning to capitalize fully upon this new source of income. Dodge recalled a series of sixty consecutive one-nighters at higher education institutions that began with the new semester. Radio play, and the Brubecks' efforts to reach new audiences, paid off in appearance fees and record sales. Max Weiss recalled that Fantasy usually had to sell approximately five thousand units to show a profit. The company soon began to move forty to fifty thousand Brubeck records a quarter and garnered huge returns. When Brubeck appeared on the cover of *Time* magazine in November 1954, Columbia used the picture for an album cover. *Brubeck Time,* the first of numerous records by the quartet organized around the theme of unusual meters, sold one hundred thousand copies. Despite the ambivalence of jazz critics, whose early enthusiasm for the pianist turned lukewarm very quickly, Brubeck became one of the most recognizable and commercially successful jazz musicians of the postwar era. During the golden years of the "classic" quartet, the group consistently won readers' polls in *Down Beat, Metronome, Playboy,* and *Billboard.*[53]

Brubeck's efforts soon opened campuses to other performers. Colleges provided the latest in a series of alternative venues to the nightclub that promised to bring a new prestige to the music, aroused changing expectations of audience behavior, and afforded new sources of profit. Early pioneers of jazz concerts played a variety of styles. Paul Whiteman brought symphonic jazz to Aeolian Hall as early as 1924. John Hammond's "Spirituals to Swing" concerts of 1938 and 1939 featured members of at least three big bands at Carnegie Hall, where Duke Ellington premiered extended works at a series of annual concerts between 1943 and 1948. All-star bands brought bebop to the Metropolitan Opera House in 1944 and Toronto's Massey Hall in 1953, and the Modern Jazz Quartet specialized in introducing jazz to prestigious classical music venues. The concert hall represents a crucial element of the "aura" that defines a piece of music as art, just as the museum or academy serves the same function for other creative endeavors.[54] In many cases the venue combined with the deportment, dress, and conduct of the musicians to encourage audience displays of restraint, respect, even reverence for the artists and their work. Yet the most profitable and enduring developments in the concert field, Norman Granz's touring Jazz at the Philharmonic (JATP) package and the annual jazz festival, provide much more complicated case studies in the relationship between a legitimate setting and artistic respect, a symbiosis negotiated by the performer and his or her audience.

In a little over ten years Norman Granz, an unpaid promoter of jam sessions in California nightclubs, became the top jazz impresario in the world and the first millionaire to make his money exclusively from jazz. Traveling groups of top name musicians billed as Jazz at the Philharmonic, after the location of Granz's first commercial venture in Los Angeles, provided the cornerstone of his fortune. Musicians and fellow entrepreneurs characterized Granz as a ruthless and tireless businessman who spared no effort to secure the best working conditions for his performers. Critics displayed a similar ambivalence toward his promotional style. Most welcomed his success in bringing jazz out of nightclubs that some enthusiasts were reluctant or, for age reasons, unable to patronize. Yet many critics grew weary of the show, in particular the poorly compatible stylists who whipped the audience into an emotional frenzy with simulated competitive exchanges. By the early 1950s, JATP tours netted stars such as Illinois Jacquet, Oscar Peterson, Lester Young, and Gene Krupa $1,000 or more per week for four or five concerts, one of the best pay checks in the business, and brought Granz approximately $600,000 to $700,000 per year. Revealing their changing attitudes toward jazz, many writers scolded Granz for his interest in profit rather than culture.[55]

Louis and Elaine Lorillard were interested in culture, in particular the idea of elevating the status of jazz. Co-founders of the Newport Jazz Festival in 1954, the tobacco heir and his Brahmin wife invited Boston nightclub owner George Wein to produce the first annual event at the exclusive Rhode Island retreat. As the inaugural festival program made clear, Newport's reputation as a leisure space for the discriminating classes helped set the tone for the event. Barry Kernfeld noted in the *New Grove Dictionary of Jazz* that "festivals . . . form a landmark in the shifting of the balance between jazz as a social event and jazz as a concert music" because the bandstand format privileges listening over secondary functions such as drinking and dancing. Typically, the sponsors organized additional educational events such as a jazz film series, photographic and artistic exhibitions, lectures, and symposia, all of which promoted an understanding of jazz as an art form by providing it with a history. Like many of the pioneering jazz concerts and even the State Department tours, which showcased the evolution of jazz from New Orleans to the present, festivals cultivated the idea of a jazz tradition of development and progress. The bandstand often communicated this message directly. The first Newport festival opened with Eddie Condon's traditional group, and progressed through the various styles of Count Basie, Ella Fitzgerald, George Shearing, Dizzy Gillespie, Gerry Mulligan, and the Modern Jazz Quartet, among others. As if to confirm their similar missions, the festival donated $3,500 in three years to the Institute of Jazz Studies, the first jazz archive and scholarly center in the country.[56]

Newport's success precipitated numerous imitations that followed a similar formula, a series of performances by large numbers of groups over several days at one location attended by thousands of visitors. By the end of the decade, nine major festivals played to over 300,000 people in the United States, and by the mid-1980s approximately seven hundred to one thousand annual festivals operated worldwide. In the early days of the jazz festival, promoters such as George Wein at Newport and Jimmy Lyons at Monterey—which hosted its first annual festival in 1958—struggled to make the concept profitable for themselves and their artists. Both festivals lost money or barely broke even in the first couple of years. Each struggled to keep up the appearance of culture and refinement while attracting sufficient people to turn a profit. Wein and the Lorillards founded the Newport festival as a nonprofit corporation, yet despite Wein's early losses—some of which apparently came out of his own pocket—he made the venture pay. After the first year, the Board awarded him $5,000 per year for four months work, plus expenses and occasional bonuses of up to $2,000. Although the Board paid some of the money retroactively in 1957, court records confirm the early date of the arrangement. Artists benefited from the boom in jazz concerts, too. Wein testified to the inflationary effect of jazz festivals on musicians' salaries in a 1960 deposition. George Shearing's quintet, for example, would not appear at a festival for less than $2,000 by the turn of the decade, as opposed to a maximum of $3,500 for a full seven-day week just a few years before.[57]

The Newport Jazz Festival Board's drive to increase revenues led to some dubious compromises with its proclaimed artistic goals. Stage managers frequently shuttled unrehearsed all-star bands on stage for short medleys of their collective greatest hits. The practice proved increasingly detrimental to the survival of the working band, a stable aggregation of players who refined and advanced their artistry through sustained live performance and experimentation. The most profitable years of the festival, which grossed about one million dollars from live music, recordings, and concessions in 1959, coincided with attempts to draw a wider audience with cabaret, folk, and rock and roll groups.[58] The earnest spirit of self-improvement that characterized its early years increasingly competed with college students' desire for unbounded pleasure, transforming the jazz festival into a prototype spring break weekend. Images of Newport in glossy magazines and the 1958 documentary film *Jazz on a Summer's Day* reflected an east coast interpretation of William Claxton's vision of the good life. The festival's promotion of this consumer vision soon came up against the limits of its ability to deliver a modest, restrained program, and the veneer of high culture had worn thin by the end of the decade. The contrast between "the gentry in the front row with their Martini shakers, [and] the sailors squatting in the back, their heads between their knees, upchucking their beer" dismayed Murray Kempton of the *New York Post*. "Was ever anything in America at once so fashionable and squalid?" he queried in January 1960.[59]

Despite its fluctuating fortunes, these early years of the music festival proved crucial to public perceptions of jazz and its fate within American culture. As the only festival of its kind for four years, Newport provided an annual focus for national media attention on the music, one spot where reporters could gather for a short period to take stock of the jazz world.[60] The high-class setting, which would have seemed incongruous a decade earlier, framed the central theme of most reports, inviting comparisons between the music's humble beginnings and its lofty status (implied by both the location and the presence of ultrasophisticated modern jazz on the bandstand). Lillian Ross's lengthy article in the *New Yorker* following the inaugural festival illustrated the irresistible comparison between crusty old Newport society and upwardly mobile jazz. A conversation between Boston arts patron Maxim Karolik and saxophonist Gerry Mulligan revealed the implied authority of highbrow venues and sponsors:

"Jazz is no longer only for the cabarets," Karolik said. "No question about it."
"You dig it, sir?" Mulligan asked.

"It's something to ponder," said Karolik. "Rachmaninoff spoke about it. It is an established fact. Jazz is America's contribution to music."[61]

Ross's fascination with the interaction between blue-bloods and hot-bloods at private society parties dismayed some critics, who wished for an exclusive focus on the music. Yet the article conveyed the way the location's cultural capital helped compensate for the music's lack of truly widespread appeal, making it pay as an art form by embracing all the attendant elitist trappings.

In this way, developments in the music and its venues attracted not only high school and college students but also young professionals who cultivated refinement. Record store owners observed an increase in jazz purchases among consumers of classical music. Jazz frequently appeared alongside established highbrow forms such as the visual arts (at the Jazz at the Museum of Modern Art series) and symphonic music (at the Boston Arts Festival). Numerous middlebrow magazines introduced jazz columns and record reviews during the 1950s. In 1958, an independent readership survey conducted on behalf of *Harper's* revealed the magazine's readers as predominantly young, well-educated, high-earning urbanites. The editors firmly believed that customers who met or aspired to this profile took an interest in jazz. Likewise, editors at *Esquire* and *Playboy* trusted that jazz features would engage the style-conscious men who read their magazines, the *Saturday Review* and the *New Yorker* made analogous assumptions about their cosmopolitan target groups, while *High Fidelity* recognized that jazz fans frequently had disposable income to spend on the latest audio equipment.[62] In 1960, *Down Beat* magazine—the leading jazz publication—conducted a reader survey that revealed 92 percent of respondents as men, with an average age between twenty four (newsstand buyers) and twenty eight (subscribers). The majority (65 percent) described themselves as high school or college students, musicians, office workers, salesmen, or engineers. No doubt jazz music's racial, aesthetic, and social "otherness" offered many of them a vicarious alternative to the stultifying white-collar existence portrayed by sociologists of the era.[63] Increasingly, however, the audience experience of jazz was mediated and made safe by the trappings of a thoroughly modern concert music.

Changes in the presentation of jazz did not end with the rise of the festival. Advancements in recording technology expanded producers' ability to showcase jazz music's artistic vitality, and led to unprecedented sales across the industry. Since the 1940s, engineers had grappled with the inherent limitations of time and frequency response on traditional 78-rpm shellac discs. In 1948 Columbia introduced $33^1/_3$-rpm vinyl microgroove discs, which became industry standard (along with RCA's

45-rpm "singles") within a couple of years. These Long Play (LP) records provided up to fifty minutes of listening on two sides, in place of the three and a half to four minute maximum on each side of a "78" or "45." The Long Play format offered immediate benefits to the top jazz artists. Musicians could "stretch out," improvising as long as they wanted without time constraints, more realistically approximating a live performance situation. LPs offered the possibility of theme albums united by a concept or vision. They rewarded consistency among songs and provided longer sequences of uninterrupted music. Together with the accompanying improvements in high fidelity reproduction (*Duke Ellington Uptown in Hi-Fi* became a favorite test record for salesmen), extended play meant the most to those artists with the broadest creative range.

Technological advances also allowed for the recording of live jazz in a concert environment. Norman Granz released the first live sides in 1945, featuring excerpts of his Jazz at the Philharmonic series. He experienced great difficulty securing a distribution deal, as record companies questioned the appeal of discs polluted with audience applause and other uncontrollable trappings of a live show. The format proved ideal for jazz, however, capturing the spontaneity of a live performance and the interaction between the audience and the improviser. Studio albums had missed this crucial dialectic in the production of jazz, and records became another linchpin of Granz's jazz empire. Long Play jazz records of the 1950s captured significant live moments previously heard only by the immediate audience on location. Dave Brubeck's 1954 album *Jazz Goes to College*, culled from three concerts, proselytized his sound at schools his band had not yet reached and outsold everything by the popular entertainer Liberace that year. By 1956 improvements in magnetic recording tape allowed engineers to capture outdoor events, including Paul Gonsalves's twenty-seven blistering choruses on "Diminuendo and Crescendo in Blue" during Duke Ellington's 1956 Newport set. The subsequent LP sold 100,000 copies, the band leader's most popular release ever. In 1957, a year when jazz record sales doubled, *Ellington at Newport* ranked among three of the four best-selling LPs recorded live on location.[64]

Of course, jazz sales came nowhere near the volume of rock and roll. The new popular music of Elvis Presley, Chuck Berry, and others set the emerging status of jazz in relief by taking upon itself many of the charges of vulgarity, permissiveness, and rebellion once associated with "America's art form." The National Academy of Recording Arts and Sciences acknowledged this trend when it founded the Grammys, an initiative by the big record labels to reward artistry and excellence in an age when most executives believed quality and record sales increasingly diverged.

Jazz played a prominent role in the formative years of the Grammys, from 1958 until the early 1960s. Although the categories reflected the founders' familiarity with big band jazz, rather than the innovative forms of the era, the televised awards reinforced the music's middlebrow appeal. The Grammy broadcasts contributed to the music's increasing small-screen exposure. Network specials including *The Sound of Jazz* (1957) on CBS and NBC's *Timex All-Star Jazz Shows* (1957–59), and local programming such as *Playboy*'s variety series, used innovative sets and camera movement to accentuate the sophisticated nature of interactive performance.[65]

Some of the most interesting redefinitions of jazz music's contested identity occurred in the movies. Several films from the late 1940s embraced a growing awareness of jazz as art. While film-makers upheld audience expectations of race, gender, and sexual roles, they often reinforced the rising status of jazz—much as the festivals did—by providing it with a history. A tuxedo-clad Louis Armstrong presented Dorothy Patrick with a copy of his autobiography in *New Orleans* (1947), suggesting that the trumpeter embodied a living tradition, while in *A Song Is Born* (1948) folklore professor Danny Kaye canonized jazz in a musical encyclopedia. Biopics of white jazz musicians usually culminated in a concert hall, the final stage in the music's evolution from rustic to cultured artifact. During the 1950s, bebop's hipster cult and its appropriation by a bohemian subculture helped foster a competing association between jazz, deviance, and criminality in films such as *The Big Combo* (1955) and *Funny Face* (1956). Yet both deviant and respectable perceptions of jazz coexisted and vied for prominence in the public imagination. *Sweet Smell of Success* (1957)—in which a jazz guitarist appeared as the one incorruptible character in a sleazy urban culture—reflected an alternative interpretation of the music that challenged its residual association with the exotic and drew strength from similar representations of jazz during the 1950s. Furthermore, the parody of pompous jazz fans in movies such as *Jailhouse Rock* (1957) provided a backhanded acknowledgment of the music's status, even as filmmakers attempted to trivialize its importance. Although modern jazz lay beyond the understanding or desire of Elvis Presley's character, with which the audience is expected to sympathize, the film affirmed the elitist and cultivated nature of jazz by opposing it to the primitive, populist rocker.[66]

Jazz music's resurgence favored all styles, as the festivals and television specials demonstrated. By the late 1950s this revival included hard bop, a redefinition of the innovations of Charlie Parker and Dizzy Gillespie pioneered by predominantly African American east coast musicians. Art Blakey, Horace Silver, the Adderley brothers, and Max Roach rejected the studied calculation of cool jazz in favor of an earthy emotionalism drawn from black church music and its secular counterpart, rhythm and blues. These influences translated into renewed attention to blues and other basic structures, which framed repetitive riff-inspired melodies, chordal voicings from gospel music, and a dominant, accentuated off-beat. By retaining—and containing—the technical advances of bebop and cool within a simpler structural and melodic framework, hard bop combined sophisticated and accessible musical devices so successfully that by the turn of the decade it had challenged West Coast jazz as the predominant mainstream style. Like cool jazz, hard bop embraced numerous musical variations. The advanced harmonic progressions and rhythmic complexities of Sonny Rollins and John Coltrane's early work satisfied the most technically demanding fan, while the lean, funky soul-jazz of Horace Silver's "The Preacher" (1956), Lee Morgan's "The Side-winder" (1963), and the Adderleys' "Mercy, Mercy, Mercy" (1966) became crossover hits.[67]

The variety of jazz forms that benefited from the success of "modern vernacular" techniques, new venues, advanced technologies, and expanded audiences underscores the extent to which an idea or ideology, rather than any shared stylistic approach, bound these divergent schools together as a national cultural entity. While innovative performers and promoters made jazz music's modernist conceptions appealing to a broad range of listeners, cultural commentators seized upon elements common to all styles and tied them to America's expressed political philosophy. Like some champions of abstract expressionism from the same period, jazz critics, academics, musicians, and entrepreneurs created a place for their art within the mid-1950s liberal consensus by equating creative individualism with a Cold War rhetoric of democratic freedom.[68] Washington's subsequent embrace of the music and its revitalized ideology marked the pinnacle of national acceptance for jazz as "America's art form."

Jazz music's popularity abroad and increasing respectability at home provided an opportunity for American officials to integrate it into a developing cultural outreach program. Yet such a strategy would have been unimaginable unless they could portray jazz as a definitively American form, encapsulating the universal values that the United States promoted during the Cold War. The government's ability to reinforce and capitalize upon jazz music's emerging prestige owed much to scholars in the nascent discipline of American studies, who created a supportive intellectual framework for interpreting the music. History and literature professors at George Washington, Harvard, Yale, and a handful of other colleges established the first American civilization courses during the 1930s, in an attempt to transcend the techniques and subject matter of their fields and chart pervasive characteristics of the American experience. Their search for the American mind in a holistic national culture received a tremendous boost from World War II. President Franklin D. Roosevelt's rhetoric of freedom cast the war with Nazi Germany as an ideological conflict, focusing attention on United States core values. His "Four Freedoms" address to Congress, illustrated by Norman Rockwell and distributed first by the *Saturday Evening Post* and then the Office of War Information, anticipated the American studies method by teasing democratic principles from American cultural practices. Ralph H. Gabriel's *The Course of American Democratic Thought* (1940), Constance Rourke's *The Roots of American Culture* (1942), Merle Curti's *Growth of American Thought* (1943), and similar texts became staples of postwar American studies programs for they proved quite adaptable to Cold War realities. Faculty could use these books to validate American exceptionalism equally well in the face of international communism as fascism, discovering democratic individualism and cultural consensus in a past once taught as a struggle between classes and factions. Aided by funding from outside sources sympathetic with the government's Cold War aims, such as the Carnegie Corporation and the Rockefeller and Coe Foundations, American studies programs multiplied after World War II. By 1948 over 60 institutions offered a bachelor's degree in the subject, and by 1973 the number had risen to approximately 250 or one in seven accredited four-year colleges.[69]

Many academics responded to America's world leadership role by attempting to craft a national cultural identity built around art forms that incorporated some reflection of American political ideals. During a distinguished career as a commentator on society and the arts, John Kouwenhoven explored "What's 'American' about America" in art, architecture, politics, and poetry. Kouwenhoven, an English professor at Barnard College and an editor at *Harper's Magazine*, characterized the United States by its fluid, extendable, and adaptable structures, a premise that led him to consider jazz as a representative American form. Drawing upon the critical writings of Winthrop Sargeant and André Hodeir, Kouwenhoven identified rhythmic propulsion, achieved by imposing polyrhythms upon syncopation, as the jazz band's defining trait. Even as a piece of music dictates a certain pattern, he explained, each performer preempts, lags behind, circumvents, and eventually returns to the beat in a process that could conceivably never end save for the limitations of phonograph technology or human endurance. Kouwenhoven proposed that this vernacular, functional aesthetic and resistance to closure typified American cultural artifacts. It linked jazz to the infinitely amendable Constitution, the Manhattan skyline, and the American gridiron street plan, as well as the process-oriented formulas underpinning soap operas, scientific production, and chewing gum.[70] Moreover, he argued elsewhere, jazz embodied democratic individualism because its rhythmic structure "reconciles the demands of group performance (the arrangement) and individual expression (the solos)." Kouwenhoven thus positioned jazz as a solution to the historical dilemma posed by Ralph Waldo Emerson between collective discipline and personal liberty, for in jazz "the thing that holds them together is the very thing they are all so busy flouting: the fundamental four-four beat."[71]

When Johns Hopkins University Press republished Kouwenhoven's essay in a compendium of his work entitled *The Beer Can by the Highway*, over thirty years after it first appeared in print, the volume included an introduction by the author's friend Ralph Ellison. The confluence between refined and vernacular antecedents in forming a fluid and flexible national culture fascinated both essayists. These concerns permeated Ellison's most famous work, the prize-winning novel *Invisible Man* (1952), as well as his widely circulated writings about the jazz and blues musicians he grew up with in Oklahoma. Ellison celebrated similar ideological values to Kouwenhoven when he described jazz as "that embodiment of a superior democracy in which each individual cultivated his uniqueness and yet did not clash with his neighbors." For Ellison, however, improvisation rather than rhythmic complexity represented the music's key feature and metaphor for the American experience. In a 1958 *Saturday Review* essay on his childhood friend Charlie Christian, famed guitarist of Benny Goodman's groups and a bebop pioneer, Ellison connected competitive individualism and mutual progress through this defining trait. "True jazz," he wrote, "is an act of individual assertion within and against the group. Each true jazz moment (as distinct from the uninspired commercial performance) springs from a contest in which each artist challenges all the rest; each solo flight, or improvisation, represents (like the successive canvases of a painter) a definition of his identity as individual, as member of the collectivity and as a link in the chain of tradition."[72]

Kouwenhoven and Ellison contributed to a broader debate over the redefinition of shared American values. As Eric Foner has demonstrated, freedom represents a popular though contested idea throughout American history, its meaning constantly reinvented in relation to a shifting spectral opposite. Cold War American studies practitioners found in jazz music's structured liberty a figurative antidote to both rigid communist totalitarianism and unfettered primitivist instinct. Furthermore, the image of jazz musicians as a harmonious group of equal individuals neatly sidestepped issues of collaborative support and creative dissonance, both arguably vital to jazz yet increasingly written out of the post-Truman Doctrine tenor of American public life. By 1947 Roosevelt's plans for collective postwar revitalization, such as the Economic Bill of Rights, were a distant memory, and congressional and business leaders had done much to replace "freedom from want" with "free enterprise" as the archetypal American promise. At the same time, superpower rivalry and the domestic red scare that accompanied American setbacks not only narrowed the boundaries of dissent but celebrated the resultant homogeneity of opinion as a virtue. African American music was drawn into a discourse about the nature of American culture within these limits.[73]

A number of influential jazz critics eagerly embraced the correlation between American arts and American exceptionalism emerging from liberal-consensus intellectuals such as Kouwenhoven and Ellison. Leonard Feather and Dan Morgenstern, both Jewish refugees from Nazi Europe, and Marshall Stearns, the English professor who accompanied Dizzy Gillespie's first tour, enlisted jazz as a token of universal cultural consensus in the battle against ideological dogmas of the right and the left. Music writers added to the concept that equated jazz with freedom an awareness that jazz offered the potential to unite diverse racial and ethnic groups.[74] In fact, these critics shared an affinity for one text in the emerging American studies canon, Gunnar Myrdal's *An American Dilemma* (1944), which posited racial equality as the unfulfilled pledge of America's democratic creed. Stearns in particular exercised a pervasive influence on the jazz scene of the 1950s through his involvement with the Institute of Jazz Studies, the Newport Jazz Festival, and the Lenox school of music and his promotion of interdisciplinary scholarship, conferences, and symposia. "Jazz," he stated, "is the result of a three-hundred-years' blending in the United States of the European and West African musical traditions; and its predominant components are European harmony, Euro-American melody, and African rhythm." Implicitly recognizing the shortcomings of the wartime melting pot, which assimilated white ethnics into the American mainstream while reinforcing the economic and social marginalization of racial minorities, Stearns argued that the jazz community—like the music—provided a model of harmonious integration. By urging Americans to copy the progressive stand of the music industry, however, he ignored an ongoing history of structural discrimination against African American performers. The musical metaphor elided these uncomfortable struggles for power, not to mention the conflicting desire among some African Americans (and whites) for social and cultural autonomy, projecting instead a rosy vision of common goals and objectives. In the words of Dan Morgenstern, who went on to edit three major jazz publications during the 1960s, jazz "symbolizes the creative union of all races and creeds which lies in the future."[75]

For many Cold War-era jazz supporters, the open market—free from racial or economic prohibition—provided an appropriate arena in which the music could flourish. During the 1930s and early 1940s, several music writers such as Charles Edward Smith and Sidney Finkelstein of the *Daily Worker* had identified jazz as a folk art operating only reluctantly within a cash-exchange nexus. The concept of jazz as folk music attracted many traditional jazz fans aligned with the political left, for whom such a designation protected the music from association with corrupt mass culture. The triumph of modern forms, McCarthyism, and the persistent condemnation of jazz as "a product of bourgeois degeneration" by Moscow largely quelled these voices by the 1950s.[76] In their place, the glossy magazines trumpeted jazz as "America's art form" precisely because it had succeeded financially in an expanding niche market.

Indeed, several attempts to employ jazz in a propaganda capacity stressed its effectiveness in promoting the virtues of capitalism. In 1963, Secretary of Commerce Luther H. Hodges confirmed that music, and especially jazz, had played an integral role in every American trade exhibition since the mid-1950s. He calculated that U.S. officials had piped jazz into pavilions at more than one hundred international trade fairs on both sides of the Iron Curtain. After attending one such event in 1956, Representative John J. Rooney affirmed the music's ability to attract foreigners to American products; the visitors "were all standing around a juke box made in Chicago listening to dance bands," he observed. According to some authorities, jazz drew an enthusiastic audience abroad because it represented economic as well as political freedom. "People in static societies must find appeal in this music," wrote Willis Conover. "Jazz suggests mobility, and it appeals to a people and a society essentially immobile."[77] Reflecting on the contrasting ways in which the superpowers scheduled and financed their cultural tours, Marshall Stearns cited Dizzy Gillespie's experience as evidence of superior American efficiency. The Soviet Union flooded foreign countries with free—but strictly supervised—talent at enormous expense, he explained in the *Saturday Review.* "The American approach was different—a sort of do-it-yourself plan with an emphasis on free enterprise." Perhaps aware of his own propaganda's significance at home, Stearns continued to stretch a point of contrast by exaggerating the band's role in setting the itinerary and implying it accepted a market-driven fee. In fact, free enterprise proved a poor basis for promoting propaganda. A congressional review of Gillespie's Middle East tour revealed losses of $84,381 and drew complaints that his salary exceeded President Eisenhower's during the tour's duration. Stearns defended the arrangements, contending that an accomplished tour reflected positively upon the American system.[78]

This evolving liberal and democratic creed helped the State Department overcome domestic opposition to touring groups. Government proposals to send modern jazz abroad ran into the same problems encountered by ill-fated tours of modern American painting, including the 1947 exhibition "Advancing American Art." Assembled by the State Department for goodwill tours of Europe and Latin America, "Advancing American Art" received tremendous reviews at home and precipitated great interest in American painting abroad. Secretary of State George C. Marshall subsequently recalled and auctioned off the exhibit, however, in the face of tabloid press and congressional attacks on the allegedly subversive and un-American content of nonrepresentational works. Conservative critics charged that the exhibits denied traditional beauty and hence appeared to condemn the environment that produced them.[79] Senator Allen Ellender of Louisiana led similar attacks on modern jazz, commenting after he listened to Dizzy Gillespie's band that "I never heard so much pure noise in all my life." He later implored his colleagues on the Senate Appropriations Committee that "to send such jazz as Mr. Gillespie, I can assure you that instead of doing good it will do harm and the people will really believe we are barbarians."[80] Ellender attempted to use his position on the committee to block further appropriations for State Department funding of "jazz bands, ballet and dance groups and similar activities" in favor of more traditional "choral groups and miscellaneous sports projects."[81]

Senator Ellender could not scuttle the State Department's touring schedule for the same reason that critics of abstract art ultimately failed to halt its export abroad. International interest in uniquely American forms of modern art and music proved too enticing to ignore, as supporters of each media enshrined artistic freedom as its defining trait. The State Department, CIA-funded foundations, and the Museum of Modern Art (MOMA) championed abstract expressionism much as the government presented jazz, as the evidence and embodiment of a superior political and economic system. MOMA's founding director, Alfred H. Barr, Jr., argued that only a liberal democracy allowed avant-garde artists the freedom to pursue any path they chose. American painters generated uncensored, controversial works that spoke frankly about the anxieties of the age. They took risks unknown in the dreary, bureaucratically ordained socialist realism of the Soviet Union.[82] This emphasis on freedom in art as a mirror image of American society complemented the official view of jazz. When asked to explain the music's worldwide popularity, Voice of America announcer Willis Conover referenced a political ideology based on the aesthetic of controlled freedom exalted by Kouwenhoven and Ellison:

[Jazz is] a reflection of our national life. . . . To me, and I think to most people, democracy is a pattern of laws and customs by which we agree voluntarily to abide: within this fixed and clearly defined framework we have freedom. Only in such a society—and ours is the best example I know—could jazz have developed. It has its own musical restrictions—tempo, key, chord structure. But within them the artist is free to weave infinite variations. Structurally, it's a democratic music. People in other countries, in other political situations, detect this element of freedom in jazz. There isn't any elaborate reasoning process involved. They can feel it—emotionally. They love jazz because they love freedom.[83]

Even more important than illustrating freedom in the arts, jazz addressed the biggest weakness in America's Cold War arsenal. The Soviet Union constantly ridiculed U.S. democracy by pointing to the unequal treatment afforded African Americans. A month before Truman launched the "Campaign of Truth," Senator William Benton reported that a key theme of Soviet propaganda centered on the premise that "America's vaunted freedom is a fraud, and our doctrine of equality is belied by racial and religious discrimination."[84] American embassy officials noted with dismay that violence and discrimination against African Americans received extensive press coverage abroad, especially in countries with nonwhite populations. While Soviet informational activities focused world attention on American race relations, foreign journalists did not need to rely on communist news agencies for material. Newspapers in Ceylon gathered information from the Reuters wire service, and stories embarrassing to Washington appeared in allied countries such as Great Britain and the Netherlands and strategic nonaligned nations including India.[85]

Legal scholars have uncovered provocative evidence that international attention to racial discrimination in the United States helped make desegregation a Cold War imperative of the Truman and Eisenhower administrations. The State Department's export of integrated jazz bands supports the claim that Washington's deep concern with world opinion precipitated otherwise unlikely political attempts to bring minority groups into the mainstream of American society and culture. Bert Lockwood argued that by introducing the human rights provisions of the United Nations Charter into legal briefs, civil rights attorneys encouraged state and federal courts to redefine constitutional provisions previously not extended to segregation. His article is suggestive, although speculative, because the relevant decisions did not refer to the Charter and any influence must have taken place "sub silentia." Mary Dudziak, however, demonstrated that Justice Department *amicus curiae* briefs in several prominent civil rights cases, including the 1954 *Brown v. Board of Education* decision, located domestic racial discrimination squarely "in the context of the present world struggle between freedom and tyranny." During the *Brown* case, Truman's administration impressed upon the Supreme Court the negative consequences for world peace of a decision upholding segregation. By adopting the government's constitutional argument, the justices granted the State Department an immediate public relations boost. Now government officials could argue, as Myrdal had, that the principle of equality had always existed in the American democratic system, waiting to be realized. They could attribute any further racial discrimination to unrepentant reactionaries. Within an hour of the *Brown* decision, the Voice of America began broadcasting the news to eastern Europe.[86]

Justice Department efforts should not divert credit from the National Association for the Advancement of Colored People (NAACP), and its role in the case. Thurgood Marshall led a talented group of Association lawyers who spent years filing legal challenges to segregation in one state after another, accumulating precedents to support an assault on the "separate but equal" doctrine. *Brown* represented the culmination of their efforts. Indeed, the black middle class, which made up much of the NAACP's membership, represented one of the few groups that could advocate civil rights reform relatively free from accusations of communist influence during the Truman and Eisenhower years.[87] Just as Dudziak explained *Brown* as an example of interest convergence between civil rights advocates and foreign policy elites, so the State Department tours represented a mutually beneficial arrangement between a government eager to demonstrate minority progress and leading critics and musicians seeking to further the worldwide acceptance of jazz as "America's art form."[88] The Eisenhower administration's desire to highlight black and white musicians cooperating as equals (and often under African American leadership) must have seemed like a civil rights triumph, an international adventure, and a financial opportunity for artists long denied critical recognition.

Yet foreign excursions also encouraged African American musicians to develop political and cultural agendas at odds with the official rationale. Louis Armstrong and Dizzy Gillespie used their tours to establish networks of reciprocal musical exchange that often furthered a diasporic rather than particularly American identity. On a 1956 visit to Accra, during which 100,000 people came to hear him play, Armstrong attributed the crowd's support to their recognition that "my ancestors came from here and I still have African blood in me." Dizzy Gillespie integrated Samba riffs into several compositions following a 1957 State Department tour that took him to Brazil and Argentina. Duke Ellington paid homage to foreign musicians and cultures he encountered on official duty in *The Far East Suite, The Latin American Suite,* and *Afro-Eurasian Eclipse.*[89] At a time many African and Asian colonies moved toward independence, these actions heightened pan-African interest within the African American press. Veteran journalist Horace Cayton celebrated Armstrong's African successes as a symbol of "the deep bonds of mutual sympathy" between black people on two continents. Singer, actor, and activist Paul Robeson—whom the State Department had prevented from traveling to promote racial internationalism—complimented Armstrong's dignified representation of African Americans during his time overseas. Tours frequently altered the musicians' perception of their homeland. After returning from Europe and the Middle East, Gillespie wrote an article for *Esquire* entitled "Jazz is too Good for Americans," in which he praised foreign listeners for rejecting his own country's preoccupation with the music's lowly roots.[90]

The opportunity to promote their music abroad only highlighted to African American performers the reality of continued discrimination in the United States. When invited to a State Department briefing before his departure, Dizzy Gillespie snapped, "I've got three hundred years of briefing. I know what they've done to us and I'm not going to make any excuses." Government officials exhibited great sensitivity to any friction between musicians' personal views and the official line of racial equality. After conducting a successful tour of West Africa in 1956, Louis Armstrong spoke out on civil rights the following year while negotiating a federally funded tour of Russia. After a performance in Grand Forks, North Dakota, on September 19, Armstrong learned that Governor Orval Faubus of Arkansas had forcibly barred African American children from entering a Little Rock high school. He immediately told a reporter that he would cancel the tour, explaining, "the way they are treating my people in the South, the government can go to hell." When he refused to recant his comments, the tour fell through.[91]

An original musical production of the period by Dave and Iola Brubeck exposed the contrast between State Department claims that jazz—and by extension democracy—brought people together regardless of race or ideology, and unabated segregation in the American South. Recorded in fall 1961 and performed at the Monterey Jazz Festival a year later, *The Real Ambassadors* centered around Louis Armstrong's experiences as a cultural envoy and featured Armstrong, Dave Brubeck, Carmen McRae, and vocal trio Lambert, Hendricks, and Ross. In "King for a Day," Armstrong proposed a basement session, the jazz equivalent of a summit conference, as his solution to international problems. World leaders would have to find a common beat and strive for harmony. "Cultural Exchange" also highlighted jazz music's conciliatory function:

Figure 4. (Left to right) Jon Hendricks, Dave Brubeck, and Louis Armstrong rehearsing *The Real Ambassadors*, 1962. Courtesy Brubeck Collection, Holt-Atherton Special Collections, University of the Pacific Library. Copyright Dave Brubeck.

Louis Armstrong [singing]:
The State Department has discovered jazz.
It reaches folks like nothing ever has.
Like when they feel that jazzy rhythm,
They know we're really with 'em;
That's what they call cultural exchange . . .

We put *Oklahoma!* in Japan.
South Pacific we gave to Iran.
And when our neighbors called us vermin,
We sent out Woody Herman.
That's what we call cultural exchange.[92]

Yet *The Real Ambassadors* did not avoid the fundamental contradiction of the government's touring policy. Like many songs in the production, the title track contrasted Armstrong's achievements abroad, which outshone the efforts of the most highly trained diplomats, with his second-class status at home. The interplay between self-important State Department officials, represented by Lambert, Hendricks, and Ross, and a resigned Louis Armstrong highlighted the incongruity:

Lambert, Hendricks, and Ross [singing]:
Who's the real ambassador?

It is evident we represent American society,
Noted for its etiquette, its manners and sobriety.
We have followed protocol with absolute propriety.
We're Yankees to the core . . .

Louis Armstrong [singing]:
I'm the real ambassador.
It is evident I wasn't sent by government to take your place.
All I do is play the blues and meet the people face to face.
I'll explain, and make it plain, I represent the human race,
And don't pretend no more.

Who's the real ambassador?
Certain facts we can't ignore.
In my humble way, I'm the USA.
Though I represent the government, the government don't represent
Some policies I'm for.

Oh we've learned to be concerned about the constitutionality.
In our nation segregation isn't a legality.
Soon our only differences will be in personality.
That's what I stand for.
Who's the real ambassador, yeah, the real ambassador?

Jazz musicians recognized the discrepancy between their work abroad and the discrimination they encountered at home. Steve Allen and *Playboy*'s Hugh Heffner carried enough weight to secure integrated groups on their television shows, but network policies mitigated against the practice. In 1951, for example, television executives replaced Charles Mingus with a white bassist during Red Norvo's appearance on the Mel Tormé show. Bell Telephone representatives kept Ella Fitzgerald's white guitarist out of camera range after the singer refused to drop him for a 1959 appearance. These accommodations typified the kind of customs that provoked Dave Brubeck to cancel a string of concerts at southern colleges in 1960, after the organizers asked him to hire a white bassist to replace Eugene Wright.[93]

For the most part, musicians kept their feelings in check and made ideal envoys. Proud to represent the United States, they viewed their role abroad as part of a gradual process of securing equality in all areas of American life. Yet as *The Real Ambassadors* demonstrated, jazz music's function as a representation of American culture necessitated a delicate compromise. At home, music critics nervously policed the issue of race in the jazz press, rigidly pursuing a line of progressive integration. A moment of indiscretion cost white band leader Stan Kenton dearly in 1956. Snubbed by *Down Beat*'s jazz critics' poll, he dashed off a telegram to the magazine complaining that white musicians had become a new minority group. Leonard Feather, the poll organizer, rebuked Kenton in an open letter that threatened to end the band leader's popular career. On the other hand, Feather took up a bet with African American trumpeter Roy Eldridge, who claimed that he could tell a musician's race from the sound of his horn on an unidentified record. Feather chose some less than typical sides to win the bet, making it clear in numerous reprints of the Blindfold Test that Eldridge "did not even guess the 50% to which the law of averages entitled him."[94]

Dizzy Gillespie's tour, no less than the *Brown* decision of 1954, helped extricate American democracy from the appearance of compromise with racial discrimination. The contrast between the democratic aesthetic of jazz and Russia's barren, state-mandated "propaganda on pirouette" played well in the domestic press. Editors gleefully contrasted Russia's heavy handed involvement with the arts (including sporadic attempts to ban jazz) with the free spirit of America's song.[95] Jazz music's complicity in these international sweepstakes soon precipitated an angry and potentially damaging dialogue within the music industry. For while the Supreme Court and the king of bop helped alleviate suspicion and ridicule abroad, both experienced massive resistance at home to the course of equality they represented. By the early 1960s, when issues of race increasingly divided musicians, critics, and fans, State Department tours and Voice of America programming appeared to many emerging players as dual symbols of their country's hypocrisy. Subsequent controversies over free improvisation provided a platform for challenging aesthetic and ideological investments in "America's art form."

Chapter 2

Free Improvisation Challenges the Jazz Canon

The idea that new venues could help elevate both jazz music's status and its profitability suffered a setback at the 1960 Newport Jazz Festival. Forcibly barred from the packed concert site at Freebody Park, thousands of drunken youths rioted in downtown Newport on Saturday night, launching beer cans, stones, and bottles at police, overturning cars, and smashing windows. Only the arrival of Marines, National Guardsmen, state troopers, and copious amounts of tear gas enabled authorities to disperse the troublemakers, arresting over 200 revelers for disorderly conduct in the process. Reacting angrily to the city's subsequent cancellation of the remaining program, the trade press quickly excused real fans from any responsibility for the disturbances. Post-riot analysis focused on the perceived wider ills of society, from communist agitation to incapable municipal authorities to the hedonistic lifestyles of high school and college age yahoos. Jazz, its defenders insisted, was not to blame.[1]

Yet festival directors cannot escape censure for the explosion that night. For several years they had aggressively lured the largest possible audience to the august beach resort with lengthy and diverse playbills, setting up competing expectations of cultural uplift and holiday indulgence. Moreover, as attendance swelled organizers paid greater attention to marketing beer, programs, and live albums to visitors than to meeting their most basic needs for seats and accommodations. By 1960 the festival had overextended itself. Unable to secure entrance, and facing another uncomfortable night on the beach, in their cars, or at overpriced hotels, thousands of disgruntled youths demonstrated their evolving sense of generational entitlement by tearing up the town.

The bloated Newport program highlighted a contradiction at the center of the board's agenda. Profit maximization hinged upon a form of self-gratifying mass consumption sometimes at odds with the notion of jazz as a modern art, and certainly in conflict with the restrained contemplation that cachet implied. Futhermore the festival's size, the presence of African American headliners, and ongoing State Department tours disguised the rapid contraction of important segments of the jazz economy. Non-jazz or crossover musicians provided the festival's top attractions. In recent years rock 'n' roll pioneer Chuck Berry, singer-dancer Eartha Kitt, and folk group The Kingston Trio had received top billing. In 1960 youths rioted for the privilege of hearing Ray Charles and Horace Silver, both closely associated with the populist soul jazz style. Bassist Charles Mingus gloated that organizers brought the disturbances on themselves "because they confused rock 'n' roll with jazz. They lost their identity with jazz." The festival still presented occasional experimental groups but, as pianist Cecil Taylor found in 1957, it often sidelined them in poorly attended afternoon sessions. Most damaging to Newport's reputation as the guardian of a progressive art form, its pay scale reflected a large disparity between popular attractions and lesser-known jazz musicians. Leading jazz innovators and exponents who lacked widespread recognition often appeared for much less money than their better-known peers and received less favorable billing. A growing number of musicians and critics concluded that commercial imperatives interfered with artistic priorities.[2]

The presence of an alternative festival in Newport that weekend, one that survived the rioting, represented a clear rebuke of the official event's policies. Staged just a few blocks from Freebody Park by musicians themselves, the counter-festival avoided the main event's overt commercialism, scale, and confrontation. The bandstand stood at the end of a long lawn on the grounds of the Cliff Walk Manor Hotel, high above the beach. During quiet interludes the audience could hear waves lapping gently against the shore and gulls crowing overhead; only occasional rain showers sent musicians and listeners scrambling indoors to a large converted dining room. Despite these idyllic surroundings, events at the Cliff Walk Manor Hotel marked a dramatic rupture with the social order. The radicalism of this "rebels" festival stemmed not from the behavior of its fans, up to 600 of whom sipped their soft drinks contentedly, but from the efforts of organizers Charles Mingus and Max Roach to conduct business independently of the music industry's entrepreneurial and promotional framework.[3]

The Cliff Walk Manor participants clearly operated outside the establishment. Elaine Lorillard, who had been dumped from the Newport Jazz Festival board during her divorce from fellow director Louis Lorillard the previous year, secured the necessary permit. Hotel owner Nick Cannarozzi defied the city council's last-minute ban on outdoor amplification, daring the police (at the time engaged in a dispute with Newport authorities) to intervene. They did not. Above all, performers who accepted an invitation from musical director Charles Mingus felt slighted by the main event's devaluation of their labor and their art. With the exception of Ornette Coleman's regular collaborator Charlie Haden and saxophonist Allen Eager (a close friend of sponsor Peggy Hitchcock), African American musicians monopolized the roster. Participants recognized the racial implications of official Newport's wage scale, which rewarded largely white name acts at the expense of largely black innovators. Festival custom, like several Jim Crow hotels in Newport, catered to the assumed predilections of the majority-white crowds that flocked to the town in early July.[4] At Cliff Walk Manor the musicians chose not to rely on anyone's good graces for recognition. They constructed the stage, set up tents to sleep in, distributed handbills, sold tickets, conducted ceremonies, played, and did almost everything else for themselves. Mingus and Roach hoped that assuming collective responsibility would ensure fair treatment, yet the organizers' inclusiveness created its own difficulties.

Charles Mingus demonstrated his ambition by recruiting participants from many musical styles and generations, including swing legends Coleman Hawkins, Roy Eldridge, and Jo Jones, bebop practitioners Max Roach and Kenny Drew, and hard boppers Kenny Dorham, Art Taylor, and Yusef Lateef. The presence of experimental musicians Eric Dolphy, Abbey Lincoln, Mingus, and Ornette Coleman carried special significance for jazz music's future. Since arriving in New York City the previous year, Ornette Coleman's wide open improvisations had placed him at the center of a fierce controversy over the musical implications of freedom. His presence on the same bill as elder statesmen Eldridge, Hawkins, and Jones, and in two extended jam sessions with Roach, Mingus, and Dorham, defied the official festival's rigid periodization of jazz. Yet although critic Whitney Balliett declared Coleman "the champion of the weekend," and marveled at the ability of several older jazzmen to improvise collectively with him, it is less clear that the experience won over Coleman's collaborators. Roy Eldridge dismissed him as a fake. "I listened to him all kinds of ways," Eldridge later told an interviewer. "I listened to him high and I listened to him cold sober. I even played with him. I think he's jiving, baby." The music infuriated Max Roach so much that he assaulted Coleman physically on one occasion and threatened to do so on another.[5] Coleman's appearance at the rebels festival challenged contemporaries to integrate his experimental style into a jazz discourse of modernism increasingly uneasy with the liberation of musical conventions. Even as Coleman played, he stoked the aesthetic controversy raging in the jazz press.

The breadth of styles and depth of talent that crossed the Cliff Walk Manor stage testified to the precarious economics of jazz for all. Ornette Coleman, however, faced the peculiar challenge of selling an unfamiliar, unsettling creative vision to a skeptical music industry largely organized around a residual understanding of jazz as entertainment. Coleman joined the rebels at the last moment, following unsuccessful negotiations over a fee with Newport Jazz Festival musical director George Wein. His presence underscored the disjuncture between a marketplace in which rock 'n' roll exacerbated the declining opportunities for experimental African American musicians and free improvisers' self-conception as artists. Two weeks after appearing at Cliff Walk Manor, as his engagement at New York's Five Spot Café came to an end, Coleman entered the recording studio to lay down the first tracks that would appear on *This Is Our Music.* The title's proprietary artistic claim implied a right to fair compensation, but Coleman found it difficult to reconcile his expectations with the customary practices of an entrenched music business.[6] The Newport counter-festival marked the opening salvo in a decade-long challenge to the aesthetic and ideological assumptions embodied in the jazz industry's commercial practices. As the festival anticipated, the debate increasingly focused on experimental musicians such as Coleman, Cecil Taylor, saxophonist John Coltrane, and a second generation of free improvisers who embodied the contradictions inherent in jazz music's reputation as "America's art form."

Free improvisation raised unsettling questions about the jazz tradition's core musical values, its identification with artistic modernism, and its place in an increasingly unstable cultural hierarchy. The resurgence of jazz in the 1950s illustrated two paradoxical features of American culture during the mid-twentieth century. Certain aspects of jazz music's ascent affirm Lawrence Levine's account of the rising status of opera and Shakespeare in nineteenth-century America, suggesting that remnants of earlier hierarchical values persisted for many years.[7] Like the old world forms, jazz became increasingly esoteric and therefore exclusive with the bebop, cool, and Third Stream styles. In a repeating pattern of custodianship, the subsequent professionalization of criticism facilitated an expanded role for nonperformers as the music's gatekeepers. Europe's enthusiasm for jazz impressed culture brokers in the classical arts and the government, much as European sanction enhanced the sacralization of highbrow forms decades earlier. Finally jazz promoters, while not nearly as successful as some turn-of-the century theater managers, took tentative steps toward pacifying audiences through the upgrade and regulation of performance spaces and venues.

At the same time, jazz music's elevation undermined the very existence of the old ranking criteria, which attributed little worth to nontraditional, nonwhite, new world artifacts. This reading conforms more closely to revisions of Levine, implying that elite attempts to separate highbrow from popular culture have always represented an incomplete, ongoing engagement. The continued popularity of dramatic realism and English-language opera, for example, suggests strong resistance to class and ethnic dominance in the very genres and period upon which Levine based his argument. This endless struggle to win consent for authority provided a defining feature of cultural guardianship throughout the twentieth century. Even as genteel Victorian conventions gave way to the dictates of modernism, left liberal commentators from the 1910s to the 1960s labored to protect high culture from the homogenizing effects of masscult and midcult with increasing frustration.[8]

The explosion of creativity known as modernism complicated efforts by cultural gatekeepers to maintain agreed-upon standards in the arts. The upheaval on both sides of the Atlantic precipitated by mature industrialization, urbanization, immigration, and war undermined Victorians' philosophical commitment to absolute truth, self-control, and the ascendancy of reason over impulse. A new willingness to consider the contingency of values, to acknowledge uncertainty about the world, manifested itself in Albert Einstein's theory of relativity, Sigmund Freud's psychoanalytical method, and the eagerness of painters, sculptors, writers, poets, composers, architects, and photographers to incorporate content and techniques from the world's previously neglected folk cultures. Artists' recourse to primitivism captured just one effort to pursue formal innovation at the expense of tradition, to "make it new," in the words of Ezra Pound.

As creative Europeans and Americans questioned their assumptions about the prerequisites for art, they frequently sacrificed realism for less representational techniques. Revealing the growing influence of Freud, modern artists painted, scored, or wrote about a less objective, rational, or ordered world of human perceptions, impressions, and the subconscious. They conveyed the subject's ambiguity by developing abstract, unpredictable styles. Cubists like Pablo Picasso fractured the picture plane, painting several different perspectives of an object or scene on one canvas to acknowledge the possibility of multiple points of view. Composer Arnold Schoenberg rejected the familiar seven-tone diatonic scale in favor of an expanded chromatic scale that sounded shockingly dissonant to unaccustomed ears. Poets William Butler Yeats, Ezra Pound, T.S. Eliot, and Gertrude Stein wrote in unconventional verse that often lacked rhyme, resolution, and orthodox structure. These artists experimented with form itself; with light and color in painting, atonal sounds in music, allusive language in poetry, and stream of consciousness in fiction. They toyed with the building blocks of their craft, the very structures that helped audiences make sense of it. As a result, critics often accused them of making "art for art's sake," self-referential, inward looking works divorced from the real world.

Many modern painters, writers, and musicians drew upon a history of bohemian rebellion. They no longer wanted to idealize their subject or uplift the audience because they lacked confidence in both the wisdom of old standards and the possibility of progress. A second strand of modernism represented a much more positive attempt to celebrate the new era. When Marcel Duchamp suggested "the only works of art America has given are her plumbing and her bridges," he encouraged native artists to address the modern landscape—particularly the city and the machine—and try to capture its vibrant energy.[9] Sculpture, painting, and photographs by Man Ray, Joseph Stella, and Charles Sheeler championed the industrial ethos. The same might be said of aleatory compositions by Henry Cowell and George Antheil, which incorporated all kinds of mechanical and environmental sounds. Whether utopian or adversarial in their approach to modern life, forward thinking artists expanded the resources of art as they tested stylistic limits.

Modernism's experimentation with the nature of representation made expert evaluation of cultural worth, and maintenance of the hierarchical order, especially problematic. Some critics attempted to authenticate works that revealed unusual conflict and complexity while treating them as autonomous, or removed from what Peter Bürger called "the praxis of life." Celebrated masters included the poets Yeats, Pound, Eliot, and Stein, the impressionist and serial composers, writers as varied as Ernest Hemingway, James Joyce, and Thomas Mann, and the impressionists, cubists, and their followers in painting. In so canonizing high modernism, left-liberal intellectuals received the support of New Critics from the 1930s on. The two groups shared formal leanings, close reading of texts, and a propensity to disconnect art from social experience. But modernism also contained the potential to disrupt these tenuous high/low distinctions, as artists attempting to reintegrate art and life worked to destroy the appearance of organic unity. Bürger defined the "historical avant-garde" by its attack on the institutionalization of art, and its attempt to subvert the audience's distanced contemplation through compelling viewers, readers, or listeners to reconcile the work with their lived experience.[10] Like John Cage, many aleatory composers, beats, abstract expressionists, and San Francisco renaissance poets of the 1950s and 1960s valued creativity "not as self expression but as self alteration." Drawing on classical and vernacular sources, they used techniques such as quotation, collage, and chance to question the very notion of a reified or "auratic" art.[11]

Jazz musicians also struggled throughout much of the twentieth century to win a position of recognition and esteem for their work.

Although jazz shared many attributes of modernism, including the integration of intellect and emotion and an emphasis on continuous reinvention, it never received equal acceptance. Instead, jazz served as the primitivist inspiration for contemporary artists working in established genres.[12] While few musicians before World War II consciously strove to separate art and entertainment in their performances, this implicit disrespect caused many champions of jazz to look toward Eurocentric models of artistic behavior, musical presentation, and theoretical criticism for legitimation. Jazz musicians of the 1940s and 1950s frequently pursued artistic credibility by approximating the historic postures and musical language of modernist symphonic performers. Similarly, leading critics recognized in high modernism's distinction between art and life a means of disconnecting jazz from its persistent identification with subcultural deviance and a rationale for professional standards of writing and analysis that distanced them from prewar hobbyists and enthusiasts. While this new emphasis on the artwork's autonomy threatened to sever the connection between jazz and its roots in African American culture, it conveniently supported the "color-blind" approach to music favored by the liberal jazz establishment and critical to its Cold War ideology. Furthermore, jazz music's modernist identity reinforced its appeal to the State Department, which (despite opposition from conservatives in Congress) cultivated a contrast between American modernism and classical Soviet forms through its touring policies.[13]

By the late 1950s and early 1960s, jazz criticism enjoyed a degree of esteem and influence among music fans and industry figures rarely enjoyed before or since. Uniformly male and almost exclusively white, its practitioners frequently supported their aesthetic judgment with authoritative invocations of supposedly universal criteria. While their commitment to a high modernist discourse varied according to training, inclination, and intended audience, sustained formalist deconstruction of musical texts reached its zenith in the pages of the *Jazz Review*. Founded in 1958, this magazine featured the writing of Martin Williams, Nat Hentoff, and Third Stream pioneer Gunther Schuller, each of whom had read widely in the modernist literary canon and absorbed the methods of New Criticism.[14] Although the *Jazz Review* only appeared until 1961, its writers played a key role in framing the debate over free improvisation and positioning it as an extension of artistic modernism. By drawing comparisons to developments in contemporary symphonic music and painting, however, champions of experimental jazz encouraged its opponents to question free improvisation's relation to the jazz tradition and challenge its place in the music's evolving canon.

Cold War constructions of jazz aesthetics enshrined freedom within the discipline of group constraints such as chords, bar lines, rhythmic meter, and pitch. A number of musicians experimented with the boundaries of these structures to great acclaim. Miles Davis—well established in the business through his bebop, cool, and hard bop work—practiced modal jazz, in which virtually static harmony relied heavily on juxtaposed scales for its progression. Tenor saxophonist Sonny Rollins took the opposite approach, expanding harmonic possibilities by playing several chords simultaneously to expand the number and range of notes he could incorporate into a measure. Composer and bassist Charles Mingus predicted a number of free form characteristics including extended solos, collective group improvisation, and mid-piece tempo changes.[15] Each band leader risked the ire of traditional critics who bemoaned a lack of melodic coherence between thematic statements. Yet by retaining virtuoso techniques, consistently crafted tones, and conventional musical reference points, experimental performers won substantial critical praise and fan approval. Rollins's *Saxophone Colossus* (1956), Davis's *Kind of Blue* (1959), and Mingus's *Mingus Ah Um* (1959) quickly assumed expert and popular status as modernist milestones for extending the practice of freedom in jazz.

Innovation and ability did not guarantee distinction in the jazz community, of course. In addition to their sizable talents, Rollins, Davis, and Mingus had established themselves as able sidemen and leaders in their own right. Before exploring new possibilities, these performers already possessed a public profile among fans, fellow musicians, club owners, record company executives, agents, and critics. They had paid their dues. Experimental musicians who lacked name recognition and heralded uncompromising new techniques faced a doubly difficult task advancing their professional careers. Cecil Taylor's work also suggested a new freedom in jazz, yet he spent much of the 1950s on the margins of the New York jazz scene. Born on March 25, 1929, in Long Island City, Taylor's musical world was shaped by the fragile contours of the black middle class. His mother, a former dancer and actress, taught him manners, enrolled him in piano lessons at age five, and expected him to become a lawyer, doctor, or dentist. His father, a skilled chef, hailed from the rural south and sang folk songs and spirituals around the house. From an early age Taylor felt the tension between his father's parochial past and his mother's bourgeois aspirations. The music he heard at home and at the jazz shows he attended from an early age became a way of holding onto black culture while living in a predominantly white suburb of Queens, New York. Perhaps it is not surprising that his musical idol, Duke Ellington, came from a similar class background and sought to combine the best European and African American traditions. Taylor often claimed that he attended the New England Conservatory of Music—one of the finest music academies in the country—after reading Ellington's opinion that future generations of jazz musicians would need such training. In Boston he assimilated the work of Igor Stravinsky, Bela Bartók, and later Arnold Schoenberg and Anton Webern, while outside the classroom he absorbed a wide variety of contemporary jazz pianists including Horace Silver, Lennie Tristano, Thelonious Monk, and Dave Brubeck.[16]

Taylor graduated from the New England Conservatory in 1953 and returned to New York, living at home and picking up gigs when he could. He attempted a jazz apprenticeship as a sideman with experienced musicians, playing engagements with Hot Lips Page and, most gratifyingly, former Ellington stars Johnny Hodges and Lawrence Brown. Taylor's evolving conception fit poorly with the traditional role of piano accompanist, however, and the jobs never lasted long. The first recording to appear under his name, *Jazz Advance* (1956), suggests both the originality and the challenge of his style, for Taylor adopted a similar approach to both lead and supporting roles. Recorded for Boston's Transition label by owner Tom Wilson, who produced four of the pianist's first six albums for various companies, *Jazz Advance* featured relatively untried musicians Buell Neidlinger (bass), Dennis Charles (drums), and Steve Lacy (soprano saxophone). Their inexperience proved both a necessity—few established musicians would play with Taylor by now—and an asset, for it enabled him to shape their understanding of time. Taylor played initially within a steady rhythmic framework provided by the bass and drums, yet his phrasing and incorporation of rests often defied the metronomic pulse and regular bar lines. His forceful attack at the keyboard, wide and sudden leaps between intervals, shifting dynamics, and unexpected accents created ebbs and surges of energy that frequently overwhelmed the stated meter and any competing instrumentalist. His solo rendition of "You'd Be So Nice to Come Home To" and the polyphonic piano-saxophone opening to "Song" constitute early attempts to liberate the music from a sounded beat and to disrupt the conventional relationship between improviser and accompanist.[17]

Taylor's eclectic melodic design reinforced his control of a tune's rhythmic momentum. The quick succession of fleeting arpeggios, block chord sequences, single-note linear solos, and scattered tone clusters further subdivided the beat and upset the expectations created by Neidlinger and Charles. Taylor's often staccato delivery produced a jagged, percussive intensity reminiscent of Thelonious Monk and subject to the same critical sniping that it did not swing. Monk's heritage clearly extended back to formative associations with Charlie Parker and Dizzy Gillespie, however. Taylor's sound values drew attention to his conservatory background. His increasingly radical alterations to tone-centered chords and melodies paralleled the development of classical music up to the mid-twentieth century. "It began on a very small basis," Taylor remarked about his harmonic sense. "At the time it began it was based on one single scale which soon became many scales, scales made up of different intervallic constructions, then chords, then diads, and then just combinations of tones, and then just intervals spaced differently, not scales at all, just groups of notes." Although Taylor believed that critics overemphasized the importance of his relationship to tonality, it underlined his connections to the Euro-American concert tradition.[18]

Jazz Advance created a small stir upon its release, helping secure Cecil Taylor's reputation as an adventurous and perhaps prescient performer. The *New Yorker*'s jazz critic, Whitney Balliett, predicted that "it could have the same revolutionary impact on modern jazz as the recordings of Charlie Parker," although he hedged his bets with the caveat that "it could go the ineffectual way of the peculiarly defiant big-brass-band works of Stan Kenton." Martin Williams displayed similar hopeful enthusiasm, suggesting "his way may well become *the* way of the future." Following its release, Taylor secured a six-week engagement at the Five Spot beginning in late 1956, which effectively put the club on the map as a home for inventive modern jazz, and an appearance at the 1957 Newport Jazz Festival. Then, almost as soon as the acclaim had begun, it stopped. Bill Coss estimated that Taylor performed for a total of thirty weeks over the next four years, working between gigs as a deliveryman, record salesman, dishwasher, and cook. Taylor reportedly told Nat Hentoff, whom he knew from their student days in Boston, that musical jobs were so scarce he held imaginary concerts in his room in order to sustain the memory of performing before a live audience. Taylor, it seems, had become almost unbookable.[19]

Taylor's press clippings from the late 1950s help account for the slowdown in offers. They describe him repeatedly as "difficult," "angry," "upsetting," and "demanding," adjectives invoked to unite his music and his personality. Taylor emerges from these reviews and interviews as a principled—if highly strung—artist, an image reinforced by his unwillingness to compromise with nightclub owners who demanded that he shorten his sets so they could turn over patrons and sell drinks or play their pianos less violently (he was notorious for damaging keys by striking them hard). He offended musicians as easily as promoters. Peers who had once just walked off the stage when he showed up for a jam session now attacked him in print. "This is just a whole lot of noise," commented singer Billy Eckstine about one recording. "It sounds like somebody trying either to tune a piano—or to chop it up." Taylor fit poorly the musical expectations and commercial exigencies of the jazz industry.[20]

While his music undoubtedly challenged listeners, as critics continually noted, Cecil Taylor resisted critical attempts to interpret his style for a broader audience and thus kept a distance from some potential supporters. As early as 1957, Harold Keith of the *Pittsburgh Courier* aligned his music with efforts by Jimmy Giuffre and the Modern Jazz Quartet (MJQ) to elevate jazz to the status of a classical American art. In his next published interview Taylor bristled at the comparison, chastising Giuffre and the MJQ for abandoning the rhythmic tension at the heart of black music. In January 1959 Gunther Schuller published the first extended analysis of Taylor's music in the *Jazz Review*, a sympathetic appraisal that stressed the similarities between his approach to tonality and the work of several twentieth-century classical composers. Schuller angered Taylor by characterizing the pianist's output as more intellectual than felt, more significant for its technical form than its emotional content. In these assessments, Taylor read a coded racial interpretation of his music. Although Schuller and Keith praised Taylor's recordings, the discussion of his work in the context of theoretical developments in western art music distanced it from the African American cultural heritage and negated Taylor's efforts to incorporate a wide variety of influences into new forms. Rejecting overtures from Third Stream promoters, and largely ignored by mainstream jazz musicians, Taylor remained an idiosyncrasy for many years, unconnected to any larger stylistic movements in jazz.[21]

Developments in Cecil Taylor's music during the early 1960s only encouraged comparisons to the modernist tradition in Euro-American concert music and broader avant-garde trends in the arts. Up until the release of *Looking Ahead!* (1959), Taylor generally recorded music based on chord changes and explicitly stated rhythms, although his live performances were considerably more adventurous. By the time of *New York City R&B* (1961), he was increasingly applying Ellington's conception of the piano as a color instrument to the entire rhythm section. On "Cindy's Main Mood," for example, he freed the bass and drums from their timekeeping function, allowing each to interact spontaneously with the playing of others and paving the way for a return to collective improvisation. Taylor's use of extended form mirrored Ellington's work since the 1930s, his complicated chord alterations echoed George Russell's compositions of the 1950s, and his free form experiments found precedent in some notorious Lennie Tristano sides from 1949. Yet his growing commitment to "the organization of sound" drew comparisons not with the jazz heritage but with the most adventurous music of the concert stage.[22]

During the early twentieth century, composers who chafed at the limitations of traditional musical resources expanded freedom in a number

Figure 5. Cecil Taylor at the piano circa 1961. Courtesy Michael Ochs
Archives.com.

of ways. One approach stressed greater prescribed complexity. The
extension of diatonic chords and scales in the work of Claude Debussy,
Maurice Ravel, and Igor Stravinsky gave way to the atonal experiments
of Arnold Schoenberg and Anton Webern. In an attempt to impose
order on the limitless atonal possibilities, Schoenberg eventually devised
a twelve-tone chromatic scale, while Webern formalized a method of
composition known as serialism that organized some or all of these
notes into fixed tone rows. Soon Pierre Boulez and others applied serial
techniques to musical values such as rhythm, timbre, and dynamics.[23]

Although tonality survived in the work of romanticists, minimalists,
and even many serialists, some American composers reacted against the
rigidity of contemporary concert music by incorporating random compositional techniques and nonfunctional resonant objects. Henry Cowell, Lou Harrison, and John Cage often emphasized percussion rather
than harmony, and utilized home made or modified instruments, found
objects, and nonelite (often nonwestern) musical ideas.[24] Cecil Taylor's
speed, precision, and overall virtuosity suggested an affinity for complex
technical experimentation at the beginning of his career, a perception
reinforced by his radical use of dissonance. Critics frequently described
his work from the 1950s as atonal and drew comparisons to those

impressionist and serial composers most strongly associated with the extension and eventual abandonment of tonality: Debussy, Bartók, Stravinsky, and Schoenberg. Yet by the early 1960s his application of collective improvisation, use of tone clusters played with the palms, elbows, and forearms, and manipulation of piano strings with bedsprings and steel mesh cloth conjured up a tradition of maverick composers stretching back to Edgard Varèse and Charles Ives. While Taylor particularly admired John Cage's openness to nontonal sounds and nonscripted performance, free improvisation represented a fundamentally different approach to music-making. Jazz elevated the performer's importance at the center of an improvised creative act. Random aleatory music deemphasized the artist and privileged chance and ambient noise. Nevertheless, Taylor's open admiration for modern dance, willingness to combine jazz performance with poetry, and musical contribution to Jack Gelber's experimental play *The Connection* in 1960 solidified his reputation as an avant-garde modernist and enhanced his alienation from most major players on the east coast.[25]

Ornette Coleman experienced a similar isolation during much of the 1950s, and might have remained in obscurity but for the publicity momentum preceding his New York City debut in 1959. Coleman's emergence crystallized the debate over free improvisation's place in the jazz canon and, like Taylor, the saxophonist witnessed supporters and detractors comparing his music with other modern art forms. Born on March 19, 1930, in Fort Worth, Texas, he grew up surrounded by music at church, school, and sung around the home by his parents and three siblings. Although his father died when he was seven and his mother could not afford to give him lessons, Coleman saved enough money doing odd jobs to buy an alto saxophone at age fifteen. After teaching himself the basics, Coleman quickly progressed through church and high school bands to professional appearances with local rhythm and blues and bebop groups. With so many men in the service or only recently returned, Coleman secured plenty of gigs despite his relative youth and inexperience. His family welcomed the extra income, yet Coleman's approach did not always suit the roadhouses and jook joints where he performed. Early acquaintances remembered that he developed a unique melodic style during those formative years, perhaps owing to an initial misunderstanding of musical theory. Coleman's search for a human or vocalized quality in his playing led him away from pitch centers determined by the chord sequence. Trumpeter Bobby Bradford, who performed with Coleman in the late 1940s and early 1950s, recalled that bebop musicians "would use the device of playing half a step above the key for one phrase, just to add piquancy, but Ornette would go out and stay there—he wouldn't come back after one

phrase, and this would test the listener's capacity for accepting dissonance." Coleman reversed one of the accepted musical practices in
modern jazz, that the chord sequence—increasingly complicated since
bebop—determined the parameters of musical exploration. Contemporary musicians such as Sonny Rollins and John Coltrane stacked chords
to increase the range and proximity of available notes. Ornette Coleman
believed that a spontaneously developing line should determine the harmonic progression. "If I am just going to use the changes themselves,"
he told the *Jazz Review*'s co-editor, Martin Williams, "I might as well write
out what I am going to play."[26]

Coleman's pioneering methods required sympathetic conspirators to
extend his principles to all instruments in the group. Attempting to
leave Fort Worth with traveling shows, he was fired, stranded, and even
beaten up for playing in such an unusual manner. Eventually settling
in Los Angeles in 1953, Coleman gradually attracted a small clique of
interested musicians, including trumpeter Don Cherry, drummers Ed
Blackwell and Billy Higgins, and multi-instrumentalist Eric Dolphy. Like
Taylor in New York, however, he faced scorn and rejection from most
members of the jazz community. His rare public appearances in traditional jazz venues met with little success. Pianist Paul Bley recounted a
long-running engagement in Los Angles that ended soon after he hired
Coleman and Cherry. "When you were driving down Washington Boule-
vard and you looked at the Hillcrest Club you always knew whether the
band was on the bandstand or not. If the street was full of audience in
front of the club, the band was playing . . . and as soon as the band
stopped they would all come back in."[27]

Unable to perform regularly, Coleman's song writing ability earned
him a much-needed break. A fellow musician recommended his compositions to Les Koenig, the owner of Contemporary records, who offered
Coleman the chance to record an album of original tunes. *Something
Else!* and its follow-up *Tomorrow Is the Question!* secured Coleman's first
national recognition and high-profile backers. *Down Beat* contributors
Nat Hentoff and John Tynan voted him "Alto Sax New Star" in the magazine's 1958 critics' poll, with Tynan contributing the first of several sensational reviews. John Lewis of the Modern Jazz Quartet engineered a
series of events to bring the saxophonist greater exposure. In 1958 he
arranged for Coleman to switch labels from Contemporary to Atlantic,
ensuring better record distribution. The following summer, Lewis
secured scholarships for Coleman and Cherry at the Lenox School of
Jazz and a place on the Monterey Jazz Festival program. After recording
a pair of albums for Atlantic on the west coast, the Ornette Coleman
Quartet accepted a two-week engagement at New York City's Five Spot
Café.[28]

The quartet's New York debut aroused a critical furor reminiscent of the days of bebop. George Hoefer's report for *Down Beat* captured the confusion and division apparent at the group's press preview:

Some walked in and out before they could finish a drink, some sat mesmerized by the sound, others talked constantly to their neighbors at the table or argued with drink in hand at the bar. It was for all this the largest collection of VIP's in the jazz world seen in many a year. . . .

This special preview for the press arranged by the Five Spot brought forth real mixed-up comments: "He'll change the entire course of jazz." "He's a fake." "He's a genius." "I can't say, I'll have to hear him a lot more times." "He has no form." "He swings like HELL." "I'm going home and listen to my Benny Goodman trios and quartets." "He's out—real far-out." "I like him but I don't have any idea what he is doing."[29]

New York had dominated jazz recording, performance, business, and publishing activities since the late 1920s. Coleman's rapid rise to prominence ensured that the city's jazz and arts community keenly anticipated his arrival. Indeed, Coleman's supporters anointed him the jazz tradition's heir apparent even before he reached the east coast. "I believe that what Ornette Coleman is playing will affect the character of jazz music profoundly and pervasively," wrote Martin Williams in his liner notes for the first Atlantic release, boldly titled *The Shape of Jazz to Come.* "I feel he's an extension of Charlie Parker," John Lewis acknowledged, "but I mean a *real* extension. He doesn't copy Parker's licks or style. He's something more, deeper than that." Frequently reproduced in the jazz press, this comparison to jazz music's last paradigm-changing figure— from a musician who had played with Parker—could hardly have failed to stir interest and discord among fans. In the months following the quartet's initial Five Spot appearance, the critical divisions over Coleman's playing and its implications for the jazz canon became increasingly clear.[30]

Coleman's most committed supporters embraced the discourses of modernism in the arts. Typified by Martin Williams, they viewed jazz as an internally consistent, self-contained art form. Modernist critics disconnected jazz from its social context and investigated the music's technical merits with the respected tools of academic analysis. Exposed to the New Criticism while a graduate student in English at Columbia University, Williams transposed its formalist reading of texts to jazz writing. As Robert Walser has pointed out, this legitimating strategy cast personal opinion in the guise of objective truth. It held a piece of music accountable to two subjective standards: how well it realized the composer's vision by resolving formal tensions and maintaining structural coherence, and how successfully it incorporated certain canonical aesthetic values.[31] New musical approaches had to meet these criteria in order to

Figure 6. Ornette Coleman holding his plastic alto saxophone, a controversial symbol of modernity, 1959. Photograph by William Claxton. Courtesy Michael Ochs Archives.com.

affirm a linear tradition, the notion that as a progressive art form jazz evolved according to the dictates of enduring principles. True to his belief in jazz as an autonomous and organic art, Williams emphasized the inevitability of Coleman's innovations. He quickly realized that playing "outside" allowed for a greater variety of phrasing and elevated the drummer from accompanist to equal soloist. By hailing Coleman as the next jazz genius, Williams reinforced his claim for rhythm as the definitive jazz trait. He bound Coleman to a pantheon of innovators in that area, including Louis Armstrong, Lester Young, and Charlie Parker.[32]

Coleman capitalized upon his acclaim as the inheritor of jazz music's legacy. His album titles predicted the *Change of the Century* and announced that *Tomorrow Is the Question!* The press release for an April 1960 concert claimed that the Quartet "have come to be recognized as perhaps the most advanced jazz modernists of our day," hinting at a paradox running through the critical response. Like Williams, the *New Yorker*'s jazz columnist Whitney Balliett acknowledged that Coleman held both an intellectual and a deeply emotional appeal. Although Balliett avoided close analysis in favor of a more descriptive prose style, he identified the modernist duality at the center of free improvisation by contrasting Coleman's "primeval" effects with his "aural puzzles." Remembering Coleman's emergence several years later, Balliett concluded that "like the best revolutionaries, he was a highbrow disguised as a primitive."[33]

Balliett's writing emphasized the importance of Coleman's "highbrow" technical achievements, which—like contemporary symphonic music—exploded the ambivalent tension between accessible and respectable musical devices. Anticipating many other critics, he recognized parallels between the advances of Ornette Coleman and Cecil Taylor, coining the term "abstract jazz" to unite their music. The term reinforced comparisons between developments in jazz and better-established art forms, as did Coleman's involvement with the classical composer and Third Stream pioneer Gunther Schuller. Coleman took music lessons from Schuller during 1960, and performed and recorded several of his tutor's works. These collaborations included "Abstraction" for alto and strings, a piece Schuller intended to underline the similarities between Coleman's "outside" playing and serial composition.[34] Whereas Taylor resisted close identification with the classical tradition, Coleman possibly saw it as a legitimation of his unusual technique. Syndicated columnist Ralph Gleason and other critics grouped Coleman, Taylor, and several emerging free improvisers under the heading "avant-garde." Although the description did not gain widespread currency for several years, it suggested a connection between free jazz and a formal western heritage. Significantly, however, neither Gleason nor his colleagues used the term as Peter Bürger has defined it, signifying an attempt to challenge the autonomy of art and reevaluate its social role. Instead, jazz writers employed "avant-garde" during the early 1960s much as Clement Greenberg did, to connote growing experimentation with and skepticism toward representation—a cutting edge extension of modernism.[35]

Attempting to place free improvisation in the context of other modernist arts, critics frequently drew connections with abstract expressionism. Artists in this movement shared a geographical location (they were often referred to as the New York School), a group of dealers and patrons, and a sense of scale apparent in their mural-sized canvases. The formal properties of their work tended to demystify representation by exposing evidence of the production method, such as visible brushwork, scrapings, and running paint. Their "allover" compositional style often lacked a central object or finished figure, allowing unconventional materials, a limited palette, and a high level of abstraction to redirect the viewer's focus from subject to process and enhance the work's ambiguous spatial perspective. Yet considerable technical and stylistic diversity separated Jackson Pollock's drip paintings from Willem de Kooning's liquid cubism or the color field paintings of Mark Rothko, Barnett Newman, and Clyfford Still. In Cold War America of the 1950s, critics such as Greenberg framed abstract expressionism also as a disengagement from the reformist New Deal agenda of American scene painting, a retreat into the psyche. Several artists explicitly embraced Jung's notion of the collective unconscious, and Jackson Pollock in particular saw his work as a means of uncovering and representing universal feelings and associations. Pollock assumes special significance as the public face of abstract expressionism. After his death in 1956, he served as the lens through which Americans slowly came to understand the movement. Pollock developed the technique of gestural painting in an attempt to free his primordial, instinctual forces. Laying a canvas on the floor so that he could walk around or across it, he dripped, splattered, poured, or flung paint in fluid, rhythmic motions. Art critic Harold Rosenberg interpreted this spontaneous act as a primary means of transcending the artist's sense of existential alienation from the surrounding world.[36]

The first generation of abstract expressionists produced mature works in the late 1940s, and the growing controversy over free improvisation ten years later coincided with their embrace by the art establishment. Ornette Coleman, who made friends with several progressive artists in New York, encouraged comparisons between his music's motivic development and organizational strategies in the visual arts. "There's a continuity of expression, certain continually evolving strands of thought that link all my compositions together," he wrote in the liner notes to *Change of the Century*. "Maybe it's something like the paintings of Jackson Pollock." The mainstream media quickly adopted this allusion to situate Coleman in a wider experimental tradition. *Time* reported that his music "at best . . . evoked an abstract expressionist painting whose dots, slashes, and blobs are miraculously knitted into a pattern." The jazz press also employed the language of avant-garde art. Martin Williams and Bill

Coss categorized Coleman's work as "non-objective," while T. E. Martin and Don Heckman (echoing Rosenberg) proposed the term "action jazz." Heckman, a composer and band leader, commented extensively and favorably on Coleman during the 1960s for *Down Beat* and *Saturday Review*. Adopting the close analysis favored by Williams, he compared the techniques as well as the effects of leading artists and free jazz musicians. "Like action painting, it is the very *act* of improvisation that becomes significant," he wrote. An anonymous *Newsweek* critic agreed. "Like their contemporaries in painting, theater, films and poetry, their art has become nothing but itself—pure sound, spontaneously created under the pressure of feeling and thought."[37]

Some of Coleman's supporters preferred to realign free improvisation more squarely with the African American musical tradition. They pointed to collective creation, vocalized inflection, and blues tonality as a reassertion of neglected formal elements of the jazz past. Suspicious of attempts to improve jazz according to academic European standards, Nat Hentoff affirmed the Dionysian spirit of the modernist paradox. "Far from being esoteric or abstract," he stressed, "Ornette's story (as a player, a writer, and a person) is as basically rawly emotional as anyone's in jazz, and more than most." In a review of *Free Jazz*, the apotheosis of free improvisation, he wrote that Coleman "plays with impregnable, blues-based sureness of direction and his customary raw passion." Well known outside jazz circles as a champion of civil rights, Hentoff later linked black music and social conditions explicitly. At the beginning of the 1960s, however, his writing still betrayed the modernist divorce between art and life. If *Free Jazz* indicated anything, it showed "that the development of jazz as a non-functional art in itself is irreversible."[38]

Coleman's champions praised his music's appeal to the mind and the heart, but his opponents saw a reflection of everything they disliked about the contemporary arts. The comparison with action painting cut both ways. "He seems to hurl his notes indiscriminately at the canvas" wrote one reviewer. In England, the *Daily Telegraph*'s Philip Larkin likened *Free Jazz* to the Jackson Pollock reproduction on its sleeve. He described the music, like the cover, as "a patternless reiterated jumble."[39] Larkin was an oddity, a traditionalist critic writing fifteen years after the arrival of bebop who regretted its transformation of jazz from entertainment to serious music. Most free jazz antagonists embraced bebop as the quintessential modern form. Leonard Feather, perhaps Coleman's most widely read detractor, had vociferously championed Dizzy Gillespie and Charlie Parker since the mid-1940s.

Bebop offered harmonic and rhythmic freedom within the discipline of stated chords and measures. Feather and other hostile critics feared anarchy in free improvisation's lack of constraints. Assessing *This Is Our*

Music for *HiFi/Stereo Review,* Peter Welding identified some common complaints:

No one can deny the emotional intensity of Ornette Coleman's music, but that is all there seems to be here—no logic, no order, no coherence, no discipline, no imagination, no taste. Why go on? Coleman has been proclaimed a bold new pioneer, a restless explorer of new areas, a dauntless iconoclast, and so on, but his music strikes me as so much belligerent and adolescent nose-thumbing—a sort of musical Bronx cheer. . . . I just can't take this pointless stuff seriously.[40]

By conceding the "emotional intensity" of Coleman's work, and contrasting it to the lack of "order" and "discipline," Welding conjured up images of the untutored primitive from jazz criticism's past, and mirrored the emphasis on instinctual process prevalent in assessments of the New York School. Unlike past evocations of the natural jazz musician, however, opponents of free improvisation openly doubted Coleman's command of musical fundamentals. In a review of the same album, *Down Beat* editor Don DeMicheal berated the "sloppy execution" and "technical abominations" of the group's performance. DeMicheal regretted the lack of conventional tone, dynamics, and swing, characteristics that led many critics to label Coleman a charlatan. In a terse rebuke of an earlier Coleman release, *Army Times* writer Tom Scanlon again suggested similarities with modern painting. Coleman's disdain for the basic structures recalled the creed of some beginning artists, he thought. Neither wanted to waste time learning their craft when they could express themselves immediately.[41]

Some detractors reasoned that Coleman deserved to share responsibility for the exaggerated publicity. Welding's review attributed his reputation as "a bold new pioneer" and "a dauntless iconoclast" to critical excess. By contrast, he presumed to speak for the ordinary fans who "can't take this pointless stuff seriously." The article implied that Coleman and his supporters held these fans and the broader jazz tradition in contempt with their derisive "adolescent nose-thumbing." Coleman's treatment by hostile factions in the jazz press mirrors a discourse linking elite taste-making and the success of abstract expressionism in popular magazine articles such as "Baffling U.S. Art" from a 1959 issue of *Life.* In it, arts correspondent Dorothy Seiberling emphasized the distance between cultural gatekeepers such as James R. Rorimer, head of the Metropolitan Museum of Art and a collector of Pollock's work, and a public bewildered and irritated by a style that few understood or embraced. That same year, observers cast Coleman as the victim of unscrupulous promoters who attempted to boost their credentials by predicting the next jazz fashion. Most of the blame fell on Martin Williams and Nat Hentoff, whom pianist/educator John Mehegan characterized as "a small group of kingmakers" and Scanlon dismissed as "the hippie branch of jazz criticism." Composer and former jazz pianist André Previn attributed their motives to fear rather than ambition. Previn held that Coleman's supporters had initially underrated Parker and Gillespie and dreaded making the same mistake again. These accusations of critical self-interest, which Feather repeated as late as 1965, only added to the dispute's acrimony.[42]

Coleman's followers personalized the disagreement too, insisting that reactionary critics and musicians had an economic stake in preserving the status quo. Those musicians who initially welcomed Coleman's advances, such as John Lewis, Gunther Schuller, and George Russell, typically already possessed an interest in applying the technical resources of western music to jazz. Most players in the bebop-derived mainstream responded with confusion or cool dismissal, and Coleman's opponents eagerly provided them with a forum. Leonard Feather's "Blindfold Test" feature in *Down Beat* invited musicians to guess the instrumentalists on unidentified records. By inserting Coleman or Taylor tunes into the rotation, Feather gained numerous opportunities to quote hostile reactions to free improvisation. "It sounds like utter confusion and madness," exclaimed traditionalist Ruby Braff after listening to Coleman's "Mind and Time." "I have never heard anything so disjointed and mixed-up and crazy as that in my life." Most participants complained that Coleman played out of tune, and mocked his purported freedom. "If that's liberty, boy, they're making an ass out of Abraham Lincoln," responded Quincy Jones sarcastically.[43]

Not surprisingly, Coleman's detractors became alarmed when his innovations began to influence a number of established musicians. None proved as controversial as John Coltrane, whose professional credentials and growing reputation made it much more difficult for critics to marginalize his music. Born on September 23, 1926, in Hamlet, North Carolina, and raised in the adjacent town of High Point, Coltrane came from a well-respected family in which religion and music proved formative influences. Both his parents were children of African Methodist Episcopal Zion ministers, and from the early 1930s they lived with Coltrane's maternal grandparents, and an aunt, uncle, and cousin, in the black professional district of segregated High Point. Coltrane's father, a tailor, played violin and ukulele, while his mother, a homemaker, sang and played piano in church. Coltrane did not take music seriously, however, until a devastating series of deaths in the family claimed his father, grandfather, and grandmother when he was twelve, and his uncle the following year. Music appears to have played some sort of compensatory function in the absence of a strong male presence and in the face of his family's declining economic circumstances, for he joined a community brass band and almost immediately developed a reputation for obsessive practicing that lasted throughout his career. Influenced by Ellington sideman Johnny Hodges, Coltrane switched from clarinet to alto saxophone in the William Penn High School band, and upon graduation in 1943 at age sixteen he determined to try a career in music.[44]

Coltrane recognized that opportunity lay in the urban north and followed an established migration path to Philadelphia. He enrolled in the Ornstein School of Music, began playing popular music professionally in local bars and lounges, and had just encountered bebop when the military drafted him, in 1945, to spend a year in a naval band stationed in Hawaii. Back in Philadelphia in 1946, Coltrane continued his musical education formally at the Granoff Studios, where he studied saxophone and theory intensively for several years, and informally by assimilating Charlie Parker's advances. Coltrane was no protégé. His musical apprenticeship lasted the next nine years, the first three primarily in show bands and rhythm and blues combos led by Joe Webb, King Kolax, Eddie "Cleanhead" Vinson, and others, the remaining time dominated by jazz performances. Coltrane's switch to tenor saxophone preceded an invitation to join Dizzy Gillespie's big band in 1949, but tours with Gillespie, Earl Bostic, and his boyhood idol Johnny Hodges afforded few openings to demonstrate the breadth of his improvisational ability. Coltrane emerged as a featured soloist and mature stylist in two extended stays with Miles Davis between 1956 and 1960, interrupted by a fruitful collaboration with Thelonious Monk in 1957. Although his playing sounded a little tentative and unsure on the first Prestige recording with Davis, he quickly integrated his rapid arpeggiated lines into this pioneering hard bop group. Rejoining Davis in 1958, he demonstrated great dexterity adjusting to a compositional style (evident on the seminal 1959 album *Kind of Blue*) that employed extended scale-based improvisation against minimal chord changes. By that time he was recording as a leader in his own right and achieving recognition by critics and fans as an original jazz voice.[45]

Working for Dizzy Gillespie, Johnny Hodges, Miles Davis, and Thelonious Monk during the 1950s, Coltrane had clearly earned his reputation as a sideman and demonstrated a commanding technique. Although he was sometimes criticized for his hard tone and running of scales, the critical darts thrown at Coleman and Taylor—alleging charlatanism and artificial promotion—did not stick. By the time he formed his own band in April 1960, Coltrane had mastered the vertical and horizontal approaches to harmonic improvisation and grown excited by Coleman's advances. The two saxophonists often discussed music during the early 1960s and Coltrane even recorded with Coleman's group, although

Atlantic did not release the results until several years after the 1960 sessions took place.[46]

Coleman's influence manifested itself when Coltrane brought sympathetic and flexible musicians into his band, especially pianist McCoy Tyner and drummer Elvin Jones. Tyner created an enigmatic sound palette by voicing chords in fourths rather than familiar triads, while his recurrent left-handed pedal point extended a practice Coltrane had used in the late 1950s and served to blur the implied pitch center. Tyner's willingness to drop out during solos allowed Coltrane to leave the chords and play in a different key for several measures, approximating the dissonance of Coleman's group. Like Coleman, Coltrane employed an array of highly distorted tonal mannerisms such as shrieks, growls, and other noise elements in the high and low registers to increase the dramatic and emotional tension. Jones's interest in polyrhythms, implying a basic pulse and adding shifting, complex rhythms on top, allowed him to anticipate and respond to Coltrane's saxophone phrasing, nurturing the seeds of a collective approach to improvisation.[47]

As much as Coltrane and Coleman employed analogous devices, they composed and played very differently. Coltrane sounded more forcefully insistent and remained closer to the chords, at least until 1965. Above all, they developed melodic ideas in contrasting ways. Even Coleman's detractors frequently admired his writing, especially the attractive themes he elaborated and rephrased until they metamorphisized into fresh new motifs. Coltrane rarely won praise for his compositions. Critics frequently complained that his solos sounded like academic exercises, probably because—as Lewis Porter has demonstrated—Coltrane's highly original organization derived from method books, scales, and practice techniques. His incantatory style, frequently rooted to an explicit modal drone, developed creative tension through cycles of thematic deconstruction and exploration. Porter has characterized Coltrane as a preacher on the saxophone, beginning with short fourth-based figures and engaging them at length. Repeating, elaborating, and restating these ideas, Coltrane moved to different tonal centers and higher notes until he reached an emotional climax.[48]

These differing musical approaches ensured that supporters of one innovator did not necessarily embrace the other. Martin Williams and Whitney Balliett, two of Coleman's foremost champions, remained unreconciled to most of Coltrane's work from the early 1960s. Peter Welding and Ralph Gleason found a passion, purpose, and energy in Coltrane's improvisations lacking in Coleman's initial recordings.[49] Yet many commentators in the jazz community identified certain similarities in the playing of Coltrane, Coleman, Cecil Taylor, and several other emerging innovators. Sympathetic observers appreciated their willing-

Figure 7. John Coltrane performing at The Jazz Workshop, Boston, 1963.
Photograph by Lee Tanner/The Jazz Image.

ness to reevaluate the music's formal boundaries. Others felt that Coltrane, like his predecessors, lacked conventional discipline.

The row over Coltrane's changing direction reached fever pitch when Eric Dolphy, who had recently left Charles Mingus's experimental band, joined the group in 1961. Dolphy's unbridled dissonance and unpredictable leaps and turns encouraged Coltrane's own free exploration, to the exasperation of several prominent critics. John S. Wilson of the *New York Times* and Leonard Feather found Coltrane's solos—which frequently lasted half an hour or longer—indulgent, monotonous, and in need of editing. His tone proved too harsh, bordering on ugly for many listeners. André Previn and John Tynan searched in vain for logical, sequential development or a recognizable tune in some of Coltrane's improvisations.[50] The controversy's flash-point occurred on November 23, 1961, when Tynan in a *Down Beat* column denounced a recent performance by Coltrane's group with Dolphy as "anti-jazz." He made familiar accusations: the band did not swing, employed too much dissonance, and lacked formal cohesion. The article reached a new level of vitriol, however, with Tynan's tirade against the "nihilistic exercises of the two horns," their melodic and harmonic "gobbledegook," and other "musical nonsense currently being peddled in the name of jazz." The review sharply and evenly divided readers. Fred Thies of Madison, Wisconsin, congratulated Tynan for taking a stand on behalf of the average fan, while Jack Howell of Canton, New York, defended Coltrane's commitment to innovation.[51]

Tynan's column betrayed his growing doubts about the course of modern jazz. Two months later, he described the musicians on Ornette Coleman's *Free Jazz* as nihilists, too, despite his acknowledged role as Coleman's first critical champion. Ira Gitler, who coined the term "sheets of sound" to praise John Coltrane's work in the late 1950s, wrote scathingly about *Live at the Village Vanguard* with Eric Dolphy.[52] If these critics saw what others missed—that the aesthetic of free improvisation made traditional standards of intonation, for example, irrelevant—they came to view the concept as ultimately bankrupt and unrewarding nevertheless. Coleman, Coltrane, and Taylor had promised to extend jazz music's continuous innovation in the direction of greater freedom, but the results proved jarring and uncomfortable to many. By attacking "a growing anti-jazz trend," Tynan underlined the tendency for critics of all persuasions to categorize several very different pioneers together. Leonard Feather reinforced the connection in the early months of 1962 when he adopted Tynan's term and repeatedly linked it to Coleman and Taylor as well as Coltrane.[53] Neither anti-jazz nor other critical nomenclature such as abstract jazz, atonal jazz, or space music gained widespread acceptance in the industry. Appropriately for such a divisive and heterogeneous art, the most popular term for freely improvised jazz among musicians, "the new thing," was both neutral and ambiguous.

The notoriety of some performers made free improvisation the most hotly debated style at the close of jazz music's mid-century resurgence. By 1962 John Coltrane, Ornette Coleman, and to a lesser extent Cecil Taylor enjoyed a rare degree of celebrity in the jazz community and beyond. Several prominent musicians from the mainstream, including Sonny Rollins and Jackie McLean, adopted Coleman's mannerisms to enhance their own techniques. A reflection of John Coltrane's hard, aggressive tone showed up in some unlikely places, including the playing of cool school veterans Art Pepper and Stan Getz.[54] Even Taylor inspired a small but fiercely committed following. Yet high profile publicity masked a decisive shift in the make-up of audiences for "outside" music. British historian and jazz critic Eric Hobsbawm voiced his concern about the gap between Coleman's acclaim and African American music's traditional community base as early as 1960. "But who has recognized him?" mused Hobsbawm:

The public at the Five Spot is overwhelmingly young, white, and intellectual or bohemian. Here are the jazz fans (white or colored) with the "Draft Stevenson" buttons, lost over their $1.50 beer. If Coleman were to blow in *Small's Paradise* in Harlem, it would clear the place in five minutes.[55]

Coleman's New York exploits won praise and adulation from arts and entertainment figures, including painters Larry Rivers and Robert Rauschenberg, conductor Leonard Bernstein, gossip columnist Dorothy Kilgallen, and composers Marc Blitzstein and Virgil Thomson. His out of town trips proved less successful. While Coleman broke attendance records at Manhattan's bohemian nightclubs, he periodically encountered the same indifference and hostility on the road that he had faced in Los Angeles. John Coltrane reportedly received a cool reception when he played at Small's Paradise in 1960 and, as expected, the band with Eric Dolphy experienced its share of disgruntled fans. Cecil Taylor struggled to find anyone who would book him for more than a share of the door receipts at a Greenwich Village coffee house or loft.[56]

In a 1959 *Esquire* article entitled "The Golden Age of Jazz," John Clellon Holmes concluded that the music now possessed "the three things essential for the full flowering of any art form: an aesthetic, a tradition, and an audience."[57] Within a few years, developments in jazz radically challenged the composition of all three prerequisites. "The new thing" tested jazz fans' willingness to accept the implications of freedom as an aesthetic principle. The controversy over individual artists obscured a larger prize: no less than the jazz tradition itself was at stake, including the unresolved question of whether the legitimate heirs to that heritage included Coleman, Coltrane, and Taylor. The narrowing audience for free improvisation illustrated experimental musicians' growing difficulty in finding suitable venues and rewards consummate with their self-image as artists. Many champions of free jazz began to view their lack of opportunity as a consequence of the music industry's racial and economic structures, rather than the intrinsic value or resonance of their work. These extra-musical developments soon interrupted and fractured the debate over modernist aesthetics, threatening the critical establishment's prestige, credibility, and ability to mediate the position of jazz in American culture.

By drawing attention to the discomforting implications of artistic freedom, "the new thing" jeopardized jazz music's identity as an autonomous modern art. Free improvisers soon imperiled the genre's canonical ideological values too. During the early 1960s, experimental musicians such as Cecil Taylor, Ornette Coleman, and John Coltrane encountered a jazz industry suffering financially from a long-term trend toward stylistic obscurity and the rise of popular alternatives. Despite contrasting experiences in the marketplace, their music and their struggles to win critical and popular acceptance inspired a second wave of free improvisers including Archie Shepp, Bill Dixon, Pharaoh Sanders, and Albert Ayler. This emerging generation's stagnant economic circumstances reinforced a growing dissatisfaction with the jazz establishment's progressive liberalism and induced them to seek greater control over their work's production, presentation, and reception.

By the late 1950s a color-blind universalism provided the jazz industry's broad ideological center. Cold War interpretations of jazz as a symbol of American freedom and democracy by Ralph Ellison, John Kouwenhoven, and other scholars had reinforced the community's integrationist wing during the decade. The concomitant rhetoric of race-neutrality, predicated upon the triumph of talent over racial difference, elicited plenty of sympathy in the music business. By downplaying the influence of biology on culture, and stressing the gradual assimilation of minority groups, it undermined scientific racism as a source of prejudice against jazz in general and African American musicians in particular. It appealed also to the many Jewish critics and entrepreneurs who had entered the worlds of art and entertainment to circumvent discrimination in the business establishment. As Ingrid Monson has noted, jazz music's construction as a language that transcends ethnic categories reinforced its stature as a self-contained modern genre. Yet color-blindness served to obscure white privilege by attributing racism to individual psychological deficiencies rather than structural inequalities in access to power and wealth. Indeed, at a time when federal housing, labor, and social security legislation excluded African Americans from valuable government protections and perpetuated de facto segregation throughout the country, the logic of race-neutrality unrealistically implied that minorities could make progress simply by adopting white customs, habits, and behaviors.[58]

The critical discourse of universalism in jazz masked underlying patterns of discrimination against African American performers. Although all musicians potentially faced exploitation, black artists experienced systematic abuse owing to their perceived lack of recourse against dishonest managers, lawyers, booking agents, and record companies. They were more liable than white musicians to be cheated of their composing and publishing royalties, shortchanged their percentage of gate receipts, and denied representation by the American Federation of Musicians. The union maintained segregated locals in almost every city outside New York until the 1950s and balked at integrating the symphonies, radio orchestras, Hollywood studios, and top nightclubs. Furthermore, jazz music's domestic resurgence explicitly celebrated the European influences and social respectability of white West Coast musicians such as Dave Brubeck and Gerry Mulligan in contrast to the deviant black style of bebop (an association solidified by the neo-primitivism of Norman Mailer and the beat writers). Thus white musicians fit promoters' image of the new jazz framed by the press and music industry, while African American artists struggled for a share of the rewards.[59]

Government failure to pursue the promise of equality compromised the authority of color-blind universalists further after 1954. Justice Department support for the NAACP in *Brown v. Board of Education* stemmed largely from government concern for the U.S. image in the world. By removing the legal basis for segregation, the Warren Court relieved pressure on American statesmen and allowed the State Department to attribute extant discrimination to local resistance. Government officials maintained that such backwardness would disappear, in the Court's phrase, "with all deliberate speed" but felt little pressure to expedite the process. The State Department acknowledged the continuation of inequality but used goodwill tours by African American bandleaders to demonstrate progress and the breadth of opportunity available to talented individuals.[60]

Government exploitation of jazz abroad only underlined African American musicians' second-class status at home, especially when federal agencies appeared reluctant to enforce civil rights protections in the South. The immediate subject of *Brown*, school desegregation, provided a case in point. Some school districts completely ignored the order while others enforced only token integration. The state of Virginia, for example, attempted to circumvent the ruling by closing many public schools and funding designated private institutions. In 1956, over one hundred southern Representatives signed a manifesto denouncing *Brown* and recommending defiance. By the fall of 1957, only 684 out of 3,000 affected school districts had begun to open their admissions policies. It is hardly surprising that Louis Armstrong, at the time he criticized Governor Faubus for blocking school integration in Little Rock, also denounced Eisenhower as "two faced" for failing to act (a statement he modified when the president sent in troops).[61]

Massive resistance precipitated a growing number of popular assaults on segregation in the South. The Montgomery bus boycott of 1956, the lunch counter sit-ins of 1960, and the freedom rides of 1961 tested southern compliance with the Court's ruling. Civil rights groups such as the Southern Christian Leadership Conference (SCLC), the Student Nonviolent Coordinating Committee (SNCC), and the Congress On Racial Equality (CORE) gave structure and leadership to a burgeoning grass-roots movement to integrate public accommodations by direct action and registering African Americans to vote. Freedom organizations drew strength from the human and material resources of southern black churches and colleges while incorporating a stream of white sympathizers. Recent accounts indicate that the southern movement experienced racial tension between black and white participants from its earliest years, although the cracks did not begin to show publicly until around 1964.[62] Within the jazz community, ethnic assertiveness and the impulse to direct action manifest itself in hard bop's reclamation of the music's black roots and programmatic demands for civil rights such as Sonny Rollins' *Freedom Suite* (1958) and Max Roach's *We Insist! The Freedom Now Suite* (1960). Around 1961, the discomfort of jazz music's color-blind gatekeepers with expressions of African American solidarity emerged in the uproar over "Crow Jim."

During the 1940s, the music journal *Metronome* invented the term "Crow Jim" to describe the belief of some critics and listeners that African Americans possessed an unmatched level of jazz feeling and skill. The strength of this romantic view of jazz in Europe, whether attributed to innate ability or cultural environment, drew stinging rebukes from *Metronome* and *Down Beat* editors. By the late 1950s, some white critics accused African American musicians of adopting the same attitude as justification for their reluctance to work with white musicians, who they blamed for appropriating and exploiting black music. In his autobiography, white saxophonist Art Pepper recalled disparaging racial slurs from African Americans in his own rhythm section, while Bill Evans left the Miles Davis group partly because of resentment from African American musicians outside the band. Several notable white performers, including Red Rodney and Buddy DeFranco, reportedly retired from jazz owing to similar experiences. In a series of articles, jazz writers Leonard Feather, Ralph Gleason, Gene Lees, and Nat Hentoff claimed an industry-wide trend toward preferential hiring of African Americans based upon race. Although some of these observers acknowledged ongoing segregation as a root cause of frustration for African American musicians, the label "Crow Jim" framed any deviation from race-neutrality as reverse discrimination and, as George Pitts noted in the *Pittsburgh Courier*, served to perpetuate the music industry's status quo.[63]

Critics' hypersensitivity to growing black particularity, at a time African American musicians faced racial slights and exclusions routinely, stemmed in part from the precarious relationship between the trade press and the rest of the music establishment. Jazz magazines played an important role in the industry's political economy. In order to make a name for themselves, and secure the attention of a booking agent or record company artists and repertory executive, musicians depended upon critics for publicity. Freelance and contracted critics wrote for a number of trade publications. Each journal drew the majority of its advertising revenue from record companies and, increasingly during the 1960s, instrument and instrumental accessory manufacturers. At the same time, record companies employed critics to write the sleeve notes for new albums while other critics reviewed those records. Issues of race aside, writers had always fended off allegations that they represented the parasites of the music business.

One publication dominated the trade press and became the focus of residual antagonisms against the critical fraternity. In continuous publication since 1934, *Down Beat* magazine had outlived a host of competitors. Its position as bastion of the critical establishment strengthened in 1961 when two rivals, *Metronome* and the *Jazz Review*, folded. The family-owned *Down Beat* enjoyed a period of growth during the subsequent decade. Its bi-weekly circulation increased by almost one third from an average of 51,750 per issue in 1963 to an average of 72,997 per issue in 1968.[64] During that period the magazine targeted a core readership of "learning musicians," an editorial euphemism for members of high school and college jazz bands. By the middle of the decade *Down Beat's* surveys showed an age profile beginning in the early teens, with a median age in the early and middle twenties, and considerable attrition thereafter. Although general sales benefited from the baby boom, African American readership remained low. Returns from news vendors, whose customer base may be expected to reflect the racial concentration of their location, indicated a smaller proportion of African Americans purchased *Down Beat* than made up the general population (although such sales ignored the number of readers who consulted the popular public library copies).[65]

Down Beat employed white editors and columnists almost exclusively, and their continued credibility and prestige within jazz depended upon the success of integration.[66] The magazine's routine news coverage of 1959 and 1960 closely monitored the desegregation of American Federation of Musicians local chapters. The following three years, however, witnessed a series of articles that attempted to diffuse interracial friction, which the editors argued would destroy jazz music's creative freedom. In a two-part feature on "Racial Prejudice in Jazz" published in March 1962, several musicians including vocalist Abbey Lincoln and her husband Max Roach discussed the nexus between art and politics with leading critics. Ira Gitler's negative review of Lincoln's album *Straight Ahead*, in which he accused her of becoming a "professional Negro" by foregrounding her racial identity, initially prompted the discussion. "Pride in one's heritage is one thing," he had written, "but we don't need the Elijah Muhammed type of thinking in jazz." Defending himself against the charge of racism, Gitler asserted that he "only implied . . . that I don't want a separation of black and white. I want to keep the two together in jazz." Some critics' obvious discomfort with black activism reflected more than a modernist desire to separate art from its social context. "Crow Jim," which *Down Beat* editor Don DeMicheal perceived as a growing trend in the jazz business, implied a devaluation of white voices in jazz writing too. At times during the debate, Roach and Lincoln appeared to support that logic. Even as Roach acknowledged jazz music's potential to communicate with a broad audience, he challenged white critics' ability to discuss it meaningfully owing to their distance from African American life. While Lincoln denied a separatist agenda, she questioned the appeal of assimilating into a dysfunctional society.[67]

In an attempt to downplay dissension over the desirability of integration, *Down Beat* organized a much more conciliatory discussion in the spring of 1963 that assumed "The Need for Racial Unity in Jazz." The panel featured three established leaders of mixed bands, critics Leonard Feather and John Tynan, and an NAACP chapter president. The article attempted to demonstrate that jazz did not belong exclusively to African Americans, and that the white musician need not consider himself or herself "an intruder or interloper." Feather expressed his desire to see white musicians join the civil rights organization in large numbers and implement its goals by creating "a truly interracial scene in every corner of the music business." By publishing Feather's comments, *Down Beat* perpetuated an editorial policy reaching back to the late 1950s of upholding the NAACP as a model of moderate racial progress in opposition to both southern segregationists and black nationalists. In a 1959 article Gene Lees had followed a similar strategy, applauding an NAACP campaign to integrate studio and symphony orchestras while comparing the "irrational" and "obviously paranoic" practitioners of "Crow Jim" to notorious proponents of Jim Crow such as Georgia Senator Herman Talmadge. The majority of readers appeared to share the editors' distaste for racial assertiveness, according to the unprecedented volume of mail that followed the 1962 features. If *Down Beat*'s expanded letters page represented the broader response, as the magazine claimed, most subscribers viewed "Crow Jim" as an unwelcome intrusion of prejudice in art.[68]

The tension between color-blind universalism and ethnic assertiveness is a recurrent characteristic of jazz communities. As Monson's ethnographic study of contemporary musicians demonstrates, these contradictory feelings frequently coexist within the same person and may be articulated in response to different stimuli. African American musicians often embrace race-neutrality as a counterweight to discrimination and in recognition of the transcendent potential of jazz performance and appreciation. When white industry figures invoke such sentiments to disguise the music's African American cultural foundation and creative leadership, however, those same musicians of color might vociferously defend its ethnic identity. Thus, while Cecil Taylor claimed that "jazz is a Negro feeling" and Charles Mingus argued "white people have no right to play it," both band leaders hired white sidemen consistently during the 1950s and 1960s.[69]

A drastic contraction of the jazz economy during this period compounded African American musicians' frustration with the slow pace of integration. The changing fortunes of celebrated entrepreneur Berry Gordy captured the evolving nature of the music industry, and its impact on minority-interest styles such as jazz. In 1953 Gordy, a middle-class music lover from Detroit, left the army and decided to go into business for himself. With a loan from his father, a plastering contractor, Gordy set up a record store dedicated to progressive jazz in a black neighborhood of his hometown. He learned a sobering lesson:

I loved jazz—Stan Kenton, Thelonious Monk, Charlie Parker—and I wanted to let people know I was modern, so I called the place the 3-D Record Mart. People started coming in and asking for things like Fats Domino. Pretty soon I was asking, "Who is this Fats Domino? What is this rhythm and blues stuff?" I listened and ordered a few records by these people and sold them. Still all my capital was tied up in jazz, but jazz didn't have the fact—the beat. I went bankrupt.[70]

After working for his father and Ford, Gordy began to produce recording sessions and sell the tapes to music industry executives in New York before setting up his own company in 1959. Motown's first record, Smokey Robinson's "Shop Around," sold a million copies within a few months of its release and showcased the techniques that earned the label a reputation as "Hitsville, USA." Gordy and Robinson developed a pop formula with enormous cross-over appeal, retaining the danceable foundation of rhythm and blues but muting its raw and often vulgar tendencies with layered gospel harmonies, clean production values, and witty but inoffensive lyrics. By 1967, Motown grossed between $20 million and $30 million per year, an estimated 70 percent from white consumers.[71]

Berry Gordy's experience revealed the two key reasons for declining jazz business during the late 1950s and early 1960s. Esoteric styles began to alienate audiences in the 1940s. Free improvisation represented the culmination of jazz music's tendency to abandon straightforward rhythms and melodies in favor of greater sophistication or obscurity. Jazz gradually lost two fundamental traits that had once helped secure popular acceptance, a steady, explicit beat and short, catchy tunes. Chuck Berry expressed a common sense of regret in his hit record, "Rock and Roll Music":

I got no kick against modern jazz
Unless they try to play it too darn fast
And change the beauty of the melody
Until it sounds just like a symphony.[72]

Berry's notoriety advertised the second reason for jazz music's faltering profile, the rise of popular alternatives. During the 1950s, jazz created a niche as a sophisticated yet accessible art. *Down Beat* reader surveys, and top-name groups such as the Dave Brubeck Quartet, found that high school and college aged listeners still formed a key segment of the jazz public. Rock and roll made devastating inroads into that audience. As Berry Gordy discovered, rhythm and blues held substantial appeal from the early 1950s, even though the major labels viewed it as crass race music. That attitude did not stop black or white youths from responding enthusiastically to rhythm and blues radio programming, and when performers such as Elvis Presley, Bill Haley, and Buddy Holly added country influences to the mix they launched a rock and roll boom at mid-decade.[73]

The major record labels' ambivalence toward the new sensation allowed for continued stylistic heterogeneity in the expanding youth market. Rock and roll existed alongside jazz, folk, calypso, and bossa nova as alternatives to mainstream popular music. Indeed, the years 1958 to 1963 witnessed a lull in rock and roll sales with some of the music's most charismatic figures—Elvis Presley, Little Richard, Jerry Lee Lewis, Chuck Berry, Buddy Holly, and Richie Valens—temporarily or permanently removed from the scene. Yet several structural developments in the music industry boded ill for the commercial future of jazz.

Pat Boone's numerous rhythm and blues covers, Philadelphia "Schlock Rock," and Motown's assembly-line sound gradually convinced the larger companies that polished rock and roll could sustain a large audience. At the same time, shifting patterns of radio airplay and record distribution increasingly focused production and sales on a narrow stylistic range of potentially huge hits. By the end of the decade, the Top 40 format dominated radio, edging out numerous specialty programs and stations. Similarly, the changing location of most record purchases from mom and pop stores to discount retailers like Sam Goody and general merchandise marts decreased the diversity of product offerings. In particular, the rise of rack-jobbers with full control over selection, displays, and return privileges reoriented retail outlets to the two hundred best-selling releases. When the Beatles' phenomenal success launched the British invasion in 1964, the majors took full advantage. Their enthusiasm inaugurated a new period of growth for rock and exacerbated the precipitous decline of jazz.[74]

By the turn of the decade, the jazz business confronted serious financial problems stemming from a structural transformation within the industry. Jazz nightclubs had traditionally provided a steady source of income for working bands. Always unstable investments, nightclubs folded in unprecedented numbers during the first half of the 1960s. Some of the nation's best-known venues closed. The recession claimed Boston's Storyville, San Francisco's Blackhawk, Philadelphia's Showboat, and Chicago's Blue Note, among others. Clubs catering to all styles of jazz suffered. In New York, the Dixieland stronghold Nick's followed the adventurous Jazz Gallery into receivership. Some clubs, such as Birdland and Basin Street East, converted to a discotheque policy in an attempt to stave off bankruptcy. At other established rooms, such as the Village Gate, jazz musicians shared the bill with comedians and folk singers.[75]

Jazz festivals struggled to find a workable balance between jazz music's cultured image and popular music's broad appeal. When Norman Granz terminated his Jazz at the Philharmonic touring package in the early 1960s, reasoning that its exuberant cutting contests failed to deliver a sufficient profit margin, the future for jazz extravaganzas looked bleak. A year after the riots, Newport authorities staged a music festival featuring show business stars such as Bob Hope and Judy Garland. When George Wein secured permission to stage the jazz festival again in 1962, he ran it as a commercial venture and reverted to crossover or non-jazz acts as headliners. The number and size of festivals burgeoned in subsequent years, but continuing events such as the Monterey Jazz Festival illustrated that the immediate future lay in moderately ambitious, carefully planned events. Financial disasters, such as the Hollywood Bowl Festival, underscored the risky nature of the undertaking.[76]

The recording business appeared to escape the pervasive down-sizing in jazz. Majors such as Columbia and independent labels like Blue Note and Atlantic continued to issue large numbers of discs. The flurry of activity masked two stark realities for performers. Jazz albums generated small sales, typically less than five thousand copies by the early 1960s according to occasional producer Nat Hentoff, and labels did not anticipate a great number of exceptions to that rule. Consequently, they limited the budget for production and promotion. The rise of rock and roll only underscored the returns available to a company that channeled resources elsewhere. Second, with a few exceptions such as Miles Davis, John Coltrane, and Dave Brubeck, jazz musicians made little money from advances or royalties. Record companies commonly charged studio time, liner notes, and other costs against future earnings. When sales failed to cover these expenses, Jackie McLean, Ornette Coleman, and other leaders learned that they owed the company large sums of money.[77]

A jazz musician interested in playing "outside" faced an additional set of problems that inhibited his or her ability to earn a living. The aspiring instrumentalist had to leave a safe local gig and travel to New York City or a large regional center in order to meet other free improvisers and put together a band. Each group hoped to play at one of the city's jazz venues, but work did not come easily for experimental combos. With rock and roll eroding the younger segment of the jazz audience, club owners at the Five Spot or the Village Gate demanded stars who drew big receipts at the door and cash tills. Too frequently they complained about the level of income generated by "the new thing." Extended improvisations with few breaks demanded attentive concentration, discouraging the rapid sale of alcohol and turnover of patrons. As a result, many of the younger musicians could only secure performances in small coffeehouses or lofts run by enthusiasts.[78]

The absence of prospects made survival precarious for experimental performers who gravitated to New York. During the early 1960s, the Greenwich Village district attracted aspiring musicians, much as it drew artists, writers, and poets, on account of its low rents and proximity to the downtown and midtown arts scene. Once there, musicians found a community of fellow iconoclasts with whom to exchange ideas, tips, and encouragement. Some of the most important contributors to the emerging free jazz movement lived within a few square blocks of the East Village during the early 1960s. Saxophonist Archie Shepp arrived in 1959 with a background in rhythm and blues and a degree in dramatic literature from Goddard College. Shepp developed friendships with many "outside" musicians, including drummer Sonny Murray and saxophonist Marion Brown, as they arrived in the neighborhood. Sun Ra brought his entire band, the Arkestra, from Chicago to the Village in 1961. Over the past ten years Ra had recruited some of Chicago's best young musicians, including saxophonists John Gilmore and Pat Patrick, trombonist Julian Priester, and bassist Richard Evans, and trained many novices. He molded them into a cohesive musical and social unit under his patriarchal supervision through constant rehearsal, informal lectures on philosophy and life, and mutual support. Members of the Arkestra shared living quarters and earnings from outside work to sustain the group between rare jobs. Tenor saxophonist Pharoah Sanders arrived from the west coast in 1962 with no money, sleeping in the subway and tenement stairwells until he tapped into the circuit of occasional gigs and revolving day jobs. Other notable residents included Ornette Coleman, Cecil Taylor, multi-instrumentalist Giuseppi Logan, pianist Burton Greene, bassist Henry Grimes, and drummer Charles Moffett. Despite the camaraderie, poverty forced many musicians to leave town. Saxophonist Albert Ayler came to New York City a year after Sanders, but despite experience working with Cecil Taylor's group in the United States and Europe he drifted back to his hometown Cleveland for lack of work. Ayler gigged and recorded sporadically on both continents before leading his own band in New York.[79]

Archie Shepp, Sun Ra, Pharoah Sanders, and Albert Ayler represented a second wave of free improvisers who drew inspiration from Coleman, Coltrane, and Taylor but lacked their notoriety. "Ornette's first dozen albums, for me, were the music of the century," remembered trumpeter Bill Dixon. "Ornette's original thing was like a comet in the sky."[80] Dixon's struggle to establish a professional identity typified the difficulties of the underground New York jazz scene. Despite extensive musical training at the Hartnette Conservatory of Music and with private tutors, Dixon's main opportunities came as a copyist or arranger for other orchestras. With trumpet-playing gigs at a premium, he worked days as a shipping clerk, record store salesman, and typist. Beginning in 1961, Dixon co-led a quartet with Archie Shepp that contrasted the saxophonist's gruff, aggressive tenor with his own grand understatement. The group recorded for Savoy in 1962, but the label only granted Dixon and Shepp one side of the resulting album, which it failed to promote. Meanwhile, the band continued to search out audiences for its free approach to improvisation in east side attics and coffee bars before Dixon left in 1963.[81]

Practically none of the second wave of free improvisers had previous experience and hence reputations with mainstream jazz groups. Any success depended upon publicity, an extremely hard commodity to

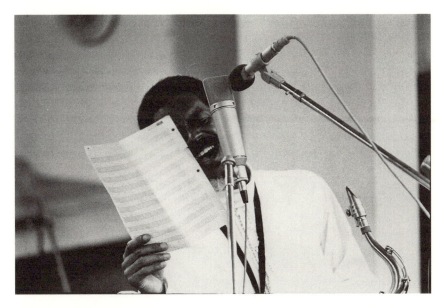

Figure 8. Albert Ayler in the recording studio during the 1960s. Courtesy Photographs and Prints Division, Schomburg Center for Research in Black Culture, The New York Public Library, Astor, Lenox, and Tilden Foundations.

come by. The outlook began to change in 1961 when ABC-Paramount established a subsidiary jazz label, Impulse! Under the direction of record producer Bob Thiele, the company cultivated a cutting-edge reputation by signing John Coltrane to the second-richest contract in jazz (after Miles Davis) and recording several "new wave" performers including Cecil Taylor.[82] Whereas Coltrane's high profile generated sales to justify his five-year, fifty-thousand-dollar advance, Thiele found that few other progressive artists on the roster aroused much critical interest. As a result, he secretly financed a new jazz publication to compete with *Down Beat* that would cover the whole stylistic spectrum and bring attention to experimental musicians in particular. Launched in the fall of 1962, *Jazz* took the name of a magazine Thiele first published in the 1940s and drew its advertising base and art direction from Impulse! Although not exclusively devoted to "the new thing," *Jazz* magazine—with a circulation that climbed to around thirty thousand copies per month—renewed the critical controversy over free improvisation and forced its competitors to respond.[83]

The debate after 1962 increasingly linked free jazz to the circumstances of its production. Experimental musicians comprised the most

Figure 9. Bob Thiele (left) and Ornette Coleman. Courtesy Photographs and Prints Division, Schomburg Center for Research in Black Culture, The New York Public Library, Astor, Lenox, and Tilden Foundations.

vocal protesters, partly because they attracted smaller audiences and fewer opportunities than any other jazz stylists. This factor should not be over-estimated, however. Innovators rarely found easy openings in any field, clubs had always offered a distracting environment, and free improvisers often did not expect great financial success. As Bill Dixon later remembered proudly, "my music *wasn't* for everyone, and neither was Schoenberg's music for everyone, and neither was Webern's music for everyone, and neither was Bartók's . . . if too many people are digging what you do, you'd better look at it again because it may not be what you think it is."[84] Dixon's allusion to composers in the western concert tradition suggested the most important reason why innovative pioneers revolted against their working conditions during the 1960s. More than any other generation of jazz musicians, free improvisers were encouraged to see themselves as artists. When they compared their treatment by white club owners, record company executives, and booking agents to the privileges enjoyed by classical performers, many attributed their inferior circumstances to racism.

Jazz had long challenged the boundaries between cultivated and popular music. During the 1930s, African American educators shaped a culture of professionalism in public schools and private instruction that infused vernacular creative achievement with discipline, pride, and a modernist reverence for innovation. Duke Ellington, Teddy Wilson, and Louis Armstrong won recognition for jazz as a virtuoso performance art while epitomizing taste and sophistication through their dress and deportment. Jazz itself became a means of upward mobility. Professional standards developed in (and in response to) urban black communities provided the foundation for its success in the broader commercial marketplace. By the 1940s, the deteriorating dance band economy strained this relationship between musicians and a broad public. Dizzy Gillespie and others tailored the nascent bebop repertory to small combos in order to take advantage of emerging club venues dedicated to jam sessions and cliques of listeners. By the 1950s, jazz music's resurgence hinged on its image as a respectable art form. Once the jazz economy declined again, experimental musicians—who experienced the recession first—inherited a reputation and identity as artists without the institutional support networks of the fine arts or (as chapter 4 will suggest) a viable community base. In addition, they saw the music industry's rewards, especially its fee scales, disproportionately favor white performers who adhered most closely to the classically-tinged West Coast and cool jazz styles.[85]

At the end of 1962, Ornette Coleman retired from jazz for two years as a result of his long-term dissatisfaction with the music business. The availability of work did not concern him. Coleman had plenty of offers but felt under-compensated for his efforts. Earlier in the year, Coleman learned that white pianist Dave Brubeck earned twice the money he received for playing to smaller crowds at the Five Spot. Coleman consequently tripled his fee, to the horror of the club's owners and his agent, and repeatedly turned down jobs that did not meet his estimation of an artist's worth. Coleman believed also that the performance environment often interfered with the integrity of his musical statements. He angrily condemned the social intimacy encouraged by nightclubs for disturbing his artistic sensibility, likening contemporary venues to bordellos. By questioning the ritual of sexuality long at the heart of jazz music's presentation and reception, Coleman not only challenged prevalent codes of masculinity in the genre; he labored to lift his music into the reified context of high art enjoyed by classical performers. Coleman attempted to provide a positive example by staging a concert of his music at New York's Town Hall in December 1962. He rented the building, paid the musicians, coordinated publicity, and played well, but the event barely broke even and Coleman withdrew in despair. "Of all the problems that a Negro is confronted with," he reflected in 1965, "none is worse than the Negro artist trying to achieve individuality and human dignity without the approval of some organization that wants to control him."[86]

Other "outside" musicians suffered for their understanding of artistic standards too. Bill Dixon refused several unsatisfactory recording offers after his experience with Savoy, and no company released a complete album under his name until 1967. By then the jazz press had virtually forgotten his early role in the movement. Some musicians felt obliged to take whatever publicity and money gigs could offer, although like Archie Shepp they resented working in "the crude stables (clubs) where black men are groomed and paced like thoroughbreds to run until they bleed." While African Americans dominated the "new thing," white musicians played important roles too and suffered similar misfortune. Steve Lacy, who pioneered free improvisation on the soprano saxophone with Cecil Taylor, sold magazine subscriptions by telephone and worked in a department store during the early 1960s. Attuned to the everyday inequalities of American life, Taylor and others recognized a subtle form of racism in white businessmen's disrespect for the conditions under which creative musicians practiced an African American art. Industry customs discriminated against the cultural form in general, whoever performed it. Club owners often neglected to tune or repair their pianos, for example, and constantly harassed Taylor for playing too loud and too long. Conditions that had once seemed tolerable for entertainment now appeared retrogressive for art, and a growing awareness of that contradiction fueled the resentment of experimental musicians marginalized by both worlds.[87]

The critical establishment's response to the financial crisis demonstrated little understanding or flexibility. *Down Beat*'s editors followed a long-established policy of economic liberalism. During the late 1950s and early 1960s, the magazine's news coverage often focused on instances when New York's cabaret licensing system denied musicians the right to freely market their talents. The city's police department issued permits to entertainers who played venues that served alcohol, and could revoke a cabaret card for any reason. A previous narcotics arrest provided the usual pretext, and many top-rank musicians such as Billie Holiday, Thelonious Monk, and Jackie McLean struggled for years to work in America's jazz capital. *Down Beat* typically highlighted the injustice of police officers denying work permission to musicians who had never been convicted of breaking the law. The journal also censured the American Federation of Musicians for failing to press the matter in court, where judges had previously insisted that the city issue cards to particular musicians.[88]

Down Beat's regular contributors had little sympathy for experimental musicians who claimed that their poverty resulted from racism on the

Figure 10. Roswell Rudd (left) and Archie Shepp. Photograph by Frank Kofsky. Courtesy Photographs and Prints Division, Schomburg Center for Research in Black Culture, The New York Public Library, Astor, Lenox, and Tilden Foundations.

part of the white entrepreneurs who ran jazz. Following the rebels protest in 1960, managing editor Gene Lees castigated Charles Mingus for complaining about discriminatory programming policies at the official Newport Jazz Festival. "Mingus apparently could not understand," commented Lees, "that the law of supply and demand, as deplorable as it may be, operates as inexorably in art as it does in business." Five years later, the magazine continued to chastise vanguard musicians for their unrealistic attitude toward the marketplace. Columnist and future editor Dan Morgenstern reported that despite extensive coverage of his January 1965 come-back concert in the *New York Times*, *Newsweek*, *Time*, and the *New Yorker*, Ornette Coleman planned no immediate follow-up gigs because he refused to lower his fee. "One hopes that this singularly uncompromising and impractical man will find a way for himself and his art in a world dedicated to compromise and practical know-how," concluded a resigned Morgenstern.[89]

Down Beat and *Jazz* argued that musicians had to preserve and expand their white, middle-class audience in order for their fortunes to improve. *Down Beat* in particular proposed a series of market-oriented solutions such as more imaginative, professional promotion and a national jazz organization to help negotiate salaries and conditions. Lit-

Figure 11. Ornette Coleman performing at the Kresge Auditorium, Massachusetts Institute of Technology, Cambridge, 1965. Photograph by Lee Tanner/The Jazz Image.

tle action resulted from these ideas.[90] The magazine also opposed any association that might reflect badly on the music and hence alienate the potential listening public. Perennially concerned about the link between jazz and narcotics, its editors condemned Archie Shepp and Cecil Taylor's musical involvement with an off-Broadway production of the drug-themed play *The Connection* in 1960. This obsession with negative publicity soon surpassed all other concerns, including performance conditions. In a March 1962 editorial on the musician's responsibilities, Gene Lees acknowledged that nightclubs represented a difficult environment yet scolded Charles Mingus again for interrupting a recent show to demand silence from the patrons. Mingus' five obligations, "to his art, to the audience, to those who hire him, to his profession, and to himself," outweighed his sense of propriety. In April 1964, Leonard Feather lamented a *Time* magazine cover story on Thelonious Monk because it seemed to identify jazz with deviance at a moment the industry could ill afford to lose business:

In crucially sensitive times like these, there are extra-musical factors to be taken into consideration—factors that could have been weighed more seriously before a jazzman was explained away to millions of Luce-minded readers as a loveable, dignified, jive-talking, honest, odd-hatted, unselfish weirdo.[91]

During the early 1960s performers, critics, and entrepreneurs struggled to come to terms with artistic and institutional changes in the music industry. They recognized the enormous stakes in the fierce contest over free improvisation's relationship to the jazz tradition and a broader modernist heritage in the arts. At a time of shrinking opportunities and growing dissatisfaction with the jazz establishment's liberal assumptions, free improvisers embodied the fate that potentially awaited all musicians and thus testified to the need for solidarity. Yet their esoteric practices and growing assertiveness also threatened jazz music's viability as a respectable and accessible art form that its Cold War champions had cultivated so carefully.

The Newport rebels festival demonstrated the difficulties and possibilities facing experimental musicians determined to seize control of their futures. While thousands of African American students sat in at lunch counters and theaters across the South to protest segregation, musicians organized in opposition to an industry they perceived as unjust and demeaning. The hoped-for solidarity failed to materialize. Charles Mingus and Max Roach anticipated that collective responsibility for the festival would lead to an equitable disbursement of the rewards, yet various performers begged, borrowed, and stole from the proceeds until the profits had disappeared. Before the rebels went their separate ways, Mingus, Roach, and Jo Jones launched the Jazz Artists' Guild (JAG), a collective designed to independently produce and promote musical events while keeping artistic and financial matters in the hands of performers. Internal squabbles and insufficient attendance brought the Guild's primary commercial venture—a New York concert series featuring many of the musicians who performed at Cliff Walk Manor—to a premature close before the end of summer.[92]

JAG's failure to establish a workable economic model spoke to the fragmentation of the musicians' community and the lack of a unifying vision or leadership. Performers defied and subverted jazz music's canonical values throughout the early 1960s, yet they articulated their grievances with hesitation. Discontent with the status quo lacked focus or direction. Although artistic innovators such as Ornette Coleman and Cecil Taylor openly resented the industry's economic and racial practices, on account of their unenviable fate in the marketplace, few made a connection between aesthetic and ideological challenges to the music's Cold War identity. By mid-decade, however, emerging musicians and writers proposed an alternative critical framework that replaced free improvisation's modernist rationale with a militant black nationalism inherently hostile to existing business practices. In the short term, it encouraged "outside" musicians to resurrect self-help collectives that provided much-needed publicity and performance opportunities on the fringes of the music industry. In the long term, however, the identification of free improvisation as the cutting edge of African American cultural nationalism by the Black Arts Movement helped win a space for it—and the broader jazz tradition—in a parallel network of nonprofit institutions that ultimately revolutionized the genre's funding.

Chapter 3

Free Jazz and Black Nationalism

Amiri Baraka heard the news at the Eighth Street Bookstore in New York City during a book launch party. An increasingly acclaimed and notorious writer, Baraka—known then as LeRoi Jones—had made his name as a poet and playwright in the interracial Greenwich Village bohemian scene of the late 1950s and early 1960s. By 1965 his close acquaintances had narrowed somewhat to the more radical black men formerly associated with the literary groups Umbra and the Revolutionary Action Movement, the second wave of free improvisers, and the new African American painters. Although he had lately developed a reputation in the press as an anti-white militant, for controversial positions staked out in interviews and at public forums, he maintained close institutional and personal ties to New York's academic and publishing circles. On Sunday February 21, as the celebration got underway, he exuded a charm and ease that stemmed from his thorough integration into the avant-garde arts world.[1]

That dynamic changed irreversibly when Leroy McLucas, a photographer who had worked with Baraka and some of the younger musicians, entered the store weeping. "Malcolm is dead! Malcolm is dead! Malcolm's been killed!" he repeated between sobs. As Baraka huddled with other African American guests for support, he felt a sense of shock and emptiness sweep over him. "I was stunned, shot myself," he later recalled. "I felt stupid, ugly, useless." His response to Malcolm X's assassination was immediate and revealing, the culmination of a growing disenchantment with his attachment to the white downtown world by work, residence, and marriage. The following day Baraka called a press conference at which he announced plans to launch the Black Arts Repertory Theater/School (BARTS) in Harlem. Conceived as a combination cultural center, arts workshop, and performance space, the venue would offer an oasis of black drama, music, art, and history. Attempting to provide African Americans with a source of group identity and an antidote to political division, Baraka envisioned taking the Black Arts to the streets in public happenings that he imagined connecting artists and intellectuals to the community.[2]

Within a few days of the announcement, Baraka moved out of his family's apartment in the Village and identified a four-story brownstone on West 130th Street as the future home of BARTS. He returned to Manhattan twice the following month to raise funds for the venture, most notably on March 28 for a major jazz benefit concert at the Village Gate. Recorded by Impulse! and issued in part as *New Wave in Jazz*, the event featured appearances by some of Baraka's closest friends and acquaintances, including Marion Brown, Archie Shepp, Sonny Murray, Albert Ayler, Sun Ra, and John Coltrane. The willingness of these and other instrumentalists to offer their services throughout the spring and summer speaks to a growing desire among black artists to pursue a voyage of self-discovery, a voyage uptown to Harlem and beyond to the non-western roots of their music. That their journeys took them through BARTS reveals the intersection between an emerging Black Arts Movement for which Baraka provided a figurehead, the radicalization of free jazz musicians who played a critical part in BARTS fundraising and outreach programs, and a black power philosophy embodied by Malcolm X but dating back to the 1930s in cities all over the United States.[3]

Conventional narratives of the civil rights movement erroneously position black power as a mostly psychological phenomenon born out of frustration and disillusionment with the shortcomings of the southern campaigns for voting rights and anti-discrimination laws. Recent studies of postwar urban development suggest by contrast that civil rights leaders in northern cities had largely framed their struggle in economic terms since the ascendancy of New Deal liberalism. In Philadelphia, for example, African American leaders convinced the city's Republican mayor and City Council to adopt one of the nation's first municipal fair employment practices laws as early as 1948 and to ban racial discrimination in municipal employment, services, and contracts in the City Charter of 1951. When it became apparent that these measures had not countered growing racial inequalities in employment, housing markets, and public schools, black ministers and the local chapter of the NAACP launched a civil disobedience campaign and consumer boycott to successfully force the city and a number of businesses to reevaluate their hiring policies. By 1963, black clergy led by Leon Sullivan shifted their efforts from protest tactics to community empowerment. At a time SNCC attempted to win representation within the national Democratic party and Martin Luther King, Jr., threw his weight behind civil rights and voting rights legislation, Sullivan pioneered grass-roots self-help initiatives such as a nonprofit jobs training program and the financing of several black-owned commercial enterprises.[4]

The pattern of black activism in Philadelphia, Oakland, New York, Chicago, Cleveland, and other northern cities suggests that the trajectory of the modern civil rights movement was shaped as much by the shifting balance of resources between cities and suburbs, and the responses of an increasingly disadvantaged African American working population, as by the progress of legal and legislative challenges to voter disenfranchisement and segregated public facilities. These impulses did not exist in isolation, however. Contemporary press coverage established a false dichotomy between loyalty to King's vision and interest in various forms of black nationalism. It failed to account for the fluidity and complexity of attitudes toward the freedom movement. During the late 1950s and early 1960s, when the momentum created by *Brown v. Board of Education* and the Montgomery bus boycott had stalled, Robert F. Williams of Monroe, North Carolina, embodied this tension of purposes. Although his notoriety rested upon armed self-defense against the Ku Klux Klan, support for black economic and political self-help, and identification with Third World anticolonialism, he also picketed for integration at his local swimming pool and acknowledged the support of white liberals and leftists.[5]

Black power encompassed multiple meanings for its supporters and detractors. Despite its sensational treatment in the media, many African Americans saw black power as an extension of the freedom struggle for dignity, equality, freedom of choice, jobs, and security. Wary of integration, which threatened the continued marginality of minority groups and dilution of their cultures, Malcolm X embodied a renewed emphasis on self-determination in all areas of black life, including political institutions, economic networks, and culture. A convert to the Nation of Islam while serving a prison sentence for burglary, Malcolm X emerged in the 1950s as a charismatic spokesman for its leader, Elijah Muhammad. As head of the Harlem mosque, he denounced white oppression and timid black figureheads equally, seeking to evoke a self-belief and unity among African Americans that could serve as a platform from which to win autonomy. After breaking with the Nation of Islam in 1964, his travels in Africa and the Middle East led Malcolm X, like Martin Luther King, Jr., in his last years, to link racism with capitalism and imperialism as the chief causes of minority subjugation.[6]

Following the assassination of Malcolm X in 1965, black power activists tended to emphasize and develop programs around individual strands of his philosophy. For many adherents, black power stood first and foremost for a push toward community control of business, education, and politics in segregated inner cities. Pluralists sought the devolution of policy for schools, hospitals, and government agencies to a local level, allowing African American officials to develop objectives that addressed grass-roots needs and demands. Such initiatives would allow black leaders to develop power blocs from which to bargain in state and national politics on behalf of race interests. Furthermore, they promised to regenerate the local economy through allocation of incentives to indigenous entrepreneurs and employers invested in urban neighborhoods. Nationalist groups advocated community control also, although organizations such as the Nation of Islam, the Congress of Racial Equality in the late 1960s, and the Republic of New Africa envisioned a complete disengagement with the political system in the form of territorial separatism.[7]

A second feature of black power, self-defense, became the hallmark of revolutionary nationalist groups such as the Black Panther Party. Founded in Oakland during 1966 by Huey Newton and Bobby Seale, the organization's neighborhood patrols and police monitoring activities harnessed a tradition of armed resistance to the concept of community control. Similarly, the organization's social services, including free meals, clothing, legal assistance, and medical care, extended an established self-help ethos. The radicalism of revolutionary nationalists lay in their belief that breaking the hold of white power necessitated a socialist reconstruction of society. Recognizing that the global reach of mature capitalism linked their struggle to Third World liberation movements, the Black Panthers conceived of African Americans as an internal colony of the United States. This conflation of gun-wielding vigilantes, international socialism, and street appeal almost immediately drew government attention and repression.[8]

A third idea, cultural nationalism, proved the most popular manifestation of black power. This campaign for African Americans to take pride in a history and culture distinctly separate from white traditions underlay all tenets of the movement and provided an alternative framework to Cold War liberalism for interpreting free improvisation. Cultural nationalists attempted to employ art in a political capacity. They believed that revolutionary nationalism could not succeed on its own owing to divisions within the African American community. Several black writers attributed these conditions to the lack of a shared bond, a prerequisite to group progress. In a 1962 survey of political leadership, Harold Cruse blamed the community's disunity on the "de-racialized and decultured" black bourgeoisie, which had sacrificed group identity for "the crumbs of integration." In his widely disseminated autobiography of 1965, Malcolm X shifted the responsibility to white America. He popularized a key belief of Elijah Muhammad and the Nation of Islam, that the majority had simply written blacks out of history. Scholars, he believed, had "bleached" African American achievements, conquests, and cultures from the record.[9] When Frantz Fanon's *The Wretched of the Earth* appeared in English in 1965, it reinforced the belief that imperial powers manipulated and eradicated the subject people's past in order to nurture feelings of inferiority and rootlessness. Although he advocated violence as a cathartic response to colonization, Fanon—and the nationalists attracted to his arguments—believed that cultural unity should occur first. A sense of self-worth had to precede political action. This "revolution of the mind" required a positive reevaluation of blackness in order to shatter the hold of white psychological and cultural oppression.[10]

While Fanon's call to revolutionary action inspired Bobby Seale and the Black Panther Party, his emphasis on its cultural grounding most impressed Maulana Ron Karenga. Founder of US Organization in Los Angeles during 1965, Karenga taught his followers to eschew the assimilation of poisonous Euro-American values and embrace instead shared traditions from the distant past. He devised and preached the *Nguzo Saba*, seven principles supposedly common to various African cultures that included unity, self-determination, collective work and responsibility, cooperative economics, purpose, creativity, and faith. He encouraged African clothing and natural hairstyles, instituted language education in Swahili, and established the celebration of Kwanzaa as an African-inspired alternative to Christmas. In doing so, he attempted to provide tools for African Americans to define themselves as a people with a common heritage separate from and equal to white America.[11]

From 1964 to the early 1970s, a burst of artistic activity embraced and embodied this goal. The "spiritual sister" of black power, according to its leading theorist Larry Neal, the Black Arts Movement included the poetry, plays, and prose of Amiri Baraka, Nikki Giovanni, Haki Madhubuti (then Don L. Lee), Ed Bullins, A. B. Spellman, Sonia Sanchez, and Ishmael Reed, the criticism of Addison Gayle, Jr., and Hoyt Fuller, and the painting of William Walker and Chicago's AfriCobra. They sought to uncover or frequently to construct a myth of origins for their work in a common African past. This task required distancing black art from European precedents and defining its racial character. The notion of a black aesthetic rejected the pluralism of African American writers such as Ralph Ellison and Albert Murray, who stressed the transformative influence of black artistic values on a broader American culture and the pursuit of universal criteria of excellence. Young writers believed that distinctive stylistic features common to creative forms in the old and the new worlds, and recognizable across media, survived in various strains of purity. As an expression of psychological apartness, the movement declared that "black is beautiful" and tried to determine exactly what made it so.[12]

Writers frequently identified the rhythms of a vernacular oral tradition as the key ingredient in black art, a feature they analyzed and inserted in verse, texts, sermons, music, and speech. Many artists hoped that this trait would facilitate communication with the masses. Indeed, the black aesthetic proved difficult to define because its advocates demonstrated more concern with its utility than with standards of beauty. They sought to carry a revolutionary message to the people in the language of the people, to encourage unity in the cause of liberation, and to draw untrained initiates into the artistic movement and the wider struggle.[13] Nikki Giovanni's poem "Beautiful Black Men" (1968) illustrated many of these populist, nationalist, and Afrocentric objectives. It immediately recalled the vocabulary of the streets with its broken grammar, and the cadence of a popular song with its repetition and restatement:

i wanta say just gotta say something
bout those beautiful beautiful beautiful outasight
black men
with they afros

At the start, Giovanni identified beauty with an exclusively African American characteristic. With a lusty earthiness, she went on to celebrate a unique sense of style that—in her legend—united a diverse body of humanity. No doubt the poet intended to reclaim black men from their frequent stereotyping by the dominant culture as lazy and good for nothing. She invested them with positive traits, not to correct white impressions but for the benefit of her own people. In the final verse, Giovanni achieved this goal by introducing a group of musician-heroes, "new breed men" set-off by their African-inspired "dashiki suits" and "outasight afros." Their assured gait derived from a knowledge of their roots (evident in their "dirty toes"), signifying a sense of self.[14]

By the mid-1960s, a second generation of free improvisers and their critical champions had begun to position "the new thing" at the center of this emerging black aesthetic. Ironically, the closer musicians aligned free jazz with avant-garde modernism, the more forcefully Amiri Baraka, Larry Neal, A. B. Spellman, Archie Shepp, Marion Brown, and others attempted to uncover performance characteristics common to the black arts and distinct from European precedents. By linking free improvisation to an African past—real or imagined—they claimed jazz as the preserve of African American musicians and as speaking most directly and meaningfully to an African American audience. Thus they fused the two assaults on jazz music's canonical identity. In their interpretation, free jazz represented both a defiance of European aesthetic discipline and a rejection of integrationist ideology. In addition, revolutionary nationalist critics—including white commentators such as Frank Kofsky and John Sinclair—vehemently attacked liberal economic practices in the jazz business and trade press. By mid-decade, mutual recrimination among critics, businessmen, and fans over the meaning and ownership of jazz seemed poised to subvert the music's fragile status.

The centrality of music and musicians to the Black Arts Movement owed a great deal to a cadre of young African American writers and performers who gathered in New York City from the late 1950s to the mid-1960s. They congregated around Newark-born Howard University drop-out Amiri Baraka, who moved to Greenwich Village at age twenty-two following his discharge from the air force in 1957. His close acquaintances included former Howard students such as the poet and essayist A. B. Spellman and saxophonist Marion Brown. Through Brown, and his own political activities, Baraka met saxophonist Archie Shepp. The two horn players introduced him to the wider free jazz scene and to musicians such as Sun Ra, Sonny Murray, Albert Ayler, and John Coltrane. Baraka became friendly also with key literary figures such as Larry Neal, who moved to New York in 1964, and Askia Touré (then Rolland Snellings). Between 1964 and 1966, Neal and Touré helped edit the radical journal *Liberator*, an important forum for discussions of the new sensibility. The group participated actively in political and artistic circles for many years. Baraka maintained the greatest visibility through his controversial poems and critically acclaimed plays such as *Dutchman*, which won an Obie award for best off-Broadway production in 1964 and signaled the beginning of the cultural explosion. From their earliest collaborations, however, each member exerted an important influence over the others' thinking.[15]

These New York artists formed the backbone of the Black Arts Movement's east coast wing. Notably, they shared an interest in new performance practices that connected several art forms. While writers Baraka, Spellman, Neal, and Touré analyzed free improvisation in album liner notes and articles in the jazz and African American press, many of the younger musicians participated actively in literary endeavors. Marion Brown arrived in New York with a reputation as a writer, penned music criticism and art history, and filled a minor acting role in the original production of *Dutchman*. Archie Shepp, Sun Ra, and Albert Ayler provided musical accompaniment for Baraka's plays during the mid-1960s. Shepp, whose play *Junebug Graduates Tonight* was produced off-Broadway in 1965, recited original poems such as "Malcolm, Malcolm, Semper Malcolm" (a tribute to the slain black power leader) at musical performances and on records. Baraka produced several loft concerts in Greenwich Village during the early part of the decade, at which he sometimes read his own verse before or between sets. According to free drummer Milford Graves, these readings helped politicize many musicians and reoriented their conception of "the new thing." Yet the musicians probably exerted an equal or greater influence over emerging African American poets and playwrights. John Coltrane's exploration of nonwestern forms stimulated a widespread interest in the black diaspora in literary circles, while Marion Brown's study of jazz music's origins shaped Baraka's view of African survivals. Baraka even patterned his poetry recitation style after the screams and yelps of Albert Ayler's saxophone playing. None of these developments overcame political and aesthetic differences among creative artists, but a shared process of radicalization facilitated free improvisation's gravitation into the orbit of the Black Arts Movement.[16]

Amiri Baraka's intellectual development best illustrated the events that brought music to the forefront of the black aesthetic and made jazz—especially free improvisation—its highest expression. Baraka gained initial prominence in literary circles as a bohemian poet. Between 1958 and 1961 he coedited a number of "little magazines" such as *Yugen* and *the floating bear*, cultivated friendships with several beat writers including Jack Kerouac, Allen Ginsberg, and Edward Dorn, and published his first volume of poetry. Baraka had left Howard University in 1954 because he found the atmosphere stifling. "The Howard thing let me understand the Negro sickness," he recalled. "They teach you how to pretend to be white." His dissatisfaction with black bourgeois respectability led him initially to the artistic alienation of the beat movement, but he soon explored alternatives that resonated with his developing race consciousness. Inspired by Robert F. Williams's example of armed self-defense in North Carolina and by African anticolonial movements, Baraka made a trip to Cuba in July 1960 to survey the revolution at first hand. The visit initiated a transformation of his career, convincing him that art and politics were not mutually exclusive. The committed example of Latin American intellectuals he met in Cuba inspired him to pursue a socially engaged literature and, ultimately, an aesthetically-informed activism.[17]

Baraka maintained an uncertain relationship to black nationalism during the early 1960s. His 1961 arrests for demonstrating on behalf of the Fair Play for Cuba Committee, and in protest at U.S. complicity in the assassination of Congolese premier Patrice Lumumba, indicate a growing identification with Third World liberation struggles. Baraka's heroes from this time—Malcolm X, Robert F. Williams, Fidel Castro, and Lumumba—cultivated organic connections to extended communities of nonwhite people. Yet despite his diatribes against liberal tokenism, Baraka belonged to a small group of African American intellectuals who had assimilated the bohemian subculture artistically, socially, and romantically and acted as interpreters of the black experience for their hosts. They remained isolated from the perceived center of black politi-

Figure 12. John Coltrane (left) and Amiri Baraka in the dressing room at Birdland, New York City, 1963. Courtesy Institute of Jazz Studies, Rutgers University.

cal life in Harlem. Baraka recruited fellow Village-based black artists including Archie Shepp, A. B. Spellman, Harold Cruse, and Calvin Hicks into the Organization of Young Men (OYM), through which he envisioned bridging the gap. "We weren't certain just what we wanted to do," remembered Baraka later. "We talked vaguely about going 'uptown' to work. But what work we did not understand." He soon merged OYM with the Harlem-based On Guard for Freedom Committee but opposed demands from nationalists to exclude whites from the new organization.[18]

About the same time that Baraka started experimenting with political groups, he began submitting feature articles about jazz—especially "the new thing"—to music publications. The two events appear to be related. Baraka expressed his frustration at the black community's fragmentation, lack of cohesion, and critical infighting in a September 1961 letter to Edward Dorn:

I meet these shabby headed "black nationalists" or quasi intellectual opportunists, who have never read a fucking book that was worth anything in their damned lives . . . and shudder that any kind of movement or feeling shd come down to the "people" thru their fingers. Also, these stupid left wing farts whose only claim to goodness is that they know capitalism is bad! Shit. So where does that leave me? Fuck if I know. I have people, old men, on Harlem streets come up and shake my hand, or old ladies kiss me, and nod "You are a good man . . . you will help us." And what? So some foul mouthed prick nationalist gets up on a box and denounces me for having a white wife![19]

Baraka concluded that without some sense of cultural commonality to raise their collective consciousness, African Americans would not and could not take united action to alleviate their shared condition. As classmates at Howard, Baraka and A. B. Spellman had spent many hours absorbing literature professor Sterling A. Brown's love of jazz. Of all the art forms, they learned from Brown, jazz offered the richest tradition and the most inspiring model of black innovation and achievement. Spellman began writing for the trade press at the same time as Baraka, and proposed that music most perfectly represented the black spirit because, unlike painting or sculpture, it represented a cultural inheritance rather than an acquired art. Musicians perpetuated and promulgated the conventions of their craft within the black community, not at white-led schools and institutes.[20]

Having found a model, Baraka attempted to describe and account for an aesthetic dominated by music that united the cultural traditions of the black diaspora. He knew that African survivals offered clues to the past, yet carefully distinguished African American art from that of the ancestral continent. As black slaves in the new world struggled to come to terms with their American identity, not least the restrictions and pro-

hibitions of bondage, their cultural forms experienced significant transformation. Thus Baraka looked for a common approach to art that
separated the transnational black aesthetic from a European heritage.
He faced a challenging task because, as the previous chapter demonstrated, champions of free improvisation had framed the music as an
extension of artistic modernism and emphasized the abstract language
shared by several western genres. In his first extended article, published
by *Metronome* in September 1961, Baraka insisted that although jazz performers may have "milked" classical music for solutions to technical
problems, the cultural impetus and ultimate meaning behind the music
was black.[21]

In this way, Baraka proposed a key feature of the Black Arts Movement
very early in the 1960s. By collapsing the distinction between art and
experience, he emphasized the limits of the strictly musicological analysis of Martin Williams, Whitney Balliett, and other modernist champions
of jazz. "The major flaw of this approach to Negro music," he wrote in
a *Down Beat* article of 1963, "is that it strips the music too ingenuously
of its social and cultural intent. It seeks to define jazz as an art (or a folk
art) that has come out of no intelligent body of socio-cultural philosophy." Instead, he countered, "the music is a result of the attitude, the
stance." Baraka recognized not only a change of artistic sensibility in the
stylistic progression of jazz, but a sociological image of African American
existence in the United States. Black music represented primarily a posture toward the world. Changes in style mirrored historical discontinu-
ities in African Americans' social position. This interpretation gained
broad acceptance within the Black Arts Movement, especially among
music theorists such as Spellman, Neal, James Stewart, and Ron Welburn. It won support also among some experimental musicians. "I can't
see any separation between my music and my life," Archie Shepp told
Leonard Feather. "They can't blow up three children and a church without its somehow reflecting itself in some aspect of your cultural development."[22]

Baraka soon had an opportunity to detail the sociocultural factors he
believed separated African American from Euro-American standards.
His earlier article in *Metronome* caught the attention of William Morrow
and Company, which invited Baraka to submit a book outline. Published
in 1963, *Blues People* anchored the black aesthetic in an African tradition
of respect for artistic practice. The functional role of art in African religious life imbued the process of creation with as much or more prestige
than the finished artifact. "*Expression* issued from life and *was* beauty."[23]
Since post-Renaissance western man was a secular individual, in Baraka's
view, he valued art only for its final pulchritude, thus structural goals
triumphed over the transcendent act. Baraka conceived of black music

in the United States as the embodiment of an oppositional value system. Drawing on an African inheritance, it challenged the commodity-driven rationality of western culture. Thus African American musicians inherited two conflicting traditions, which they attempted to resolve in the blues and later in jazz. As Kimberly Benston has recognized, Baraka "interprets the evolution of this idiom as the struggle of African expressiveness to assert itself in ever-changing musical forms."[24]

The ethos of jazz as a "non-matrixed" language became a key tenet of the movement's musical theory. As James Stewart elaborated, black art had "little concept of fixity" and thus did not value preservation or perpetuation. The operation or "the accomplishment of creating" mattered more than the end product, a "temporary residue" of the artistic act.[25] Ironically, this emphasis on action and process recalled the modernist discourse linking free jazz and abstract expressionism. In Baraka's hands, the same feature evoked an anti-modern critique of enlightened reason rooted in black music's resistance to capture, exploitation, or eradication. The primacy of the oral tradition in cultural transmission had become a virtue during slavery, when owners attempted to strip slaves of the physical representations of their heritage. In a discussion of African survivals rooted in Melville Herskovits' study *The Myth of the Negro Past*, and the observations of his friend Marion Brown, Baraka identified those jazz styles that encapsulated the African approach to art.[26] He recognized the most complete statements of black American identity in blues and bebop. Unlike the commercially-influenced swing, cool, or hard bop styles, Baraka argued, their melodic and rhythmic lines transcended excessive structural constraints and most closely approximated human vocal effects. In addition, the physical isolation of wandering bluesmen and deviant bebop cliques enhanced the separatism inherent in their music.[27]

As Baraka struggled to relate free improvisers such as Ornette Coleman and Don Cherry to the black tradition, he began to realize how much they shared both the musical emancipation and the social alienation of earlier "roots" styles. As he wrote to Dorn in May 1961:

My bear note was simply to place the two of them. As stylists. As forces &c. To my mind, going back to Bop (which I sd [sic] of Ornette) is genius. Bop and Blues I think are the only two complete musics to come out of Shade music! Completely autonomous![28]

In *Blues People*, Baraka proposed that free improvisers survived assimilation, socially as well as musically, by self-consciously assuming roles as artists. Society stigmatized free form musicians, he believed, because they resisted easy commodification. Baraka also heralded "the new thing" as a renewal of an African American approach to music making.

Figure 13. Marion Brown in an undated publicity shot, probably mid-1960s. Photograph by Bill Stephens. Courtesy Photographs and Prints Division, Schomburg Center for Research in Black Culture, The New York Public Library, Astor, Lenox, and Tilden Foundations.

Its natural emotiveness and negation of form recalled the same undiluted expressiveness as Blind Lemon Jefferson and Charlie Parker.[29]

Critics generally praised Baraka's attempt to provide an intellectual and historical context for the development of jazz. Many of the music's aspiring canonizers, including Nat Hentoff and Joe Goldberg, increasingly despaired of the modernist bifurcation between art and life and welcomed the new approach.[30] Baraka faced severe criticism, however, from those who had championed jazz as a national art form. Ralph Ellison argued that *Blues People* ignored the cross-pollination between black and white influences that formed a common American culture. According to Ellison, Baraka unrealistically asserted the survival of a pure strain of the African impulse that defied acculturation, when in reality African Americans had always helped shape mainstream music. Albert Murray agreed, contending that the blues idiom "represents the most comprehensive and the most profound assimilation. It is the product of a sensibility that is completely compatible with the *human* imperatives of modern times and American life."[31]

Blues People suggested that the black aesthetic's critique of western culture was incompatible with the black bourgeoisie's pursuit of material advancement. This construction of jazz and blues as a contrary force cast black middle-class distance from its musical heritage as evidence of cultural "passing." To get ahead, Baraka implied, African Americans must deny their roots. He interpreted this rejection of the blues and jazz tradition as a racial transgression, minimizing the role of aesthetic taste and the music's social origins as determinants of its reception. Similarly, Baraka attributed musical innovation to an anti-commercial, anti-assimilationist stance rather than economic or artistic motives. White musicians existed on the margins of this interpretive scheme, rebels against their upbringing who chose to absorb a foreign culture. *Blues People* did not account for the presumed rebellion of jazz pioneers such as Sidney Bechet, Duke Ellington, Fletcher Henderson, and Miles Davis against their middle-class upbringing. For Baraka, authenticity seemed wedded to an idyllic conception of the folk, evident in his evocation of the blues to represent the African American impulse in music. It would take several years for him to seriously explore alternative class orientations to the jazz and blues tradition.[32]

Discussing Baraka's work in relation to the wider Black Arts Movement, Saunders Redding challenged the notion of a viable black aesthetic. He argued that attempts to reclaim an African heritage floundered on a poor historical understanding of African cultural norms. Too few champions of Afrocentric traditions appreciated the diversity of the continent's languages, religions, arts, or fashions. Redding believed that scholars deceived themselves by attempting to recover a homogeneous cultural impulse where none existed. Charles Kiel agreed, signifying on Herskovits to accuse Baraka of fashioning his own "myth of the negro past." Redding, Kiel, and other reviewers identified accurately a lack of comparative nuance in *Blues People*'s survey of African customs, yet it is unlikely that Baraka deluded himself about the extent of similarities between tribes, regions, and nations. The process of creating what one commentator described as "an Africa of the mind and the imagination" remains the most important aspect of his writing on the history of African American music. By constructing a romantic ideal of pure jazz, Baraka offered African Americans a common source of identification, pride, and "roots." The symbolic value of myths to a "functional, collective, and committing" art (a phrase popularized by Maulana Ron Karenga) played a critical role in fermenting an African American consciousness. As Lorenzo Thomas has proposed, the Black Arts Movement attempted to rework an ideology previously administered by jazz music's white guardians. Privileging black voices in jazz criticism by insisting on familiarity with the music's social and cultural context, Baraka contested ownership of jazz music's meanings and reclaimed it as a talismanic expression of black culture.[33]

The Black Arts Movement's nationalism finally crystallized during 1965. The splintering civil rights movement, the spread of Fanon's ideas, and in particular the assassination of Malcolm X radicalized and clarified the goals of its leading participants. The former Nation of Islam minister had inspired many key figures in the arts. His speeches transformed Sonia Sanchez from an integrationist CORE worker to a poet striving for a mass black audience. His vision provided the common bond between activists Amiri Baraka, Larry Neal, and Askia Touré. Malcolm X's death, apparently at the bidding of a Nation of Islam faction, underscored the destructiveness of internal strife and the need for a liberating racial unity. As a result, African American intellectuals increasingly dedicated their efforts toward African American people. Larry Neal opened a 1968 essay, widely anthologized as the black arts manifesto, with a statement of resolve: "The Black Arts Movement is radically opposed to any concept of the artist that alienates him from his community." Elsewhere, he reiterated the need for black performers to reject protest politics aimed at reforming the establishment, white audiences, and prevalent aesthetic standards in favor of an art that strengthened black America through promoting self-actualization.[34]

Once again, Amiri Baraka signaled the changing movement's implications for jazz. Baraka had not completely defined his separatism in 1963. The remnants of his beat philosophy surfaced in *Blues People* when he suggested that both black and white bohemians could identify with "the new thing" on account of their shared familiarity with the conventions of western nonconformity. By 1965 he had severed his links to the white establishment by marriage, residence, and prestige, and replaced this distinction between the artist and the lay audience with an antipathy between black culture and the white observer.[35] In a December panel discussion organized by *Jazz* magazine, entitled "Jazz and Revolutionary Black Nationalism," Baraka told pianist Steve Kuhn: "The music you play is the white man's music. If somebody listens to your music and can't tell you're white, it's either because A) they don't know enough about jazz to know you're white, or B) you're imitating black." When Frank Kofsky suggested that he could detect a revolutionary conscious-ness in the work of Archie Shepp and Albert Ayler, Baraka retorted that the difference between a white sympathizer and a black musician was "the difference between a man watching someone have an orgasm and someone having an orgasm."[36]

Baraka, Neal, and Touré made a symbolic break with their integration-ist pasts when they established the Black Arts Repertory Theater/School during 1965. A bold attempt to build a community institution dedicated to bringing black arts to black people, it featured concerts by Cecil Tay-lor, John Coltrane, Sun Ra, Archie Shepp, Albert Ayler, Pharoah Sand-ers, Jackie McLean, and Milford Graves, courses in black history and literature, and drama and poetry workshops. For several months BARTS secured funding for expanded summer programs from Harlem Youth Opportunities Unlimited (HARYOU), an agency funded by the Office of Economic Opportunity as part of President Lyndon Johnson's War on Poverty. For eight weeks, 400 students took lessons in black studies and African American drama. BARTS advertised its programs with open-air demonstrations in parks, playgrounds, and vacant lots. As organizers sealed off a city block, residents and bystanders gathered to hear experi-mental jazz, a revolutionary play, or a poetry reading. "Each night throughout that summer we flooded Harlem streets with new music, new poetry, new dance, new paintings," Baraka recalled, "and the sweep of the Black Arts movement had recycled itself back to the people."[37]

The BARTS experiment did not last long. Baraka's public repudiation of nonviolence, advocacy of territorial independence for Harlem, and growing notoriety in the press soon ended government support, although not before the organization had wrung an estimated $200,000 or more from HARYOU. Lacking economic or institutional support in Harlem, BARTS struggled to overcome internal strife and resentment from local nationalists, who regarded the poets and musicians as invad-ers from downtown. Police closed the operation within a year, after find-ing a stash of guns in the BARTS brownstone offices, by which time Baraka had retreated to Newark and a disaffected volunteer had shot and wounded Larry Neal. Despite its brief life and rapid disintegration,

BARTS helped inspire longer-lasting community projects throughout the country, including an estimated 800 black theaters and cultural centers and a supportive network of Black Arts festivals and conferences. It attempted also to position jazz musicians, particularly free improvisers, as key figures in transforming the historical and spiritual consciousness of African Americans and providing a basis for overcoming such disunity in the future.[38]

Reflecting on his experience with BARTS, Askia Touré later remembered "we would serenade the people on the streets of Harlem, and it made the authorities nervous as hell. We went all over Harlem and brought to its neglected, colonized masses the messages of Black power, dignity, and beauty."[39] Nationalists insisted that music helped carry these messages, despite its minimal use of words or visual images. They looked to jazz music's aesthetic features for evidence of a nonwestern heritage, which might support a unifying cultural agenda. Free improvisation's stylistic traits, especially collective creation, Afro-Asian inferences, and vocalized instrumental lines, appeared to embody a black aesthetic. Yet in the hands of a second wave of experimental musicians such as Albert Ayler and Roscoe Mitchell, these same performance techniques became tools for pursuing a concept of pure sound anticipated in the work of classical composers including John Cage and Karlheinz Stockhausen. Attempting to close down alternative readings of free improvisation and to confirm its African American—rather than contemporary modernist—lineage, black arts theorists insisted on the revolutionary implications of the musicians' intent. In particular, Baraka and Neal emphasized the role of ritual in conveying messages of black solidarity and communal uplift. Thus they fused a western romantic understanding of the artist with the function of an African griot, in order to forward the goal of African American liberation.

Free improvisation provided an attractive symbol for the Black Arts Movement because a number of stylistic characteristics appeared to distance jazz from its European influences and reassert neglected elements of the African American past. Critics as diverse as Martin Williams, Nat Hentoff, Amiri Baraka, and James Stewart compared Ornette Coleman's group improvisation with the practice of New Orleans musicians in the early years of the century.[40] Like many pioneer jazz ensembles, Coleman's group imposed a degree of order during the performance. The latitude afforded individual musicians improvising collectively contrasted sharply with the rigid scores and hierarchical leadership expected of classical music orchestras. Even aleatory compositions frequently abdicated compositional choices to chance rather than to spontaneous creativity by the performers.[41]

Free jazz instrumentalists explicitly paid tribute to music outside the Euro-American tradition, evoking rather than reproducing directly African and Asian strains. Poet Ronald Milner described John Coltrane as "a man who, through his saxophone, before your eyes and ears, completely annihilates every single Western influence." Although Milner exaggerated, Coltrane frequently looked abroad for solutions to technical problems. In one month of 1961 alone he recorded pieces influenced by African, Indian, English, and Spanish folk music. Coltrane wanted to free his group from harmonic constrictions but, as the 1960 recording with Coleman's band showed, he felt uneasy abandoning modes and scales completely. By approximating the Indian tamboura's sustained drone, using a pedal point or repeating bass, he found a way to maintain a tonal center while obscuring functional harmony. Coltrane's interest in Indian music, fueled by a lengthy correspondence with sitar expert Ravi Shankar, may also have influenced the length of his improvisations, his choice of scales, and his characteristic melodic development.[42]

The distinctly nonwestern sound of Indian ragas, and their association with spirituality, attracted John Coltrane and Eric Dolphy much as it appealed to pop groups such as the Beatles later in the decade. Coltrane's "India," and his chanting on the album *Om* (1965), suggest that jazz musicians' fascination with nonwestern cultures extended beyond the black diaspora. The decline of European empires helped inspire a new appreciation for varieties of world music rooted in alternative cultural values. Experimental musicians placed the idea of Africa at the center of the emerging black aesthetic, however. From 1961 until his death in 1967, Coltrane mimicked African methods on albums such as *Africa/Brass* (1961) and *Kulu Se Mama* (1965). His friendship with Nigerian drummer Michael Babatunde Olatunji encouraged this interest. Like many free improvisers, Coltrane sometimes used additional bassists, drummers, or percussionists to achieve complex rhythmic textures and additional layers of sonority. Malachi Favors Maghostut of the Art Ensemble of Chicago researched African music extensively, too. Favors encouraged fellow Chicagoans to fashion their own "little instruments" in order to create dense layers of overlapping pulse.

Another distinctly non-European technique formed an integral component of "the new thing," drawing the attention of friendly and hostile critics alike. Free improvisers, especially saxophonists, tended to simulate human speech patterns on their instruments. Nat Hentoff, Amiri Baraka, and others again drew parallels to the "singing horns" of New Orleans jazz. Indeed Baraka, drawing once more upon his discussions with Marion Brown, identified this vocal quality as a key African trait that slaves transferred to the New World. As the pitch of each syllable altered the meaning of words in Africa's tonal languages, careful attention to melodic inflection proved essential to preserving the intent of vocalized references in instrumental lines.[43] This quality reemerged during the 1960s in works such as Coltrane's *A Love Supreme* (1964), in which each instrument improvised around a four-note phrase that reproduced the cadence of the title. Coltrane chanted "a love su-preme" over the figure, erasing any doubt as to the correlation.

Although generations of jazz performers had vocalized instrumental lines, free improvisers exhibited a much greater range of emotions than their predecessors, including anger, passion, and rage. They sacrificed the qualities of intonation and coloration esteemed by European art music in order to produce a harder tone. And by freeing themselves from chord and pitch restrictions, they incorporated a wider range of expressive sound effects. In this way, Archie Shepp's gruff tenor and Pharoah Sanders' high register squeals could imitate not only the human song but the human cry and shriek as well. In a related development, bandleaders frequently discarded or radically altered the role of the piano. The keyboard limited a group's capacity for microtonal (vocally-inflected) increments, and the piano's traditional role of feeding chords inhibited the scope of a soloist's melodies. Ornette Coleman dispensed with the instrument after his initial Contemporary album, Coltrane's pianist McCoy Tyner usually dropped out during the leader's extended improvisations, and Cecil Taylor adopted tone clusters as a means of eliminating the dominance of any given pitch.

John Coltrane's frequent African and quasi-Asian references demonstrate the preoccupation of many performers with the musical and mystical potential of Third World cultures. The opening section of "Africa," recorded by the John Coltrane Quartet in conjunction with a supporting orchestra during 1961, displayed several musical characteristics prized by black nationalists.[44] During the introduction, pianist McCoy Tyner's pedal point combined with two basses to suggest an "eastern" drone, while Elvin Jones' drumming evoked shifting polyrhythms rather than standard time. Arranger Eric Dolphy used the remaining instruments to further blur musical boundaries. The massed brass and reeds enhanced the indistinct tonality of Tyner's repeating figure before Coltrane's tenor saxophone entered the mix. In the background, the orchestra's snorts, gurgles, and screeches continued to obscure the pitch center. Although Coltrane planned his thematic statement in advance—as alternate takes demonstrate—and contained it within the chords, he produced a startlingly strident and penetrating tone. Upon leaving the predetermined melodic sequence, Coltrane's first solo anticipated the harmonic dissonance that dominated experimental jazz by mid-decade.

Despite these self-conscious efforts to incorporate nonwestern influences, the similarities between modern jazz and other Euro-American

Figure 14. Pharoah Sanders in the recording studio, December 1970. Courtesy Michael Ochs Archives.com.

aesthetic practices provide the biggest stumbling block to Baraka's portrait of an art breaking free from cultural colonization. At the time, Saunders Redding noted the indebtedness of Black Arts poetry to the beat tradition, hippie culture, and free speech movement. More recent cultural histories have identified "a will to explore and record the spontaneous creative act" as a definitive feature of avant-garde art between 1940 and 1960. Scholars such as Daniel Belgrad have argued that abstract expressionism, beat literature, modern dance, and bebop jazz embodied the process of improvisation—so key to Baraka's Afrocentric scheme—as an alternative to the "epistemology of objectivity" that supported rigid cultural distinctions.[45] Although the arbitrary nature of this time frame obscures the longstanding importance of spontaneity to African American music and other media, such studies have reaffirmed that a shared approach linked jazz with several disparate genres.

The most compelling challenge to Baraka's thesis, however, lay not in comparing the usual suspects of recent cultural criticism but by juxtaposing free improvisation with developments in western musical modernism. In an era when racial identity increasingly confirmed musical legitimacy, performers often appeared reluctant to acknowledge a common pool of resources and inspiration. The first generation of free improvisers, however, all possessed considerable familiarity with contemporary concert music. Taylor's conservatory training, Coleman's lessons with Gunther Schuller, and Coltrane's studies at Granoff studios provide just a few examples of jazz innovators' exposure to an alternative heritage. Their rejection of harmonic tyranny in favor of an abstract language of unspecified tones and subtle shadings of color found precedent in Schoenberg, Webern, and Boulez. Indeed, the atonalists, serialists, and aleatory composers predicted nearly every liberalization of structural constraints practiced by free improvisers, from flexible phrase and section lengths to the atmospheric rather than metronomic application of rhythm and percussion instruments.[46]

By the mid-1960s, a second wave of free improvisers began to assemble these elements in a way that appeared closer to developments in classical music than to the jazz tradition. Following Cecil Taylor's example they attempted, in the words of saxophonist Albert Ayler, "to escape from notes to sounds." In conventional works, sound enhanced the musician's projection of a theme. In the new music, sound itself became the subject of development and experimentation.[47] John Cage established this goal in his revolutionary manifesto "The Future of Music: Credo," delivered first in 1940. "Wherever we are, what we hear is mostly noise," he told an audience in Seattle. "When we ignore it, it disturbs us. When we listen to it, we find it fascinating. The sound of a truck at fifty miles per hour. Static between the stations. Rain. We want to capture and control these sounds, to use them not as sound effects but as musical instruments."[48] During the 1920s and 1930s, Henry Cowell and others had manipulated pitch, timbre, and duration using tone clusters, prepared pianos, and elastic form. In addition to exploring similar territory, Cage questioned the very notion of musicality by incorporating chance noises through the use of electronic radios (*Credo in US*) and structured silence (*4'33*). His desire to undermine the composer's agency, and with it the romantic idea of the artist as genius, reflected a growing interest in oriental music and eastern philosophy. A quarter-century after Cage's Seattle address, Karlheinz Stockhausen confirmed the realization of its objectives: "Sounds previously classified as noise are now being incorporated into the vocabulary of our music, just as the apparently random scrawls, lines, and blobs of abstract painting have become accepted parts of modern art." The same sensibility that Stockhausen recognized in fine art music and painting appeared in jazz. Don Ayler, trumpeter in brother Albert's band, gave specific instructions for following their music. "One way not to [listen], is to focus on the notes and stuff like that. Instead, try to move your imagination toward . . . the pitches, the colors. You have to watch them move."[49]

Some of the richest improvisations emerged from the South Side of Chicago, where Muhal Richard Abrams had directed the Experimental

Band since 1962. Under his tutelage, young musicians developed an expressive vocabulary facilitated by free forms. The Roscoe Mitchell Sextet's *Sound* (1966), for example, explored fully the implications of its title. The lead track dispensed with conventional timekeeping, using percussive instruments to create dense, indeterminately-pitched textures. Solo voices—a trombone, recorder, clarinet, or saxophone—rose from and returned to static supporting tapestries. The lack of an explicit beat and accumulation of layered sound typified the Chicago aesthetic and also featured prominently on John Coltrane's *Ascension*, recorded in June 1965. The session brought together the first wave of innovators, represented by the leader's classic quartet, and younger musicians such as Pharoah Sanders, Marion Brown, Archie Shepp, and John Tchicai. Coltrane's simultaneous abandonment of the beat and the chordal framework contributed above all to the churning turbulence of the final takes. Coltrane and Mitchell produced albums that—along with Cecil Taylor's *Unit Structures* (1966) and Muhal Richard Abrams's *Levels and Degrees of Light* (1967)—signaled new sonic directions for jazz. Strikingly original in execution, their conceptual departures did not lack precedent. As Ronald Radano has pointed out, "with free jazz, black music and modernism achieved a level of structural syncretism, in which likenesses from both musical worlds encouraged stylistic merging."[50]

Although Amiri Baraka admired European avant-garde music by John Cage, Morton Feldman, and others, the Black Arts Movement's mythology ensured that cultural nationalists denied any significant cross-fertilization between the two traditions. Ron Welburn dismissed similarities between free improvisation and the "spiritually alienated" music of the serialists as "irrelevant." James Stewart conceded that jazz music's focus on "the operation of creating" converged with the practices of cubists, abstract expressionists, and performance artists. Yet Stewart insisted that the transfer of ideas moved in one direction, as white bohemians tapped an African American creative approach to revive their dying tradition.[51] In a 1969 *Ebony* article about the recently deceased saxophonist, A. B. Spellman claimed that "a man like Coltrane was playing *about* something consciously black, no matter how abstract his formulation may be." Although Coltrane expressed few overtly political opinions, and gave equivocal answers when pressed on controversial current events, music theorists returned to Baraka's emphasis on the attitude behind the performance. James Stewart declared the rejection of dominant cultural standards a revolutionary act in itself. Regardless of the musician's rhetoric, Stewart equated the new music's "inner dynamic" with nationalist tenets. In a war for control of black minds, Lindsay Barrett added, embracing the black aesthetic was "like wielding a Coltrane solo as a club."[52]

In a *Negro Digest* column of 1968, Larry Neal identified a second avenue of communication between black artists and the community: "The only thing which is fundamental to good art is its ritual quality. And the function of ritual is to reinforce the group's operable myths, ideals, and values." Comparing African American performers to the religious functionaries who preserved and passed on tribal traditions, Neal encouraged them to strive for "the kind of energy that informs the music of John Coltrane, Cecil Taylor, Albert Ayler and Sun Ra—the modern equivalent of the ancient ritual energy." The purpose of such art, he told the magazine's readers, lay in its ability "to shake us out of our lethargy and free our bodies and minds, opening us to unrealized possibilities."[53] Neal, Spellman, Baraka, and other young black intellectuals refined a mythology that cast musicians in a priestly role, reinforcing timeless values of communal support and individual transcendence shaped by an African past.

John Coltrane's music and persona played a critical role in redefining concepts of spirituality and black masculinity in the search for an elevated consciousness. Coltrane's blistering tone, speed, and musical attack, reinforced by powerful drummer Elvin Jones, provided the energy basis of which Neal spoke. The furious interaction between these two musicians heralded a muscular assault on jazz music's conventions. In particular they destroyed bebop's clever conceits, including its light, swinging groove, Tin Pan Alley quotations, slick exchange of fours, clever signifying heads, and ambiguous passing notes; everything, in short, that Scott Saul has identified as "bebop's ironic pose." As Saul notes, Coltrane replaced the hipster's flash and display with an inner-directed search for sanctification. The minimal chordal movement and expanded duration of Coltrane's modal work suspended the listener's grounding in time. Coltrane's frequent use of the drone or vamp contributed to the incantative effect. His repetitive melodic deconstruction and restatement, within cycles of unresolved harmonic tension, reinforced the sense of inward searching that recast jazz music's phallocentric thrust and parry with an inner strength rooted in vulnerability.[54]

Coltrane's personal example reinforced his reputation for integrity. A 1957 spiritual awakening stemming from heroin detoxification provided the defining inspiration for his autobiographical album *A Love Supreme* (1964). The forty-minute, four-movement suite acknowledged both the composer's reliance on a divine being and his perception of God's mercy and deliverance. The recording's explicit exposure of Coltrane's ritualistic journey into the self through the section titles ("Acknowledgement," "Resolution," "Pursuance," "Psalm"), accompanying prayer poem, and conversion testimony helped make it his most successful album, selling half a million copies in five years. The humility and generosity of spirit reflected in the record's tribute manifest itself also in Coltrane's conciliatory response to his fiercest critics and constant willingness to help younger experimental artists secure gigs and recording contracts. After Impulse! released *A Love Supreme* in early 1965, Coltrane followed the second wave of free improvisers away from traditional harmonic, melodic, and rhythmic frameworks toward the exploration of soundscapes in releases such as *Ascension* (1965) and *Meditations* (1965). As the titles imply, Coltrane linked the act of musical liberation with a mystical universalism. "My music is the spiritual expression of what I am—my faith, my knowledge, my being," he told a *Newsweek* reporter in 1966. "I'd like to point out to people the divine in a musical language that transcends words. I want to speak to their souls."[55]

If Coltrane led by example, Chicago's Association for the Advancement of Creative Musicians (AACM) self-consciously attempted, in the words of its charter, "to stimulate Spiritual growth in Creative artists . . . to uplift the public image of Creative Musicians," and "to uphold the tradition of elevated, cultured Musicians handed down from the past." Members of this performers' collective such as Muhal Richard Abrams, Roscoe Mitchell, Joseph Jarman, and Malachi Favors Maghostut embraced the parallel with Africa's legendary griots. Those musicians who had played with the Experimental Band viewed the act of collective improvisation as a highly ritualistic performance. Abrams taught his pupils to regard experimental music making as a spiritual quest, in which participants learned to cast off the cultural restrictions represented by functional harmony. By trusting and supporting each other, they found their own paths to artistic resolution.[56]

Nobody valued the relationship between ritual and myth, or believed in their contribution to shaping the future, more than Sun Ra. A self-described "myth scientist," Sun Ra's extensive reading convinced him—along with Malcolm X, Frantz Fanon, and many African American thinkers of his generation—that white historians manipulated the past to serve their own racist ends. Sun Ra displayed a lifelong passion for challenging conventional wisdom. He constructed a series of overlapping mythologies, including the possibility of communication with other worlds and his own alien origin. His band, the Arkestra, exploited a number of performance techniques to sustain the legend of interplanetary travel and extra-terrestrial knowledge. These devices included elaborate stage costumes (for example, Sun Ra's gleaming headgear and spangled capes), unique handmade instruments such as the sun harp (a small box with steel reeds that made a tinkling sound when plucked), repetitive chants ("we'll take a trip to space, the next stop mars"), dazzling light shows, and regular processions through the audience. Sun Ra's unconventional antics undermined accepted interpretations of the

Figure 15. John Coltrane in a contemplative pose, a common image from the 1960s. Courtesy Michael Ochs Archives.com.

world and questioned the validity of objective truths. By appropriating the identity of a space traveler, he encouraged listeners to escape the limits of their immediate environment and to believe in the possibility of assuming unprescribed roles.[57]

The Black Arts Movement embraced free form musicians in this mythical capacity as seers and truth tellers. Spellman's poem "Did John's Music Kill Him?" (1969) recalled Coltrane in the role of scribe, uncovering and rewriting the past:

Figure 16. Sun Ra in a publicity shot released by Impulse! for which he recorded from 1972–1973. Courtesy Institute of Jazz Studies, Rutgers University.

> . . . *little old lady*
> had a nasty mouth. *summertime*
> when the war is. *africa* ululating
> a line bunched up like itself
> into knots paints beauty black

Baraka's pioneering work of the early and mid-1960s inspired a black poetry circuit that elevated John Coltrane to sainthood after his death. In her poem "How Long Has Trane Been Gone" (1969), Jayne Cortez— who had once married Ornette Coleman—urged its intended black audience to revere their history and heroes even as memories faded. Establishing John Coltrane as the "True image of Black Masculinity," she cast the artist as a role model, a patriarch, and a comforter. African American poets did not wait until death to celebrate free improvisers— Cecil Taylor, Sun Ra, and the other members of Coltrane's band all received their share of dedications. Coltrane remained the movement's inspiration, however, drawing tributes from some of the most notable talents of the era, including Haki Madhubuti, Sonia Sanchez, and David Henderson. Coltrane's iconic status derived in part from his ability to transcend material culture and embody a universal spirituality that later infused the counterculture. Coltrane rooted his music sufficiently in past jazz styles and popular show tunes—at least until 1965—to remain familiar, yet his sincerity and striving distanced him from jazz music's detached modernist cool.[58]

By contrast, many of jazz music's middlebrow critics failed to grasp the implications of these ritualistic costumes and performances. Sun Ra's cosmic philosophy, which appeared frequently in album liner notes and promotional materials, confused many reviewers. Don DeMicheal wanted less poetry and more personnel information on the sleeve to *Jazz in Silhouette.* Confronted with similar mystical pronouncements, Bill Mathieu sensed a "put-on" while Martin Williams found the philosophical statements distracting. Reporting on the Arkestra in concert, *New York Times* critic John S. Wilson dismissed the props as "gimmickry" and "superficial eccentricities." Similarly, Whitney Balliett and Philip Larkin mistook Archie Shepp's stage persona for comic theater.[59] Critical hostility convinced free improvisation's radical champions that African Americans played and appreciated "the new thing" best. The music's small audience at mid-decade represented a beginning, rather than an obstacle to community acceptance.[60] More important, music theorists such as Baraka, Neal, and Spellman provided a basis for reinterpreting the African American artistic tradition by fusing the two main assaults on jazz music's canonical values. Cultural nationalists took free jazz, a travesty of accepted norms of musical discipline, and turned it into a symbol of racial distinction.

Between 1964 and 1966, Baraka, Neal, Spellman, and other writers constructed and articulated an Afrocentric, nationalistic, and separatist ideology that claimed free improvisation as the contemporary manifestation of a residual black aesthetic. Tracing the roots of an ethnic musical impulse from its African origins to the experimental present, these sympathetic observers attempted to uncover performance characteristics common to the black experience and distinct from European precedents. Cultural nationalists envisioned art serving a vanguard function in the black freedom struggle. By providing a source of cultural commonality, they attempted to overcome divisions within the black community and to provide a foundation for the freedom struggle. Critics rightly questioned Baraka's understanding of African customs and his underestimation of acculturation in the United States. They usually ignored the value of constructing an African past—real or imagined—to the Black Arts Movement's attempts to provide a basis for African American unity.

It is impossible to overestimate the confusion, anger, dissension, and alarm that militant champions of free improvisation caused within the jazz industry. Amiri Baraka became the focus of hostility for many fans. His explanation that "the force and spirit . . . of jazz is through a black understanding of the world, black interpretation of the world, black definition of the world" immediately alienated thousands of listeners who prided themselves on their commitment to cultural pluralism.[61] Reader response to Baraka's January 1965 *Down Beat* profile of Archie Shepp demonstrated the fractious nature of his criticism. Baraka's contention that Shepp expressed "the weight of black" in his playing proved particularly divisive. Joyce Derkin, a Canadian reader, betrayed a hurt experienced by many committed fans. "I love jazz, yet I get the feeling that I am being put down because I am white," she wrote. David Lahm of Indianapolis responded with sarcasm: "When Archie Shepp's dug his way out from that pile of thank-you letters, perhaps he'll have time to express his gratitude to us ofays whose rather gracious gift of oppression made his music possible." Some fans came to the author's defense. Arturo Martinez Rodriquez of San Clemente considered the article "beautiful," but he held a minority opinion. Oblivious to the ways in which color-blind liberalism worked to obscure white privilege, readers sometimes responded furiously to suggestions of their complicity in ongoing discrimination. Jerry Guild of Brooklyn called Baraka's column "a venom-filled thrust from his dagger of hate," while a Philadelphia reader found "*Down Beat*'s placating, fawning obsequiousness to the militant loud-mouth Negro . . . nauseating."[62] The turmoil caused by such a small group of radicals anticipated the controversy surrounding outspoken black power leaders in the mid to late 1960s, and the cracks they produced in Lyndon Johnson's Great Society. By demonizing liberal

white critics, businessmen, and fans, cultural and revolutionary nationalists exposed a bitter rift in the jazz world that threatened to destroy the
music's identity as "America's art form."

By mid-decade, jazz music's status hung in the balance. The old
canonical values that had taken root in the Cold War consensus, and
facilitated jazz music's elevation in the cultural hierarchy, had suffered
severe blows. Baraka and his cohorts aggressively challenged the music's
integrationist basis, while revolutionary nationalists such as Frank Kofsky
and Archie Shepp repeatedly exposed the inability of economic liberalism to provide a livelihood for experimental performers. The Black Arts
Movement lionized these musicians, yet fans continued to argue acrimo-
niously over their merits. More than any other factor, the size and composition of this listener base shaped the subsequent fate of free
improvisation. On the one hand, the music's ambivalent reception
helped legitimate a divorce between its aesthetic and supposedly political values. At the same time, musicians' self-definition as artists combined with an increasingly elitist audience and support from young
African American intellectuals to pry open new opportunities for support and prestige outside the commercial marketplace.

Chapter 4

The Musicians and Their Audience

The Cellar Café, a basement coffee house with a capacity of about 90 on New York's West 91st Street, seems an unlikely venue for a jazz festival. Yet for four days beginning on the afternoon of October 1, 1964, it hosted more than twenty groups and soloists playing varieties of free improvisation to overflow crowds. Many listeners stayed around for late night panel discussions on the state of the industry featuring experimental musicians such as Cecil Taylor, Archie Shepp, and Steve Lacy. Billing the event as "The October Revolution in Jazz," producer Bill Dixon set out to demonstrate that "the music is not ahead of the people—all it needs is a chance to be heard."[1] Although few participants made a living playing "outside"—headliners included Jimmy Giuffre, Paul Bley, and Sun Ra but most were virtually unknown—regular performances and a stable audience maintained the style's visibility and forwarded its credentials as a vital creative expression. The listener profile mattered little at first. Yet cultural nationalists within the jazz business soon realized that their ability to cultivate an African American audience for "the new thing" would prove crucial in legitimating claims of black ownership. If they hoped to win critical and institutional control of black music from its traditionally white champions, Amiri Baraka, Larry Neal, A. B. Spellman, and others had to link the revolutionary arts to an African American consciousness. They faced a challenging task. Critics and performers found it much easier to rally intellectual support for John Coltrane, Ornette Coleman, and Albert Ayler as purveyors of a black aesthetic than to win the patronage of fans in sufficient numbers to sustain careers in music. This realization had profound implications for the fate of free improvisation in the jazz canon and the future of jazz in America's cultural hierarchy.

By all accounts, including record sales, availability of work, and the reluctant testimony of musicians, jazz attracted a small, predominantly white, middle-class, and educated audience during the 1960s. West 91st Street was hardly on the New York City club circuit, however, and "The October Revolution" did not appeal to a commercial jazz crowd. Those in attendance "listened attentively and receptively," according to Mar-

tin Williams. The gathering consisted of "mostly youths, obviously attentive (in some cases nearly frighteningly so)" added Dan Morgenstern,
who doubted many would pay downtown prices and stand for jazz club
distractions such as chattering customers, persistent waiters, and noisy
cash registers.[2] Dixon's hopes of creating an underground public for
free improvisation rested on combining the intellectual and bohemian
segment of the jazz audience with a community-rooted African American base. He had every reason to believe that African Americans aspired
to and enjoyed higher levels of participation in jazz activities than
whites, despite their numerical relation to the overall cadre of enthusiasts. A varied music scene persisted into the 1960s in many black neighborhoods, and experimental musicians often found a niche by
combining their music with familiar or provocative trappings. Yet at a
time of aesthetic innovation and exploration, deindustrialization and
suburbanization precipitated the decline of performance venues in
downtown entertainment districts and inner city communities. An October panel on "The Economics of Jazz" confronted the reality that as
practitioners of the most demanding and perhaps obscure music, free
improvisers felt the squeeze first and hardest. Another midnight discussion forum, "The Rise of Folk Music and the Decline of Jazz," struck an
equally ominous note. The availability of radical, accessible alternatives
that spoke directly to the baby boomers' anxieties and aspirations,
including folk and especially soul and rock later in the decade, further
reduced the listeners and venues for jazz recording and performance.

During the mid-1960s, free improvisers adopted a number of strategies to counter or compensate for the music's precarious existence and
reconnect with jazz audiences, while remaining faithful to their aesthetic
vision and heritage. Experimental musicians generally resisted the sug-
gestion that their art held little appeal for the music-loving public.
Instead, they maintained, inadequate publicity and promotion ham-
pered their efforts to communicate with a wider audience. Although the
history of jazz is replete with unilateral attempts by musicians to improve
their position in the industry, the 1960s witnessed an unprecedented
number of collective self-help efforts. Two endeavors pioneered by
experimental musicians represent opposite approaches and very different outcomes. The Jazz Composers Guild, an interracial New York City
cooperative established by Bill Dixon following "The October Revolution," attempted to introduce a second wave of free improvisers to a
wider audience through sponsoring concerts and engaging in collective
bargaining with record companies. Despite the acrimonious dissension
that accelerated its rapid demise, the organization focused renewed
attention on the burgeoning movement. The Association for the
Advancement of Creative Musicians (AACM), founded in 1965 by four

of Chicago's veteran experimental performers, engaged in similar self-promotion, although it entertained much more ambitious goals to serve the South Side black community through training, education, and moral example. Both groups encouraged the formation of similar cooperatives during the next decade, and the AACM continued its work into the twenty-first century, yet their very existence underscored the marginal position of free jazz in the marketplace.

Amiri Baraka, Larry Neal, A. B. Spellman, and other black nationalists accepted only reluctantly the music's failure to fulfill a genuinely populist function. Unwilling to concede that its abstrucity inhibited wider acceptance, champions of free jazz hoped that greater social commitment in the art itself would facilitate connection with the masses. Increasingly, they excoriated the black bourgeoisie for failing to provide mechanisms that developed, nurtured, and propagated African American talent. This call for community aid structures both acknowledged and challenged a hierarchy of expression within the black aesthetic and a stratification of the black public sphere. By the latter half of the 1960s, musicians such as Archie Shepp, Cecil Taylor, and Bill Dixon had come close to exhausting popular and institutional support in both black communities and the integrated jazz scene. One role still open to them, the romantic artist, offered a model for reconciling their commitment to artistic integrity with rejection by the music establishment. Yet by embracing it they risked distancing themselves from the evolving jazz canon and the communities they came from. The challenge for free improvisers lay in uncovering sources of prestige and funding that could sustain their complex music without sacrificing their identity as guardians of African American culture.

The size and composition of jazz audiences during the 1960s proved critical to the musicians' economic survival and the cultural identity of their music. Yet attempts to reconstruct an audience profile for this period encounter a problematic paucity of evidence. Statistical data based upon sampling or other controlled, scientific methods does not appear to exist before 1982. That year, and again a decade later, the National Endowment for the Arts (NEA) included jazz as one of seven "benchmark" categories in a Survey of Public Participation in the Arts conducted by the United States Census Bureau.[3] The reports uncovered a young, urban, white, and well-educated audience from high-income households, although participation rates among African Americans and men exceeded their representation in the adult population (especially among the most dedicated listeners). Indeed, nearly half (49 percent) of African Americans surveyed in 1992 wished to attend more jazz performances compared to less than a quarter (22 percent) of whites. As arts patronage correlates positively with education and income, areas in which African Americans as a social group lag behind whites, improvements in overall minority socioeconomic standing would likely produce even higher levels of black participation. These findings suggest that race serves as an important predictor of interest in and commitment to jazz, yet they also confirm the parameters of jazz music's distinctly limited appeal. While nearly one-third of adult Americans listened to jazz on the radio, television, records, or at a live performance during 1981–82, only 26 percent of them liked the music. This response underscored the possibility of passive involvement in jazz activities and the pervasiveness of jazz-influenced music that falls outside many canonical definitions. Jazz music's appeal grew significantly between 1982 and 1992. In the latter survey, one-third of all Americans "liked jazz," while 5 percent (up from 3 percent) liked it "best of all" musical genres. However, only 10 percent of adult Americans (19.7 million) witnessed a live performance in 1991–92, no more than the total attendance for classical music, and 80 percent of participants in all jazz activities were white. Although African Americans comprised 34 percent of respondents who considered jazz their favorite genre, at a time they made up around 11 percent of the general population, such committed enthusiasts represented less than 2 percent of people questioned. At the end of the twentieth century, jazz appeared to have a minority-rich but relatively small base.

Such recent findings may support historians' suspicions about the evolving shape of jazz audiences in earlier years and help identify trends to trace. Yet to project this evidence back in time would ignore the extent to which changes in jazz and its cultural identity have themselves affected the music's reception. The NEA's inclusion of jazz as a highbrow genre, alongside classical music, opera, musical and dramatic theater, museums, and ballet, confirms that the music's status—and one would expect its audience—has changed significantly since Ornette Coleman, John Coltrane, and Cecil Taylor first appeared on the national scene. In lieu of quantitative information, music historians rely upon personal testimony and anecdotes to define the jazz audience prior to 1982.[4] In order to recreate an accurate profile, scholars must combine the observations of musicians, critics, club owners, and other contemporary witnesses with a variety of opinions on and investments in free improvisation. No individual source is valid by itself. Taken together, and compared to musicians' working habits and record sales, a range of informants establish a feasible—if impressionistic—composite.

By the early 1960s, the demise of jazz nightclubs, disruption to music festivals, and decline in record sales reflected an erosion of the relatively affluent segment of middle-class high school and college students and young professionals who had bolstered jazz music's core audience during its mid-century resurgence. Stories of critically acclaimed recording artists drawing unemployment benefit for long periods, depending upon their wives for support, or fleeing to European residencies circulated in the trade press and among musicians. Critics at *Down Beat* and *Jazz* urged performers not to neglect or alienate their paying customer base by engaging in hostile or deviant behavior.[5] Meanwhile, the perceived reluctance of black audiences to embrace modern forms in large numbers continued to frustrate African American musicians. Pianist Billy Taylor's article, "Negroes Don't Know Anything About Jazz" found echoes in the sentiments of drummer Art Blakey. When asked if African Americans viewed jazz musicians as heroes, Blakey replied that "the Negro people never even heard of Charlie Parker." In 1966, trumpeter Freddie Hubbard added that black audiences "had better wake up, and I mean this in all sincerity, because we created this thing, and they can't even accept it. Colored people can't dig Charlie Parker; they're so busy listening to cornball crap."[6] These comments undoubtedly exaggerated African American indifference to sophisticated musical styles, which were nurtured in black musical circles, reflecting both the musicians' elitism and a strategy of challenging potential customers to sponsor jazz as a matter of race pride. Nevertheless, they reveal a growing uneasiness with the ability of black audiences to sustain creative performers.

Free improvisation attracted an even smaller, more exclusive quantity of listeners than alternative styles. Young experimental musicians experienced great difficulty winning the fans of successful modernists such as Dave Brubeck, Miles Davis, and Maynard Ferguson. Of all the innovative "outside" players, only John Coltrane established a sizable following, and he had made his reputation playing in the bebop tradition with Davis and Thelonious Monk during the late 1950s. For the most part, Ornette Coleman, Cecil Taylor, Albert Ayler, and Archie Shepp attracted a core audience of intellectuals, bohemians, cosmopolitan explorers, and adventurous students. In New York, the city that eventually lured most ambitious experimental performers, the bars, lofts, and coffeehouses of Greenwich Village and Manhattan's lower east side became the hub of free jazz activity. Following a New York teaching sabbatical in the summer of 1960, British historian Eric Hobsbawm lamented the gulf between the downtown jazz scene and its neighborhood antecedents. Writing in the *New Statesman*, Hobsbawm drew a rather simplistic distinction between the proletarian fans of Harlem-based organ combos and the estranged hipsters attracted to Ornette Coleman's music at venues such as the Five Spot and Jazz Gallery.[7] Yet audience reaction to Coleman's out-of-town trips seemed to confirm his limited appeal. Chicago jazz promoter Joe Segal recalled disgruntled customers leaving their drinks at the bar in their haste to leave one gig at the Sutherland Hotel during the early 1960s. Donald Garrett, a member of the Sutherland's house band at that time, remembered fellow musicians lining up in front of the stage, adopting the posture of an execution squad, and firing imaginary rifles at Coleman on their way out. Chicago's own musicians often found South Side night spots such as McKie's Disc Jockey Lounge and Birdhouse closed to their experimental groups or, increasingly, just closed. Although AACM members scheduled regular performances at community centers and church halls, they found some of their most enthusiastic supporters at the University of Chicago. During the late 1950s and early 1960s, Sun Ra's Arkestra played for students in Chicago and Montreal before moving to the east coast. In New York, the band frequently worked bohemian locations such as the Charles Theater, a favorite of avant-garde film makers, the Café Bizarre, and Slugs Saloon. Nat Hentoff, one of the few critics to pay attention to the audience for free improvisation, consistently stressed the music's appeal to writers, painters, intellectuals, and students.[8]

Any assessment of urban music scenes in the early 1960s risks underestimating the fluidity and complexity of the audiences and their tastes. In addition to showcases that featured nationally known jazz bands, each city possessed a network of nightclubs, social clubs, hotels, and cocktail lounges that hosted professional and semi-professional local groups playing a diverse array of styles from Dixieland to the most experimental forms. In Chicago, for example, piano trios, swing orchestras, and New Orleans combos predominated in North Side clubs while modern jazz groups from the east coast generally appeared in busy South Side venues such as the Sutherland, McKie's, Birdhouse, and Roberts' Show Lounge. Local musicians including Johnny Griffin, Ira Sullivan, and Ramsey Lewis often found an audience at smaller South Side rooms such as the C. & C. Lounge, the Coral Club, the Wonder Inn, and the Archway Lounge, while rehearsal bands and jam sessions, the latter often organized by Joe Segal, provided opportunities for aspiring and experimenting professionals at the Pad, the Poodle, and the Gate of Horn.[9]

As Sun Ra's career in Chicago during the late 1950s demonstrates, there was always a place for the exotic in this diverse musical environment, and experimental musicians often tapped into a persistent interest in spirituality and pan-African sentiment among African American listeners. Free improvisers reached audiences most successfully when they combined "outside" improvisation with familiar musical signposts. Sun Ra played free compositions alongside imaginative arrangements of pop songs and swing standards. Albert Ayler's tunes frequently sounded like nursery rhythms, spirituals, or marches on the verge of collapsing in on themselves. John Coltrane reached into his past in rhythm and blues bands for earthy honks and ecstatic screeches. Many musicians turned their concerts into elaborate stage shows, often with interactive, multimedia events to stimulate, captivate, and transport those in attendance. Members of the Art Ensemble of Chicago wore African-inspired garments and face paint, Sun Ra led the Arkestra in chants and processions through the audience during elaborate light shows, and Archie Shepp read poetry to music. Concerts by the most imaginative free improvisers looked back to the variety of traditional revues and forward to spontaneous happenings simultaneously. Drawing on multiple genres for insight and accompaniment—Cecil Taylor's incorporation of dance and poetry recalled the Black Mountain College collaborations between John Cage and Merce Cunningham—"the new thing" extended a black bohemian tradition of modernist experimentation.[10]

The potential and limitations of multi-media, avant-garde art in promoting self-awareness and liberation among the working classes is apparent in the ambiguous impact of the Black Arts Repertory Theater/ School (BARTS). In his autobiography, Amiri Baraka claimed that BARTS attracted "huge audiences, really mass audiences" for its outdoor events in Harlem during the summer of 1965. Baraka demonstrated a keen awareness of what it took to draw a crowd, and typically the show began with an outrageous piece of street theater. On one occasion a gun-touting black actor began proceedings by chasing a fair-skinned actor around the block; on another, Sun Ra, Albert Ayler, and Milford Graves led a cacophonous procession of free improvisers in a parade up 125th Street. Yet many accounts indicate that the new music did not hold listeners' attention for long. Later in 1965, Shepp himself conceded to Larry Neal that "it will be a long time before the Black artist and the Black community can really stand next to each other . . . I think it would be very difficult for Cecil [Taylor] or Ornette [Coleman] or myself to go up to Harlem and expect to be accepted right away—as good as our intentions may be." During the late 1960s, Baraka, Neal, and Spellman edited an infrequent music journal, *The Cricket*, designed to provide an African American critical and historical perspective on the new music for black readers. In it, Spellman and others bemoaned the lack of interest in free improvisation among African American listeners in Atlanta, Harlem, Cleveland, Detroit, Chicago, and other cities with large populations of color.[11] These ruminations suggest a growing concern about the relevance of both avant-garde music and its intellectual supporters, who posited an organic relationship with the black masses as part of their nation-building function.

Mainstream jazz musicians exacerbated this anxiety by regularly exposing the distance between free improvisers and African American audiences, as Ron Carter, Johnny Griffin, and Betty Carter demonstrated in interviews with jazz drummer Arthur Taylor. Betty Carter believed that "you can go uptown and ask ten people on the street who Archie Shepp is and they won't be able to tell you. Ninety percent of his audience is white." Ornette Coleman "avoid[s] black people," according to Carter, while "Sun Ra has got whitey going for it. He couldn't go uptown and do that." This personal invective may reflect Carter's own diminishing prospects at the time; out-of-favor jazz artists often blamed experimental musicians for the decline in business, and these comments mirror a common view that too much critical attention to experimental music ruined the prospects for mainstream performers. As harsh as these criticisms may be in view of Sun Ra and Archie Shepp's active involvement in BARTS, free improvisation sometimes alienated the most culturally aware African American listeners. Sherry Turner described a late 1960s benefit concert headed by drummer Milford Graves at which "titters of embarrassed laughter" disrupted the opening routine, and eventually "the laughter drowned out almost the entire performance." Graves was not entertaining white college students (in fact, his duet with Don Pullen had drawn an enthusiastic response at Yale University in 1966); Turner reported that "the audience wore, as usual, full bushes, dashikis, and African dresses." In a classic strategy of rationalization, the writer endorsed the actions of poet Askia Touré, who took the microphone to lecture the assembly on "the natural head's processed mind" following Graves's performance. Like many cultural leaders, Touré and Turner blamed the people for failing to "open their minds" rather than holding the artist accountable for effective communication.[12]

Unfortunately for experimental musicians, their growing interest in free improvisation coincided with the devastation of urban jazz nightspots in the midst of industrial decay and ongoing flight to the suburbs. Chicago's postwar music scene featured an estimated 75 jazz clubs on the South Side alone, in addition to thousands of private social clubs that frequently hired church halls and community centers for musical events. These venues ranged from the 6,000-seat Savoy Ballroom on South Parkway to after-hours operations such as the Congo Club, strategically located next to the Regal Theater. In the space of two years during the early 1960s, most of the best-known jazz showcases eliminated live music or shut their doors altogether. Martin Williams reported similar developments in New York City.[13] The new jazz connected with an interdisciplinary, boundary-crossing ethic that appealed to aesthetic adventurers but attracted tepid support among jazz promoters seeking to maximize returns from a shrinking consumer base. In separate reviews, Dan Morgenstern and Leonard Feather noted that a showcase of free form musicians attracted the lowest turnout at the 1965 Newport Jazz Festival. Feather described the response to Cecil Taylor, Archie

Shepp, Paul Bley, and the Jazz Composers Orchestra as "a pathetically meager crowd. One of the smallest attendances I have ever seen at Newport." As the entertainment paper *Variety* scathingly acknowledged, free improvisation was an underground movement. "Jazz Mugged By 'New Thing'" screamed one headline, "Latest Idiom Poison at B[ox] O[ffice]."[14] Herm Schoenfeld, who wrote the accompanying article, unfairly blamed free improvisers for scaring jazz audiences away from New York's Birdland—few experimental bands played there. Similarly, an afternoon time slot undoubtedly contributed to the small audience at Newport. Yet the article and festival schedule reflected the predominant view of club owners and booking agents that free jazz lacked sufficient followers to make a profit. Record company executives agreed; avant-garde jazz albums sold poorly. Companies usually cleared under three thousand copies according to industry sources. Alfred Lion reported that his Blue Note label considered a "new thing" record successful when it broke even financially. Jerry Wexler at Atlantic confirmed that "in spite of a noble attempt to represent a broad spectrum of jazz and jazz-tinged music, it was rhythm and blues and rhythm and blues only that paid the rent."[15] Over the course of a decade, the implication of that equation for the production and marketing of free improvisation, and the need for experimental musicians to find alternative support mechanisms, became increasingly apparent.

The growing obscurity of jazz styles since 1940, and the emergence of accessible alternatives such as rock and roll and Motown, provide the most convincing explanations for jazz music's declining popularity by the early 1960s. During the following decade, developments in jazz, soul, and rock music accentuated both of these trends. Ornette Coleman, John Coltrane, and Cecil Taylor pioneered an expressive, collective approach to improvisation by playing outside conventional chord, bar, pitch, and tempo constraints. They placed a greater emphasis on sounds rather than stated melodies, rhythms, and harmonies. This experimentation with form disoriented even experienced jazz fans by removing conventional reference points. Listeners found it harder to anticipate and identify those moments of climax and transition that create tension and provide release. While harmonic stasis and expansive soundscapes reinforced the sense of spiritual searching, the absence of easily identifiable structures and crisp execution confounded the expectations of many modern jazz fans. *Down Beat* reader R. D. Murro described the reaction to a 1963 free form concert:

If it had any musical worth at all, it definitely was not evident to the majority of listeners I viewed in the audience. I watched as they restlessly fidgeted about,

Figure 17. Cecil Taylor performing during the mid-1960s. Photograph by Joe Alper. Courtesy Michael Ochs Archives.com.

trying to find something to grab on to as they were submerged in this sea of nothingness. . . . If the devoted followers of good jazz are themselves unable to find any worth in it, these listeners will inevitably be lost, and jazz will have succeeded in bringing about its own destruction.[16]

Those writers who attributed jazz music's faltering profile to its esoteric characteristics tended to blame the artists for abandoning their audience. Robert Sylvester wrote in the New York *Daily News* during 1964 that "all the music and all the fun went out of [jazz] as it was taken over by the advanced 'artists' who would rather play for each other and for the silly cult critics from the silly butcher paper magazines." The argument that modern jazz musicians, starting with Dizzy Gillespie and Charlie Parker, self-consciously adopted anti-commercial postures has appeared frequently in literature both praising the music's supposed "progress" and regretting its disengagement with African American audiences. Yet the first generation of modernists sought to exploit rather than escape the marketplace. Gillespie and other bebop pioneers took pride in their status as professionals, and attempted to transform the emerging idiom into a viable—if marginal—commodity.[17] Similarly, free improvisers and their supporters constantly cajoled promoters into providing greater exposure and rewards for their services. The identity of romantic artists tempted Taylor, Coleman, and other experimental musicians only when it appeared that few other career options remained open.

Robert Sylvester's comments indicate that the seriousness with which free improvisers attacked musical problems often dismayed potential fans. Hostile critics frequently attacked "the new thing" as "humorless" and self-involved, ignoring the wit and spirit of play at the heart of some of the most "outside" work by the Art Ensemble of Chicago, Sun Ra, and others. Some listeners concluded that its neglect of formal constraints made experimental jazz "boring" and "incoherent." At mid-decade, Tom Scanlon exposed a latent anti-intellectualism felt by many enthusiasts when he wrote that "too much angry, pounding, repetitious noise—dripping with self-conscious intensity, squealing with emotional immaturity, and scowling with intellectual pretentiousness—passed for jazz."[18] Even champions such as Nat Hentoff and David Hunt conceded that the music of Ornette Coleman, Albert Ayler, and Archie Shepp required an educated, committed audience to decipher the challenging text. Less sympathetic observers blamed its obscurity on a lack of talent, especially among second wave performers such as Shepp, Pharoah Sanders, Sun Ra's Arkestra, and the AACM.[19] The latter accusation rang especially hollow. Ra recruited several novices in order to mold their sense of musical possibilities, but he hired skilled graduates of Walter Dyett's Dusable High School music program such as Pat Patrick and John Gilmore too. Similarly Muhal Richard Abrams opened the Experimental Band to seasoned professionals and beginners alike, and trained all his musicians in the art of listening and responding to each other. At heart, many modern jazz fans missed the tautly held groove and virtuoso dexterity that free improvisation often deemphasized in favor of cerebral esotericism or unchained expressiveness, and attributed their absence to a lack of ability or respect for tradition. As Bill Halpin of New Jersey wrote to *Down Beat* in 1963: "I, for one, will stick with . . . the old swinging jazz and leave these new things to those who are supposed to understand them."[20]

Free improvisation's opacity encouraged jazz fans to seek authentic entertainment elsewhere. The maturation of soul and rock music in the middle and late 1960s provided sophisticated alternatives to both "outside" experimentation and the early decade's formulaic pop. Soul built upon the insistent propulsion of 1950s rhythm and blues, with the addition of syncopated bass lines and more prominent brass and reeds. Singers drew heavily upon the gospel tradition of emotional display, call and response, handclaps, and tambourines. Three performers pioneered this raw, energetic blend and turned soul into the popular music of black America, and a considerable crossover force, by 1965. James

Brown's "Please, Please, Please" (1956), Sam Cooke's "You Send Me" (1957), and Ray Charles' "What'd I Say" (1959) suggested an unaffected eloquence that made their music appear the epitome of lived experience. The country-soul of Percy Sledge, Bobby Bland's blues-soul mix, the gospel moans and shouts of Solomon Burke and Aretha Franklin, and the Impressions' smooth lyricism each extended the style in innovative directions.[21]

These artists shared a reputation for raising African American consciousness through their songs and performances, at a time free jazz players struggled for recognition. Soul soon surpassed its musical definition. According to one edition of *Webster's New World Dictionary*, soul represented "a sense of racial pride and social and cultural solidarity, often with opposition to white, middle-class practices and values." Ironically, whites played key roles in the music's creation and dissemination. The white-owned American, Goldwax, and Stax/Volt studios in Memphis, and the Fame and Quinn Ivy studios of Muscle Shoals, Alabama, produced the "blackest" varieties of soul. Integrated groups of southern musicians such as Booker T and the MGs played on huge crossover hits including Otis Redding's "I've Been Loving You Too Long" (1965), Wilson Pickett's "In The Midnight Hour" (1965), and Aretha Franklin's "Chain of Fools" (1967). Although soul singers could not compete regularly with Motown and British invasion groups on the charts, their biggest successes depended upon black and white purchasing power. Even the hip black DJs who popularized soul's style and argot usually did so at white-controlled radio stations.[22]

Despite the intimate involvement of whites in its ownership, production, and to a lesser extent consumption, soul represented a group identity and racial essence above all. Its evocative regional sound carried particular resonance among African Americans. Soul connected with the collective memory of black people in a way experimental jazz did not. It affirmed shared roots in the church and the South. While whites continued to consume music by black performers during the 1960s, African Americans increasingly limited their selections to black singers. At the end of 1963, white artists sang one third of all the hits on *Billboard*'s Rhythm and Blues chart. By the beginning of 1965, only three records by white performers made the listing, including a novelty song.[23]

Soul projected a sense of racial unity by urging listeners to share in a celebration of ethnic heritage. Records attempted to reproduce the communal bond between performers and a live audience, itself a reflection of black church rituals. Singers stirred the same fervor as Sunday preachers, eliciting the emotional involvement of their secular congregations through clapping, testifying affirmations, call and response vocals, and soul dances. In contrast to the studied concentration demanded by free improvisers, their raw energy, sweat, and physical commitment to an audience endeared soul men and women as cultural icons. Although explicit message songs did not appear in great numbers until the late 1960s, numerous lyrics demanding "Respect" heightened black pride before Aretha Franklin took Otis Redding's anthem to the top of both charts in 1967.[24]

At a time soul cut deeply into the African American audience for jazz, other musical developments lured away white listeners. The generation that embraced rock and roll in the 1950s grew up demanding more complex experimentation and greater social awareness in music.[25] These qualities continued to attract some white listeners to jazz, but during the 1960s rock's coming of age decimated the jazz industry. At the beginning of the decade, simple blues-based harmonic progressions and rhythmic patterns dominated rock and roll music, while themes of romance and adolescent rebellion defined the genre's lyrics. The Beatles did not stray far from this formula with early songs such as "I Saw Her Standing There" (1963) and "Can't Buy Me Love" (1963). Yet within a few years the Beatles pioneered rock's greater musical sophistication and social consciousness. By introducing idiosyncratic harmonic variations and unusual instruments such as the flute, sitar, French Horn, and strings, the group expanded rock music's range of textures and effects. Heavily influenced by the electronic experiments of John Cage and Karlheinz Stockhausen, The Beatles took advantage of studio technology to create alternative sound worlds by recording feedback, backwards-playing tape, and continuous tape-loops among other innovations. Songs such as "Nowhere Man" (1965), "Eleanor Rigby" (1966), and "Taxman" (1966) examined social concerns with wit and insight, while several tracks on their self-titled 1968 release openly explored sexuality. Other British acts such as the Rolling Stones and the Who engaged increasingly complex and reflective material in the second half of the decade.[26]

John Lennon and Paul McCartney's embrace of more meaningful themes reflected in part the influence of American singer-songwriter Bob Dylan, who they in turn inspired to explore electronic music. Dylan conquered and transformed the folk music movement in the early 1960s by stretching the popular song form to accommodate longer numbers, addressing serious topics such as nuclear war and civil rights for a broad audience, and introducing a poetic sensibility into his lyrics. Although journalists and academics have compared Dylan's work to writers as diverse as Walt Whitman, Arthur Rimbaud, T. S. Eliot, William Blake, and Franz Kafka, the beats remain his most immediate influence. On "Subterranean Homesick Blues" (1965), for example, Dylan's delivery of the stream of consciousness verses recalls Jack Kerouac or Allen Ginsberg (who appeared in Donn Pennebaker's accompanying film) imitating an improvising jazz musician. Indeed, jazz critic Ralph Gleason recognized in 1966 that Dylan had succeeded in bringing modern verse to a new audience where previous experiments had failed. "The jazz and poetry guys of the 1950's . . . woke up 10 years later and here is this squirrelly little kid who has done the things they wanted to do . . . to get poetry into the streets, to the people and on the jukeboxes."[27] Dylan's move away from topical songs to more abstract, ambiguous material in 1964 and 1965 facilitated the importation of an overtly modernist aesthetic into popular music. His adoption of an electric supporting group on the 1965 albums *Bringing It All Back Home* and *Highway 61 Revisited*, and during his appearance at that year's Newport Folk Festival, underlined rock music's growing collage of influences. Dylan's blend of folk songs, the blues, rock, and poetry inspired the Beatles, the Doors, and the west coast folk-rock movement epitomized by the Byrds and Crosby, Stills, and Nash.

At the same time Dylan captivated a wider market by amplifying his prophetic visions, Cream—featuring guitarist Eric Clapton—led a transatlantic blues revival that expanded the form's youth audience. The band infused traditional structures with the improvisational dexterity and inventiveness of modern jazz musicians, inspiring the same adulation among devoted fans (to which the popular graffiti "Clapton is God" and shouts of "Give God a solo" during concerts attested). Bassist Jack Bruce admitted "it was like jazz playing in a rock setting."[28] It took blues guitarist Jimi Hendrix another year to achieve notoriety in America, yet his eventual success demonstrated the potential appeal of sound over notes. Unlike Albert Ayler, Roscoe Mitchell, and other jazz musicians working in similar territory, Hendrix opened the door to popular acclaim by combining distorted soundscapes with steady rhythms, repetitive vocal melodies, and extravagant showmanship.

From 1965 to 1970, folk-rock, the blues revival, jazz-style improvisation, and countercultural philosophy came together in the San Francisco-based acid rock movement. Jefferson Airplane, Big Brother and the Holding Company, the Grateful Dead, and Country Joe and the Fish captured the "irreverence . . . edge . . . and the feeling of spontaneity" associated with jazz so well that critics Ralph Gleason and Nat Hentoff debated whether "America's art form" could retain a separate identity.[29] Acid rock surrounded an experimental ambition reminiscent of jazz with straightforward rhythms, and aligned itself with topical concerns such as mind-expanding drugs, permissive sexuality, and the generation gap. Largely a product of white middle-class anxieties, the counterculture and its music provided an easier source of identification for most baby boomers than the underground jazz scene. A junior at

Cornell gave voice to her generation's shifting musical tastes in 1967. "We were pretty much turned off jazz in the beginning of the sixties," she explained. "The cult was always too exclusive. The guys in the cult always made sure you could never be part of something. Folk music and the subsequent rock renaissance welcomed everyone—and everyone forgot the little about jazz that they knew." Jazz music's subculture was the province of initiates able to negotiate its complex racial and musical codes. While rock stars idolized black musicians, white audiences shared with their heroes a mediated distance from the source and a mutual journey of self-discovery. Rock music's inclusive spirit facilitated its mass appeal and generational resonance.[30]

The music of the counterculture gained national prominence in 1967 as product quality improved, a supportive business framework emerged, and the press took notice. In May the Beatles released *Sgt. Pepper's Lonely Hearts Club Band*, a psychedelic album that reflected Paul McCartney's impressions from a trip to Haight-Ashbury. A critical and artistic triumph, *Sgt. Pepper* harnessed the group's song writing skills and technological innovation to a unified concept that extended from the thematic material to the album design to the promotional work. San Francisco's own bands, including Jefferson Airplane and the Grateful Dead, received considerable air play early in 1967, reflecting and encouraging changes in radio programming that proved vital to the movement's success. Top 40 play lists dominated AM and FM radio until the mid-1960s, when the Federal Communications Commission ordered stations in urban markets to separate the content of each frequency. San Francisco's KMPX pioneered a new format for FM stations by emphasizing longer tracks and a broader range of musical forms, a move supported by record companies that recognized the financial advantage of promoting material from albums rather than singles. June's Monterey Pop Festival, inspired by and formatted after the Monterey Jazz Festival, exposed top San Francisco bands to thirty thousand fans and numerous record company executives and reporters.[31]

Monterey and the much-anticipated "Summer of Love" focused national attention on the Bay area musicians and their intimate connection to the counterculture. As *Time* reported in June, "the sound is also the scene. With its roots in the LSDisneyland of the Haight-Ashbury district, the music is a reflection of the defiant new bohemians." Corporate media and advertising soon caricatured the hippy image as it had the beatnik a decade earlier, yet widespread youth and adult interest provided new opportunities for commercial ventures to sustain the music. Bands moved gradually from the ballroom circuit to the burgeoning rock festival tour. Over 2.5 million fans attended thirty rock festivals in the two years after Monterey, culminating in huge audiences at Newport (actually staged in the San Fernando Valley), Woodstock, and Altamont during 1969. In October 1967, Berkeley drop-out Jann Wenner launched the first professional publication devoted exclusively to rock. With the intimate assistance of Ralph Gleason, *Rolling Stone* achieved a level of insightful criticism and market orientation unknown in previous fan magazines.[32]

Ralph Gleason's involvement in *Rolling Stone* illustrated the appeal of new rock forms to critics, advertisers, and fans who had once looked to jazz for sophisticated musical art. Although few converts abandoned jazz completely, Nat Hentoff, Frank Kofsky, John Sinclair, and other writers also turned their attention to rock. Most significantly, the mainstay jazz magazines bowed to economic exigencies and followed suit. In early 1967, *Down Beat*'s owner decided to use the occasion of an imminent staff change to introduce rock features. As incoming editor Dan Morgenstern recalled:

The advertisers had been pressuring the magazine, which is to say the publisher and the advertising manager, for a long time already to include rock in its coverage. And it became evident that if *Down Beat* did not do this, a good deal of the instrument advertising, which was the cornerstone, [would disappear] . . . I knew that was a compromise we had to make. At that point it seemed like it was a matter of the survival of the magazine.[33]

Down Beat's competition made similar content changes. In August, *Jazz* took the name *Jazz & Pop* and extended its coverage to include rock, folk, and blues. Denying a "sell-out of jazz," editor Pauline Rivelli declared her intention to enlarge the music's audience. In a November column, Rivelli justified the magazine's shifting subject matter by addressing changes in rock music itself:

There was a time when popular music, or rock and roll if you will, reflected the mentality of a retarded 17-year-old. But no more. The rock musician of yesterday either grows up, as the Beatles have done, or else he falls into obscurity. . . . What we have been talking about above can be boiled down in one terse phrase: popular music has grown up.[34]

Rock music's maturation, and the emergence of soul, provided popular sources of inspiration and identification that relegated free improvisation to the margins of the music world. Experimental musicians conceded only reluctantly that the abstruse nature of their art prevented it reaching a wider public. Instead, they countered, inadequate promotion and exposure inhibited efforts to build a viable support network. During a panel discussion at the 1965 Newport Jazz Festival, Archie Shepp berated impresario George Wein for providing Frank Sinatra top billing while excluding musicians who worked more squarely in the jazz tradition. When Wein pointed out that Sinatra guaranteed the festival's success, Shepp replied "of course he made it, and I would make it too if you gave me the same publicity you gave to the Beatles and those people."[35] With so many commercial outlets closed to them, experimental musicians in New York and Chicago—the two largest centers of free jazz activity—formed self-help collectives to provide performance opportunities for struggling artists, honor past traditions, and shore up their community base. Despite contrasting legacies, both groups sustained the music's profile, nurtured the careers of unknown instrumentalists, and provided examples for future collaborative efforts. Their struggles for survival, however, underlined the jazz industry's uneasy accommodation of free improvisation and the music's tenuous ties to black America.

Self-help initiatives occurred fairly frequently in jazz prior to the mid-1960s, as individual musicians attempted to take greater control of their careers. Artists such as Fletcher Henderson doubled as booking agents in the 1920s and 1930s. Duke Ellington and other composers established publishing companies to maximize songwriter royalties. Some musicians even promoted their own shows. A lack of resources or business acumen often undermined the success of these ventures. Following his self-produced Town Hall concert of 1962, Ornette Coleman's efforts to establish a publishing company and a jazz club over the next two years failed. Dave Brubeck, Dizzy Gillespie, Charles Mingus, Max Roach, and other performers founded independent record labels in order to give musicians greater choice over when and what they recorded and a larger share of the profits. Despite their frequent artistic successes, these labels usually collapsed owing to distribution and cash flow problems. El Saturn Research, perhaps the longest-lasting musicians' label, issued seventy-one albums and twenty-six singles by Sun Ra's Arkestra between 1956 and 1988. Yet Saturn pressed records in very small quantities, often no more than fifty at a time.[36] Musicians organized in numbers only rarely. Sun Ra's Arkestra operated more like a commune than a collective. Over a period of four decades, a nucleus of members lived together in Chicago, New York, and Philadelphia, pooling income from outside jobs to support the band's work. The short-lived Jazz Artists' Guild provided a closer precedent to later groups, although it fell apart amid internal disagreements after organizing several concerts at a small Manhattan theater and recording an album entitled *Newport Rebels*.[37]

On the surface, the Jazz Composers Guild achieved little more than the earlier collective it resembled in name. Trumpeter Bill Dixon had led a band with Archie Shepp in the early 1960s, and wrote compositions and arrangements for the New York Contemporary Five. Following his successful promotion of "The October Revolution," and consultations with his friend Cecil Taylor, Dixon invited Taylor, Shepp, Sun Ra, and

Danish saxophonist John Tchicai to join an interracial organization that also included white musicians Roswell Rudd, Jon Winter, Burton Greene, Mike Mantler, Carla Bley, and Paul Bley. The Jazz Composers Guild differed from previous initiatives in the scope of its intended activities. Dixon conceived of the Guild as a collective bargaining unit. Buoyed by momentum from the October festival, its members planned to withdraw their music from commercial venues and studios. By cultivating audiences through self-produced concerts and records, they hoped to force entrepreneurs to negotiate with the Guild and offer contracts favorable to the group as a whole. Spokesman Burton Greene stated that "our idea is to corner the market, to take this music off the market for as long as is necessary to establish the kind of relations with the business people that are needed to give the music its proper outlet. Meanwhile, we'll generate our own activities."[38] Recognizing that band leaders benefited most from the publicity that accompanied gigs, the organization distributed gate receipts to supporting musicians first. Its most rigid statute mandated that no individual could accept a job without the approval of his or her peers. By emphasizing fundamental economic restructuring, Guild members sought to replace the competitive self-promotion inherent in the music industry's star system with an ethic of mutual self-help that reflected free improvisation's collective aesthetic.

As Bill Dixon has insisted correctly, the Guild raised the profile of free improvisation—especially the second wave of musicians—at a time the jazz and magazine press paid little attention to the form.[39] John Coltrane had retreated from the experimentation that marked his collaborations with Eric Dolphy, and would not reemerge as a leading force in free jazz until later in 1965. Ornette Coleman chose not to perform publicly in the United States between the end of 1962 and January 1965. "The October Revolution" and subsequent activities forced the music business to concede that free improvisation continued to attract support among listeners and musicians. Two of *Down Beat*'s most respected reporters, Dan Morgenstern and Martin Williams, wrote enthusiastic articles on the series. Almost immediately after the October concerts, the magazine published a four star review of a Savoy album featuring Dixon's septet on one side and Archie Shepp and the New York Contemporary Five on the reverse. Peter Welding heralded the disc, which featured several founder members of the Guild, as "an introduction to the work of a number of the most exciting young New York avant-garde jazzmen." Follow-up concerts at Judson Hall in December and the Contemporary Dance Center in Greenwich Village during the spring generated a new flood of publicity. John S. Wilson reviewed two performances in the series "Four Days in December" for the *New York Times* and advertised future shows. *Down Beat*'s avant-garde expert Don Heckman, a participant in the October series, reported on all four winter concerts while A. B. Spellman and Whitney Balliett wrote extended reviews for *The Nation* and the *New Yorker* respectively. *Down Beat, Jazz*, and the *New York Times* continued to report on Guild events during its existence.[40]

The collective's success in drawing renewed attention to experimental music partially explains its collapse. Organizational activities generated a number of job offers for individual musicians, who accepted without consulting other members. Archie Shepp's negotiations with Impulse! records proved especially divisive. Social conflicts played a role in the organization's demise too. According to some reports, African American musicians perceived that whites chafed under their leadership. Sun Ra exacerbated the friction when he tried to persuade other musicians—including Carla Bley's husband Paul—to exclude women. Dixon himself left in the spring, dismayed by a lack of commitment among his fellows, and the Guild folded in April or May.[41] Bernard Stollman, an attorney who had offered the organization legal advice, helped sustain the momentum behind free jazz by continuing to promote "the new thing" actively. Stollman had worked on the estates of Charlie Parker and Billie Holiday, and through music industry contacts he began to manage clients such as Ornette Coleman and Cecil Taylor. In the wake of publicity generated by the Jazz Composers Guild, Stollman's ESP record label eventually signed a host of "outside" musicians including Ornette Coleman, Milford Graves, Sonny Murray, Albert Ayler, Sun Ra, Paul Bley, Marion Brown, Burton Greene, the New York Art Quartet, and Pharoah Sanders. The first set of albums, shrewdly cross-promoted with a Town Hall concert of ESP artists, generated numerous reviews and reignited the dormant avant-garde debate in the spring of 1965. Stollman's controversial releases coincided with a decision by Impulse! producer Bob Thiele to revive the label's reputation as a home for experimental jazz. His action resulted in part from John Coltrane's embrace of freer forms and sponsorship of several younger musicians. Albert Ayler, Marion Brown, Pharoah Sanders, and Archie Shepp all recorded for Impulse! on account of Coltrane's recommendation.[42]

Paradoxically, the nature and limits of the Guild's success rather than its outright failures provided salient lessons about relations between free improvisers and the listening public. Dixon's bold attempt to transform experimental musicians into a collective bargaining unit defied the creative individualism at the center of virtuoso performance and the cutthroat practices of a contracting jazz industry. The Guild's inability to attract corporate suitors or follow through plans to acquire a building and a record label surprised few observers. Participants had greater difficulty accepting that increased exposure and growing reputations did not translate into a viable career in music. Even those performers who left the Guild to pursue individual offers found that they could not make a living playing free jazz. Archie Shepp, whose contract with Impulse! led to several albums, many performance opportunities, and widespread publicity, supported his family as an English teacher in the public schools, a social worker, and by collecting welfare. Bernard Stollman became a very unpopular figure in the jazz underground because ESP's artists, who often recorded without advance payment, rarely received royalties. Bob Thiele faced similar resentment on account of the disparity in returns garnered by top jazz artists and second wave free improvisers at Impulse![43] Reflecting on the composition of listeners at "The October Revolution," Dan Morgenstern's prescient remarks anticipated the form's future:

The new music needs special handling. Above all, if it is to survive, it needs to be subsidized, either by private foundations or by government grants. The new jazz players are as deserving—if not more so—than the painters, poets, classical musicians, and writers who are now among the recipients of such aid. The fact that the two fountainheads of the new jazz—Cecil Taylor and Ornette Coleman—are not working steadily, or hardly working at all, is the clearest proof that this is the situation. This music cannot, and for its own future and sanity, should not, compete with [Dave] Brubeck, [Cannonball] Adderley, [Oscar] Peterson, and jazz tinged vocalists in the marketplace.[44]

In contrast to the Jazz Composers Guild, Chicago's Association for the Advancement of Creative Musicians has won widespread recognition as a valuable and thriving self-help organization for over four decades. The AACM's sheer longevity has drawn accolades from jazz critics and civic leaders, and in the long run its cultural nationalism has proved less threatening to the music establishment than the economic self-determination preached by Dixon and Shepp. An important part of its mythology centers on passing the legacy of "Great Black Music" to younger generations of South Side musicians.[45] This community focus and its apparent racial solidarity helps separate the organization from market-oriented ventures such as the Jazz Composers Guild, with its petty disputes over exposure and inclusiveness.[46] Nevertheless, the terms on which the group has survived illustrates the fragility of commercial and community support and the increasing role of arts funding in supporting experimental black music.

A grass-roots network of black churches and neighborhood political and arts organizations in Chicago likely inspired its founders, yet the AACM most closely followed a west coast precedent. In 1961 Los Angeles trombonist and pianist Horace Tapscott founded the Underground Musicians Union, later renamed the Union of God's Musicians and Artists Ascension (UGMAA). A former sideman with Lionel Hampton, Tapscott dedicated UGMAA to instilling an awareness of and respect for African American culture among young people and providing them with a positive creative outlet. Tapscott recruited graduates of the renowned Jefferson High School music program into the organization's signature experimental ensemble, which he opened to beginning and established musicians alike. The orchestra pioneered concerts in non-traditional public sites, including community centers and public parks in South Central Los Angeles, even playing outdoors during the Watts riot to try to calm the disturbances. Unlike many collectives, UGMAA survived to see multiple generations of alumni, represented by Sonny Criss, Charles Lloyd, and David Murray, establish themselves in the music business.[47]

The AACM filled a similar need to UGMAA in Chicago and repeated its early history. Both organizations sought to reconnect a heritage of adventurous black music with urban communities increasingly stripped of commercial jazz venues. The AACM traces its origins to the Experimental Band, a rehearsal group that came under the leadership of pianist and clarinetist Muhal Richard Abrams in 1961. A decade older than many other members, Abrams had played professionally since 1948. His reputation as the driving force behind legendary Chicago band MJT + 3 secured work as a sideman with visiting jazz and blues musicians, touring opportunities with name acts such as Woody Herman, and solo spots as an intermission pianist at local nightclubs. Abrams and Donald Garrett, former bassist with Sun Ra and an active figure in Chicago jazz, composed and arranged for the younger and largely inexperienced musicians such as Roscoe Mitchell, Joseph Jarman, Kalaparusha Ahrah Difda (then Maurice McIntyre), and Troy Robinson. Numerous testimonials indicate that Abrams provided instruction in the techniques of free improvisation, a model of self-reliance, and a sense of belonging to a purposeful entity.[48]

In May 1965, Abrams founded the AACM with three other Chicago musicians: former Arkestra trumpeter Phil Cohran and occasional Experimental Band contributors Steve McCall (drums) and Jodie Christian (piano). They immediately invited the rehearsal band members, and as many sympathetic musicians as they knew, to join. The group embraced Abrams' commitment to musical development, collective self-help, and mentoring African American youth. Its first challenge involved finding performance opportunities for approximately fifty instrumentalists, many of whom played rarely in public. One dollar weekly dues sponsored Saturday concerts by the AACM Big Band, an extension of the Experimental Band open to all members, and six or seven other aggregations. The more popular groups, such as Cohran's Artistic Heritage Ensemble and Christian's hard bop quintet, found a few gigs in nightclubs and bars. Mostly they played at church halls, colleges, and community centers alongside the Big Band and groups led by Mitchell, Jarman, and Anthony Braxton.[49]

The AACM's commitment to institution building extended beyond the search for gigs to embrace far-reaching social ambitions aimed at bringing cohesion, pride, and self-determination to South Side neighborhoods through the regenerative potential of the arts. While struggling musicians often turned to the AACM for employment opportunities, its emerging leadership placed this goal within a broader holistic effort to create a suitable environment for creative exploration. According to this vision, meaningful communication required an internal transformation in which collective musical practices nurtured self-respect and consideration for others, while mythical Afrocentric traditions and black nationalist sentiment offered a context for rethinking cultural norms.[50] In 1966, Abrams indicated that the group wished "to set an example of high moral standards for musicians and to return the public image of creative musicians to the level of esteem which was handed down from past cultures." Aware of jazz musicians' reputation for selfishness, cynicism, and self-abuse, Abrams convinced his peers that their interests were closely tied to the community's fortunes. Over the years, AACM bands played benefit concerts for the South Shore Community Arts Center, the Black Theater Alliance, Kuumba Workshop, and many other neighborhood arts ventures.[51] Members took greatest pride in the AACM school, at which they tutored inner city students in composition, theory, and instrumental techniques. Founded in 1968, the school enrolled up to seventy students in ten-week courses, meeting in a variety of rented spaces on the South Side. Students ranged in age from six to forty years old, although the association gave priority to the youngest and to those who could not afford to study elsewhere. Instruction reflected the organization's goals to pass on the heritage of African American music and to encourage personal growth among African American youth. The school's mission statement announced:

Our curriculum is so designed as to elicit maximum development of potential within the context of a training program that exposes youngsters to constructive relationships with artistic adults. Widest encouragement is given to music for leisure and educational purposes; and we are continually seeking new ways of relating music to the needs of individuals and the community for increased skills, improved study habits and cultural enrichment. Superimposed over our training framework is our keen desire to develop within our students the ability to value *self*, the ability to value *others* and the ability to utilize the opportunities they find in society.

The AACM financed the school through its fund-raising efforts. It did not charge tuition, frequently loaned students instruments to play, and

Figure 18. Muhal Richard Abrams in a publicity shot for Delmark Records, June 1967. Photograph by Terry Martin. Courtesy Photographs and Prints Division, Schomburg Center for Research in Black Culture, The New York Public Library, Astor, Lenox, and Tilden Foundations.

only introduced a fee for materials in 1979. During the 1970s it graduated several notable musicians who have taught at the school themselves, including Mwata Bowden, Douglas Ewart, and George Lewis.[52]

The historiography of the AACM frequently contrasts its prosperity to the rapid demise of New York-based collectives such as the Jazz Artists' Guild and the Jazz Composers Guild, comparing the Chicagoans' group consciousness with the individualistic spirit that doomed east coast efforts. The AACM not only survived, it encouraged musicians in St. Louis to form a similar organization—the Black Artists Group (BAG)—with which it exchanged concerts.[53] Most writers attribute midwestern unity to the absence of a highly competitive commercial jazz scene, which allowed musicians greater freedom to practice, communicate, and work out their art together.[54] The AACM's noble goals, impressive rhetoric, and consistent message reinforced this impression of solidarity. Yet its precarious relationship to the black community and the market-place challenged the organization's cohesion, unity, and survival from its earliest days.

Personality conflicts disrupted the first Experimental Band in 1961, but musical differences caused the greatest friction. Several older musi-cians resented Abrams' inclusion of inexperienced players such as Mitchell and Jarman who, some claimed, played "outside" because they had not yet mastered fundamental musical techniques. One Experimen-tal Band veteran, who wished to remain anonymous, claimed that "everybody that plays so-called free music that I know has wanted to play bebop . . . I know very few who have really been into what they call free music. They just seem frustrated by not being able to play [chord] changes." David Baker and Leslie Rout encountered similar dissension when they interviewed the first generation of AACM members on sepa-rate occasions.[55] In part, the argument over standards reflected differ-ences in musical taste. The Experimental Band initially drew upon hard bop influences before adopting the multi-sectional compositional style, overlapping instrumental voicings, and indistinct tonality favored by Abrams, Jarman, Mitchell, and Robinson. Similarly, the AACM took its musical lead from free improvisers, which eventually disillusioned musi-cians such as Eddie Harris, Jodie Christian, and Phil Cohran who pre-ferred a more popular hard bop or even rhythm and blues foundation. Musical taste itself reflected a deeper crisis over how to connect with a black audience and Afrocentric heritage. Critics of the dominant aes-thetic questioned whether the absence of an explicit rhythmic pulse reflected the traditions of black music and doubted free improvisation's ability to reach African Americans in their own neighborhoods. Cohran, who became a spokesman for those musicians favoring a more accessible approach, recalled the turmoil that centered on Abrams's former stu-dents:

We had a conflict with[in] the AACM because they were playing out . . . and it was all the way out. It didn't relate to nothing. . . . They didn't come from the heritage of the community. . . . I always had a problem with them calling it black music. . . . I found them very offensive because they didn't care to communicate. They wanted to communicate with something outside of the people, and to hell with the people, and [they] often criticized the people for being ignorant and backwards and a whole lot of other things. . . . But there's a collective wisdom in [the people] that is greater than anything I know, and I respect that.

By 1968 Harris and Christian no longer met with the AACM and Cohran had established the Affro Arts Theater, an interdisciplinary performance and educational space on the South Side that featured soul as well as rhythm and blues music.[56]

The AACM's community focus sometimes conflicted with the career aims of its members, a reality underlined by its success reaching beyond Chicago's black neighborhoods. Jarman's informal jam sessions at the University of Chicago student lounge paid immediate dividends, as appreciative collegians founded the Society for Contemporary Music to sponsor regular concerts by AACM groups at Noyes Hall and Mandel Hall. Producer Chuck Nessa convinced Bob Koester's Delmark label to make the first records by AACM groups. Roscoe Mitchell's *Sound* (1966), Joseph Jarman's *Song For* (1967), and Muhal Richard Abrams's *Levels and Degrees of Light* (1967) each reflected new approaches to the construction of sound that deemphasized the frantic blowing of many east coast free improvisers. Koester recorded saxophonist Anthony Braxton's first two albums in 1968, while Nessa established his own company to record trumpeter Lester Bowie and the Roscoe Mitchell Art Ensemble. Chicago-based *Down Beat* magazine published frequent reviews by sympathetic writers. Like free improvisers in New York, however, AACM members soon found that exposure did not lead to financial success. Indeed, their distance from New York prevented contact with industry networks that might have secured a greater following. The organization's biggest challenge lay in retaining a sufficient number and quality of musicians to continue its outreach programs. In 1969, two of the AACM's most visible bands—the renamed Art Ensemble of Chicago featuring Mitchell and Jarman, and Anthony Braxton's trio with Wadada Leo Smith and Leroy Jenkins—left for Europe within a month of each other. Both groups settled in France to pursue performance and recording opportunities and a chance to earn a living in music. During the 1970s, an increasing number of AACM musicians departed for New York including, in 1977, founder members Muhal Richard Abrams and Steve McCall.[57] It is a measure of his selflessness that Abrams stayed so long to develop young talent, despite owning the best musical credentials of the group. Before leaving, Abrams and others—who returned to support the organization periodically—successfully nurtured a second generation of leaders.

Isolated in a city no longer known for its thriving jazz scene, the AACM struggled to remain solvent.[58] At first, the leadership resisted pursuing institutional support on the grounds that doing so would violate the orga-

Figure 19. The Art Ensemble of Chicago at The Warfield, San Francisco, November 1982. (Left to right) Lester Bowie, Malachi Favors Maghostut, Famoudou Don Moye, Joseph Jarman, and Roscoe Mitchell. Photograph by Tom Copi. Courtesy Michael Ochs Archives.com.

nization's self-help ethos. It is unclear when that position changed, although BAG's successful petitions to the National Endowment for the Arts and the Missouri Arts Council may have played a role. In 1972, Joseph Jarman revealed that the AACM had continually applied for foundation fellowships and civic grants to no avail, although several musicians won individual awards. During the next decade, concerted efforts to secure outside funding paid off as sponsorship from endowments, municipal and state arts bodies, corporations, and an international fund drive helped sustain concert programs and pay administrative costs. Yet the AACM always faced an uncertain future, its fortunes tied to the inconsistency of arts funding. School instructors rarely received any remuneration, the school itself closed down temporarily in the early 1980s, and unforeseen circumstances—such as a crippling robbery in 1983—threatened the organization's very existence. The AACM's survival owed a great deal to its members' commitment, the school's ability to nurture dedicated musicians, and the eagerness of young African Americans to learn about black music. The increasing reliance of the school and its graduates on support mechanisms outside the marketplace, however, pointed to the future of experimental African American art in the United States.

The material conditions that birthed musicians collectives during the 1960s forced Black Arts Movement writers and the performers they championed to reconsider the relationship between free improvisation and increasingly stratified African American communities. At the time "outside" experimentation peaked in the late 1960s, metropolitan areas that housed the overwhelming majority of African Americans in the north and west experienced accelerated economic polarization. Deindustrialization and the spreading low-wage service sector decimated the central cities African Americans had occupied since World War II, even as the slow-growing black middle class took advantage of civil rights era gains in employment and housing opportunities to distance themselves from increasingly rundown urban spaces. Ironically, the destruction of Jim Crow removed the most obvious unifying focus for black communities and, by making integration appear more achievable, created a wedge between those seeking to move out and assimilate and others hoping to revitalize the places they lived through the redistribution of resources.[59]

Increasing class fragmentation within the black public sphere injected the nationalist agenda of constructing a shared cultural heritage with great urgency, even as it made the task of unifying black America behind it more challenging. It is unsurprising that Amiri Baraka looked back to the 1940s, the decade of his adolescence, as a golden age in which African American neighborhoods experienced tremendous social and cultural solidarity and "the most advanced concepts of the music were worked out in the community."[60] Remnants of this close relationship between musicians and the people, and the universal view of music it supposed, still surfaced in the black press during the early 1960s. Despite extensive coverage of jazz in papers such as the *Chicago Defender, New York Citizen-Call, New York Amsterdam News,* and *Pittsburgh Courier,* writers rarely idealized the music as a self-contained art form. Instead, African American journalists typically integrated material on jazz musicians and entertainment figures in gossip columns and record reviews. The humorous rating systems in the *Citizen-Call* and *Courier,* for example, applied equally to rhythm and blues wailer Eddie "Cleanhead" Vinson and Miles Davis. Even in serious features, the *Amsterdam News* and *Defender* frequently avoided the word jazz to distinguish instrumentalists exploring the legacy of Armstrong, Ellington, and Parker. Experimental music stretched the boundaries of this anti-hierarchical model to breaking point. George Pitts of the *Courier* or the *Citizen-Call*'s Louise Davis Stone assumed reader familiarity with a broad and often sophisticated musical tradition, but free jazz rarely intruded into the commentary. When it did, writers sometimes showed the same puzzlement found in the trade press, although less outright hostility.[61] Black papers generally reported African American accomplishments in any field and, in view of free improvisation's notoriety in *Down Beat, Metronome,* and the *Jazz Review,* may have avoided dismissing it outright.

Cultural nationalists such as Amiri Baraka, Larry Neal, and A. B. Spellman continued to promote free improvisation's revolutionary potential, advocating greater realism in the music as a means of overcoming its limited appeal. In 1966 Pantheon books published Spellman's *Four Lives in the Bebop Business,* which assessed the impact of institutional racism on the careers of Ornette Coleman, Cecil Taylor, Jackie McLean, and Herbie Nichols. In a review for *Negro Digest,* Larry Neal captured the Black Arts Movement's response to the widening gap between African American artists and audiences. Neal allowed that Coleman and Taylor often appeared to depart from the jazz tradition. In explaining their failure to build a community base, however, he skirted the music's challenging aesthetic framework and instead blamed a lack of social commitment among the performers:

In order for this music to become revolutionary, it must extend itself into the Black community in a manner which, heretofore, it has failed to do. It must mean to the community what the Supremes, the Impressions, and James Brown now mean. And it must have a direct bearing on the political and social life of the community. The struggles of the community must somehow be mirrored in the music, and in a manner that is readily felt by the people. Currently, the only things revolutionary about the "new music" are its technical innovations. And these are not enough.[62]

Neal did not define what form this new realism ought to take, although his sentiments echoed statements by other creative artists that black musicians needed to enunciate the concerns of their race. In 1965 Archie Shepp sounded a note of desperation when he told a reporter, "we can't let the audience escape. We must bring into our music every stench of the streets, every tragedy, don't let them rest." By 1968 he admitted to having lost almost all contact with black listeners. The difficulty cultural nationalists experienced in articulating a means to bridge this divide highlighted their ambivalence about the role of the arts in the freedom struggle. On the one hand, writers envied the popularity of vernacular musical forms in African American neighborhoods. In October 1966, Askia Touré declared that jazz had abandoned the black community and that rhythm and blues reflected the people's aspirations. A. B. Spellman admitted that "the man standing in line for the Otis Redding show at the Apollo almost certainly never heard of tenor saxophonist Albert Ayler, and wouldn't have the fuzziest idea of what he was doing if he did hear him." On the other hand, young African American intellectuals cherished the exclusive character of free improvisation as confirmation of their cultural taste and leadership. In addition, the complexity and elitism of experimental jazz challenged the accepted superiority of Euro-American art music on its own terms.[63]

Amiri Baraka's 1966 essay "The Changing Same (R&B and New Black Music)" illustrated best the Movement's desire to reconcile experimental free jazz with the masses through the power of myth. Baraka treated both rhythm and blues and free improvisation as legitimate expressions of "roots" music. They derived from different class positions and sensibilities but shared central values of the black aesthetic. The variations between the styles, he contended, "are merely indicative of the different placements of spirit." Free form instrumentalists sought "a middle class place," a position Baraka defined not in terms of their education and training but according to the music's emotional content. Experimental musicians engaged in self-conscious reflection, while rhythm and blues artists conveyed pure expression.[64]

Baraka maintained that the spiritual source of all black music united the disparate forms. Although many rhythm and blues performers had long since left the church, their music transcended an oppressive material environment. James Brown projected a practical and earthy spirituality ("Money won't change you . . . but time will take you out") while free jazz exhibited a mystical and intellectual religion. Baraka recognized the contemplative nature of "the new thing" in a number of features: in album titles such as Coltrane's *A Love Supreme, Meditations,* and *Ascension;* in tone color, mood, and resilient energy; and in the most secular artists' obeisance to ancient African spirits. Similarly, in Baraka's conception, rhythm and blues spoke of a physical, sensual, and social love while free improvisers deliberated on the idea of loving. Baraka hoped that the strength of these shared values would overcome the artificial opposition between the different styles. These forms would then resolve into a Unity Music:

which is jazz and blues, religious and secular. Which is New Thing and Rhythm and Blues. The consciousness of social reevaluation and rise, a social spiritualism. A mystical walk up the street to a new neighborhood where all the risen live. . . . The Rhythm and Blues mind blowing evolution of James-Ra and Sun-Brown.[65]

Baraka's attempt to unite populist and esoteric forms of black art on the basis of innate extra-musical qualities both acknowledged an aesthetic hierarchy within African American culture and challenged its relevance. Recognizing the fluidity and complexity of the black community's tastes, Baraka, Touré, and Neal (whose work shared an emphasis on the catholicity of the black aesthetic) hoped that anchoring rhythm and blues and free jazz in similar cultural values would enhance their own proximity to the black working class and legitimate their status as organic intellectuals.[66] This attempt to connect with an African American public usually took place at the expense of the black bourgeoisie, which the Black Arts Movement typically cast as a collection of assimilationist strivers. In his review of *Four Lives*, Larry Neal held the black middle class responsible for failing to support and recognize African American artists. As a result of this neglect, Neal argued, African Americans lacked the opportunity to develop an appreciation for "the new thing," and musicians fell prey to the shifting interests of white fans.[67] Harold Cruse forwarded the most compelling indictment of established African American leaders for abdicating their responsibility to promote black norms, values, and standards. In *The Crisis of the Negro Intellectual* (1967), Cruse argued that the black middle class had invested its hopes for status and position in integration and shunned any cultural form that evoked racial distinction or nationalism. Consequently the black artist, who Cruse accepted as the community's true intellectual voice:

has never really been held accountable to the black world for his social role . . . [because] the black world cannot and does not support the Negro creative intellectual. The black bourgeoisie does not publish books, does not own or operate theaters or music halls. It plays no role to speak of in Negro music, and is remote from the living realities of the jazz musician who plays out his nights in the effete and soulless commercial jungles of American white middle-class café culture.[68]

Cruse and Neal overstated the dearth of black middle-class support for jazz. In 1959, for example, the NAACP awarded Duke Ellington its prestigious Spingarn Medal "for the highest achievement by an American Negro during the previous year or years." In 1964 the Harlem Cultural Council established Jazzmobile, Inc., which presented outdoor concerts on the back of a flat-bed trailer and lecture-concerts and workshops in local schools throughout Harlem, Bedford-Stuyvesant, and the South Bronx.[69] Yet experimental musicians benefited little from this interest. Marginalized in their own neighborhoods, free improvisers had pause to reconsider their relationship to the black community and much mythologized sacred function. Cecil Taylor confided to Joe Goldberg that neglect by African American institutions and leaders encouraged jazz performers to reconcile their music with a national artistic heritage and, in effect, follow the black middle class' purported disengagement with social responsibility:

The jazz musician is quite apart, because the black bourgeoisie is interested in identifying with Sammy Davis and Sidney Poitier. They consider Billie Holiday a drug addict, that's all they know about her. . . . The Negro middle class, as best I can see, is very busy trying to emulate the white middle class. *I'm a part of the*

tradition of the American artist. That's the only thing to hold onto. It's the most vibrant
and alive thing that there is to hold onto.[70] (Emphasis added)

Taylor's comments encapsulated the dilemma of free jazz performers.
A lack of sustained organizational support in either black or white
America left experimental musicians at the mercy of the marketplace.
They attempted to survive as artists in an entertainer's milieu, their only
model the romantic construction of the composer as an outsider driven
by personal genius. This ideal emerged in early nineteenth-century
Europe, before commercial exchange mechanisms compensated for the
declining aristocratic patronage system. At a time of great dislocation
and transition, the romantic musician, writer, sculptor, or painter cast
off the rational formal constraints prized by Enlightenment thinkers
in favor of uninhibited emotional individuality.[71] Free improvisers
educated in the classical concert tradition frequently identified with the
isolated and iconoclastic figures of western lore. "I'm an artist," proclaimed Albert Ayler in 1966. "I've lived more than I can express in
[be]bop terms. Why should I hold back the feeling of my life, of being
raised in the ghetto of America?"[72] Just as African American experimental music incorporated African and Euro-American sources to form a
syncretic musical modernism, free improvisers' professional self-conception increasingly drew upon the legends of both the African griot and
alienated artist. Yet at its center, a fundamental contradiction existed
between these two models. The romantic posture implied a distance
from the masses, while cultural nationalists theorized black music as a
repository of the community's values. Throughout the late 1960s, experimental musicians struggled to find institutional forums in which they
could remain true to their creative principles, make a living, and retain
their identity as representatives of the people.

Chapter 5

Jazz Outside the Marketplace

On January 18, 1969, Howard Klein, Assistant Director of Arts Programs at the Rockefeller Foundation, arrived in the small college town of Yellow Springs, Ohio, for a jazz ensemble performance. He must have wondered how an unorthodox bandleader who barely made a living in New York City, America's cultural capital, would be received in the heartland. He had met pianist Cecil Taylor at the Foundation's New York offices a few months earlier and had come away from their meeting convinced that the commercial nightclub environment irreparably harmed jazz music's artistic integrity. For some time the Rockefeller Arts Program had sought ways to support diverse performers and audiences traditionally excluded from its activities. Klein had traveled over six hundred miles to explore whether Antioch College could provide a model solution.[1]

Cecil Taylor appeared with saxophonist Jimmy Lyons and drummer Andrew Cyrille in a concert jointly sponsored by the Music Department and Afro-American Studies Institute (AASI), a student-run organization that had recently secured the addition of several Black Studies courses to the curriculum. The promoters hoped to convince the Rockefeller Foundation to fund an innovative residency program under Taylor's leadership in which predominantly African American jazz musicians would experiment and perform, teach interdisciplinary workshops with film makers, dancers, actors, and musicians, and take jazz groups into inner city schools in nearby Dayton and Cincinnati. The brainchild of assistant music professor John Ronsheim, a former classmate of Taylor's at the New England Conservatory of Music, the project supplemented Antioch's liberal arts mission with a social commitment to attracting nontraditional students and making connections with the surrounding community.

The event left Klein in little doubt as to Cecil Taylor's artistic dedication or embrace by the students. When he entered the Antioch auditorium that evening, Klein found the 800-seat theater filled beyond capacity as the audience spilled onto the stage and into the aisles. After an opening number that lasted for a remarkable one hour and fifteen minutes ("the equivalent length of a Mahler symphony," he noted in his report), "the audience rose in unison with cheers and applause." After a brief intermission the group evoked a similar response with another lengthy improvisation. Klein attributed Taylor's success to his unique blending of artistic qualities and traditions. "To me the music was on a level of communication seldom heard in the work by many so-called serious composers," he marveled. "This is to say that C[ecil] T[aylor]'s jazz is thoroughly sophisticated, utilizes the most avant garde musical devices, is highly structured and yet presents that fabulous vitality of spontaneity without which music often seems academic." The next morning Taylor impressed Klein with his calm logic and ambitious vision during a long discussion of the pressing need for an independent creative sanctuary. As the pianist spoke of bringing fellow musicians such as Ornette Coleman, Don Cherry, Bill Dixon, and Sonny Murray to campus, Klein imagined the potential for supporting an indigenous American art form, every bit as serious and needy as Euro-American concert music, while appealing to previously neglected listeners.

Despite Klein's enthusiasm for the project, his report to the Rockefeller Foundation carried some warnings. Although he did not consider Taylor a black nationalist, Klein worried that the workshops might become segregated along racial lines. Taylor's view of jazz as an African American art and reluctance to work with Gerry Mulligan, who had been recommended by *New York Times* critic John S. Wilson, raised the specter of "Crow Jim" (a concept Klein clearly had been briefed about). The Afro-American Studies Institute's ability to win concessions from the Antioch administration further complicated the picture. Its head William Brower, who Klein described as "extremely bright and a natural leader," supported Taylor's residency in avowedly nationalistic terms. "The proposal is good," he suggested during Klein's meeting with student representatives, "because its central core is black music and it helps promote the reconstruction of black people in that they are a nation." Indeed, the Rockefeller Foundation rejected Antioch's initial application for support largely out of fear that the AASI would "capture" the project and exclude white students and instructors. Taylor accepted an appointment at the University of Wisconsin-Madison instead, and the Rockefeller Foundation only backed the project—and secured Taylor's services—after Antioch's trustees abolished the AASI and secured matching funds from the National Endowment for the Arts.[2]

The struggle for sponsorship of Cecil Taylor's Antioch residency illustrates the complex interplay between intellectual and institutional forces that mediated jazz music's place in America's cultural hierarchy. For a short time during the 1960s, free improvisation and its supporters challenged the accepted criteria for appraising jazz music and its worth.

Unable or unwilling to dismiss "the new thing" out of hand, critics attempted to divorce its aesthetic and supposedly separatist values. They discovered that designating the music as "avant-garde" jazz marginalized its innovations within the jazz canon and accentuated the validity of more structured and disciplined approaches to experimentation. Yet free improvisation's contribution to American culture goes beyond a momentary challenge to the evolving pantheon. The music's fluid identity during the late 1960s interacted with changes in access to education, arts funding, audience composition, and the career choices of leading experimental performers to open new opportunities for free improvisers to reconcile their artistic imperatives, cultural heritage, and material needs outside the marketplace.

During the late 1960s and 1970s jazz moved into the nonprofit arena, particularly those public sectors most susceptible to political pressure, accumulating a new level of prestige that attended academic recognition, government funding, and to a lesser extent private foundation and corporate sponsorship. Musicians working in many different jazz styles benefited from these sources of income and status, but free improvisers pioneered in each field for several—sometimes contradictory—reasons. Developments in experimental music corresponded with creative assumptions in the European tradition, enabling champions of jazz to argue for its inclusion on the basis of a commitment to artistic modernism. Free jazz performers had demonstrated their inability to survive in the marketplace and thus appeared less compromised by commercial imperatives and more worthy of subsidy than other musicians. Finally, the Black Arts Movement's embrace of free improvisation as a uniquely African American form enhanced the music's appeal to universities and endowments that faced mandates to democratize the arts and education. Taking advantage of these trends, experimental performers extended the emerging grants economy and transformed the funding of jazz.

Like symphony orchestras, ballet and opera companies, theater and dance troupes, and art museums, jazz musicians continue to rely heavily on commercial sources of income, although to a much greater extent. By the end of the 1970s, academic, public, and philanthropic support remained considerably and consistently lower for jazz than for orthodox highbrow genres. This pattern has many explanations, including the accumulated status of European-derived forms that advocates of African American art struggled to match, the continued individualism of jazz performers that denied them access to organizational grants, and the greater viability of jazz in the marketplace. The music's ambiguous relationship with the established sponsors of high culture makes it difficult to assess whether jazz further subverted America's cultural hierarchy, as many of its supporters insist, or merely facilitated a reordering of aesthetic values.[3] It is clear, however, that free improvisers validated a legacy of black artistic and intellectual achievement through their association with nonprofit philanthropic and educational institutions, and that they frequently pioneered the diversification of exclusive artistic programs.

By defying its dominant aesthetic and ideological values, free improvisation drew an immediate reaction from the jazz industry. Dismayed by the Black Arts Movement's efforts to invest the music with radical meanings, many established critics attempted to reorient the debate over its merits. Their approaches lacked uniformity, however. While writers such as Leonard Feather dismissed "the new thing" as "jazz anarchy," Ornette Coleman, John Coltrane, and Cecil Taylor cultivated sufficient support among musicians, critics, and fans for their reputations to survive scorn or silence. John Coltrane won four *Down Beat* Readers' Poll awards in 1965 after the release of *A Love Supreme*, and Ornette Coleman won two awards in 1966, including "Jazzman of the Year" in recognition of his return to public performance.[4] Nor should one assume that only cultural nationalists embraced the musical goals of experimental performers. Martin Williams, Dan Morgenstern, and Whitney Balliett had offered early support to one or more of the pioneering innovators. The second wave of "outside" players—Albert Ayler, Archie Shepp, Pharoah Sanders, Marion Brown, the AACM musicians, and others—proved more problematic either because they sympathized openly with separatist politics or they extended modernist experimentation in disquieting directions.[5] Thus tentative supporters of free improvisation joined with opponents (who gradually realized the music would not simply disappear) in two endeavors: to separate free jazz from its association with nationalism and to locate it at the edge of the tradition.

Fierce debate over free improvisation's musical merits did not necessarily harm the jazz business. Indeed, it provided the record companies with free exposure for both traditional and progressive artists on their rosters. In an attempt to engage a wide audience, the trade press carefully printed opposing sides of aesthetic disagreements. In-depth features on an experimental musician frequently followed a particularly virulent attack on the movement by a nervous critic. Similarly, letters to the editor usually reflected a balanced response to an issue. When a prominent *Jazz* magazine writer attacked Willis Conover's programming for the Voice of America, the letters page carried a series of severe rebuttals from leading industry figures in a subsequent issue. Although controversy energized readers, individual critics had much to lose from the emergence of free jazz. They had invested their reputations in a set of values that represented personal tastes and outlooks. To mitigate the divisive impact of their caustic attacks on free improvisation, jazz writers employed indirect methods also to relegate the style to the far reaches of the jazz tradition. Leonard Feather's "Blindfold Test" feature in *Down Beat* invoked the authority of established performers to marginalize experimental music. "It's a little too far out, a little distorted to my ear," Tyree Glenn responded upon hearing Ornette Coleman's "Lonely Woman." "It's certainly not the type of jazz that I was brought up on." Throughout the 1960s, Feather gleefully—and extensively—quoted Miles Davis and other established stars dismissing records by Coleman, Cecil Taylor, Archie Shepp, and other experimental artists.[6]

Critics couched their discussions of free improvisation in language that often united diverse musicians in a common category and distanced that group from mainstream performers. During the early 1960s, writers used "avant-garde" as one of several terms to describe the experimental music of Coleman, Coltrane, and Taylor. From about 1964 on, the phrase came into widespread use to locate free jazz on the perimeter of musical developments. Separated from any discussion of its historical social function, columnists and record reviewers employed "avant-garde" as a favorite linguistic device to signify a tenuous regard for convention. Experimental performers displayed considerable ambiguity toward the label. Archie Shepp rejected it in favor of "black classical music," aligning his art with a race-specific tradition. The AACM preferred "Great Black Music."[7] Jazz artists recognized that the term offered the legitimacy of a collective identity, with overtones of European-style vanguardism. Yet it suggested also that "the new thing" represented the outer boundary of creative expression, the limit of accepted musical discourse that threw canonical values into stark relief.

Jazz magazines made a consistent effort to understand the new music and interview practitioners, yet they adopted similar tactics to frame nationalist performers and critics as outsiders. When the experimental band leader George Russell charged *Down Beat* with "exploiting the popular delusions and madness of crowds," he referred to a controversy between himself and Archie Shepp upon which the journal capitalized fully. Following a July 1965 feature on his music, Russell accused staff editors of using an off-hand comment as an eye-catching headline. The phrase, "the avant-garde is the last refuge of the untalented" enraged Shepp, who demanded—and received—space to respond in print. Russell recognized that by publishing both articles, *Down Beat* piously portrayed itself as an impartial party while fueling petty divisions among experimental performers. Disharmony among musicians reinforced the impression of disharmony in the music. *Down Beat* achieved more than kudos by giving Shepp an unabridged right of reply, which appeared in December as "An Artist Speaks Bluntly." The magazine's careful attention to context and layout ensured that the article's unregulated expansion from free jazz to worldwide leftist politics sat uncomfortably amid same-page reports of Louis Armstrong's International Award of Merit and Duke Ellington's latest Hollywood project.[8]

Down Beat employed a combination of subtlety and insistence to detach cultural nationalists from the jazz mainstream. *Blues People* made Amiri Baraka one of the most authoritative writers on contemporary jazz, and the magazine offered him a series of regular but infrequent columns. When "Apple Cores" first appeared in 1964, however, *Down Beat* billed Baraka as "one of the most provocative spokesmen for the 'new jazz,'" so that readers knew his views represented the fringe. As Baraka defined his separatist position more clearly, *Down Beat*'s rebuttals became increasingly forceful. In June 1966 the magazine published an article in which *Negro Digest* contributor Brooks Johnson denounced "neo-neo Toms" within jazz. Johnson labeled Sun Ra and unnamed others "paranoid," and accused them of abdicating mainstream jazz to white performers in a misguided attempt to isolate free improvisation as a uniquely African American style. This reductionist view of experimental jazz allowed Johnson to portray its practitioners as the victims of ambitious black activists such as their "pimp" Baraka. While deracinated "neo-Toms" surrendered their identity to accommodate white tokenism, Johnson argued, "neo-neo-Toms" sacrificed genuine artistic contributions for a rhetorically-protected sphere of "black music." By suggesting that nationalist sentiment served as cover for poorly conceived art, Johnson conflated musical and political radicalism while allowing that "genuine, enlightened" music might still revitalize the jazz tradition. Editors employed an African American writer to protect the magazine against accusations of racism and to add credibility to its attack on black nationalism. "Let me say I'm black and proud of the fact," added Johnson with stilted indignation, "but I really don't think I enjoy hearing music supposedly representative of me that is based in ignorance and a talent void." In an October 1966 follow-up article, Johnson attempted to invalidate the political pronouncements of "outside" musicians by questioning their musical qualifications once more. "Currently there is a perversion of black pride in jazz," he asserted. "It's easier to be a racist than a good trumpeter."[9]

A tragedy and an artistic rebirth heralded the demise of cultural nationalism as a paradigm for interpreting jazz and ensured that "the new thing" represented one more stylistic alternative rather than the logical extension of modernist development. John Coltrane, inspiration and hero to the Black Arts Movement and one of the few experimental musicians to enjoy crossover appeal, died of liver cancer in July 1967. Although many talented performers continued his legacy of relentless musical exploration, none possessed a similar combination of ability, passion, humility, and spirituality that made Coltrane both an icon of integrity and a marketable commodity. Indeed, Coltrane's recordings in the last two years of his life demonstrated that few musical barriers remained unbroken, and by the late 1960s innovation had passed to a younger generation of musicians willing to blend free improvisation with firmer structures. Ironically, veteran trumpeter Miles Davis—Coltrane's former employer—led the recording sessions that heralded the emerging fusion style. His albums *In a Silent Way* (1969) and *Bitches Brew* (1970) showcased key features of the new approach, including rock time signatures, electronic instruments and effects, and impressionistic melodies. Record companies packaged young, fashionable artists in the manner of rock stars. Their ranks included many white musicians, and black performers typically displayed race pride in pan-African symbols—dress and song titles, for example—rather than diatribes against oppression at home. Free improvisation's failing resonance among white and African American fans, and the critical press that spoke to their interests, demonstrated the urgent need for experimental musicians to uncover supplemental or alternative sources of support. They found them in the academy and, to a lesser extent, in government, foundation, and corporate funding agencies during the late 1960s and 1970s. At a time when these institutions faced mounting pressure to transform public access to the arts, jazz musicians—sometimes ambivalently—attempted to win both the symbols and spoils of legitimation by the custodians of traditional high culture. Paradoxically, both the music's residual association with cultural nationalism and parallels between free jazz and the Euro-American concert tradition opened doors in the non-profit sector.

The enormous growth in American higher education after World War II provided a platform for jazz music's changing fortunes. In 1939, less than 1.4 million students attended colleges and universities; in 1947 enrollments rose to 2.3 million at 1,800 campuses, and by 1986 they had reached 12.4 million at 3,300 establishments. Spending throughout the sector jumped from $2.2 billion in 1950 to $21 billion in 1970 to more than $97 billion in 1990.[10] The 1944 GI Bill, an attempt to ease the reintegration of veterans into civilian life, accounted for initial increases in the student population. The program's enormous popularity, the increasingly bureaucratic and technological character of government, business, and industry, and unprecedented postwar prosperity sustained institutional expansion. Even after veteran attendance declined in the late 1940s, overall enrollments rose again from 1952 as a greater proportion of high school graduates from more diverse backgrounds than ever chose to continue their studies. As the baby boom approached college age in the late 1950s, educators anticipated a "tidal wave" of applications.[11]

A revolution in federal policy enabled the boom generation to pursue academic goals in such large numbers during the 1960s and 1970s. The GI Bill's success strengthened the hand of advocates such as American Council on Education head George Zook, who favored universal access to higher learning. Zook chaired the President's Commission on Higher Education, which suggested in 1947 that 49 percent of Americans could benefit from two years of college while 32 percent had the ability to complete a four-year course of study. In 1940, by comparison, less than 16 percent of high school graduates enrolled in colleges or universities. The Soviet launch of an unmanned satellite in 1957 provided the political momentum to achieve this goal. Sputnik alarmed Congress and the country by challenging America's technological superiority at the height of the Cold War and directly inspired the National Defense Education Act of 1958. The act established a loans and graduate fellowship program designed to nurture scientific expertise, but which effectively provided aid to students in all disciplines. From that point on, successive presidents and Congresses expanded federal assistance to universities and students. During the 1960s, college and university enrollment grew from 3.6 million to 7.9 million students, and the number of higher education institutions increased by one-third while their average size tripled. By 1968, student aid programs accounted for one-third of all federal higher education spending, the same proportion as sponsored research. The college population included 32 percent of eighteen to twenty-one-year-olds, the goal of Zook's 1947 report. Even after the last boomers left college in the late 1970s, enrollments continued to grow as female, minority, adult, and part-time students attended in greater numbers.[12]

As policy-makers embraced the goal of universal access to higher learning, academics and administrators reassessed the relevance of the classical curriculum for a new generation of students. "General Education" experiments at Columbia and Chicago between the wars suggested a precedent by proposing, in varying degrees, a restructuring of course requirements to provide greater interdisciplinary emphasis and a broader base of social and intellectual skills. In 1945, Harvard's "Redbook" report endorsed the role of education in imparting shared knowledge and developing well-rounded citizens. In addition, business and government needs for college-certified employees encouraged vocational studies with practical applicability. Many universities responded to these rather different demands by establishing a greater range of non-major distributive requirements in the arts and sciences, and increasing the professional orientation of most major programs. These changes held great significance for the growth and development of artistic disciplines.[13]

College music departments expanded rapidly following World War II to accommodate increased enrollments. The curriculum remained fairly orthodox, however. By the end of the 1940s, only five colleges (including two music academies) provided jazz courses for credit, while ten more tendered noncredit electives. By 1960, forty colleges offered jazz instruction, about half for credit. In accordance with broader curriculum trends, institutions frequently justified these classes on vocational grounds. North Texas State College committed to a dance band major in 1946; yet, despite the experimental nature of its laboratory bands, the word "jazz" never appeared in the course catalog. When the Music Inn at Lenox, Massachusetts founded a School of Jazz in the 1950s, it targeted practicing and aspiring professionals.[14]

The precipitous growth of jazz studies occurred during the 1960s. By the end of the decade 135 colleges and universities allowed jazz instruction for credit, 165 on a noncredit basis. Miami Beach hosted the first national college jazz festival in 1967, and the following year the Music Educators National Conference recognized the National Association of Jazz Educators as an auxiliary organization. By the mid-1970s, approximately 400 colleges provided at least one jazz course for credit, while several prominent institutions established graduate degrees. Jazz programs swelled as a direct result of the demand from high schools for trained stage-band directors and the desire of student-musicians to maintain their creative activities in college. Jazz-oriented stage bands multiplied in high schools after World War II under the influence of music education graduates familiar with swing styles, a proliferation of jazz study materials, and the need to occupy unprecedented numbers of adolescents. Thus university administrators added jazz courses in response to professional pressure from their students' potential employers. For this reason, college music departments rarely afforded jazz equal standing with European classical music. Throughout the 1960s, jazz teaching usually fell to a single instructor, and the music frequently lacked official status as a major or even an accredited course of study.[15] In 1965, Indiana University music professor David Baker described jazz as "the academy's neglected stepchild," owing to a general ignorance of the criteria by which to assess the music or the pedagogical tools available to teach it.[16] Jazz served valuable vocational or recreational purposes, but few faculty considered it an appropriate subject for academic pursuit.

Baker's concern with the content of college music programs coincided with widespread demands for curricular change during the 1960s.

Huge increases in financial aid attracted students from a wide variety of economic and social backgrounds to American colleges and universities. Protesting against the concentrated departmental major and core requirements, students demanded courses relevant to their social and ethical concerns, especially in the areas of feminism, environmentalism, and Black Studies. The new antagonism reflected both student alienation on large, impersonal campuses and a growing view of the administration as part of the problem. Institutional collaboration with the House Un-American Activities Committee, local police, draft boards, and scientific research for the military precipitated widespread strikes, building occupations, demonstrations, and sometimes violent protests led by free speech, civil rights, antiwar, and countercultural activists.[17]

The birth of Black Studies programs at colleges and universities throughout the country represented a triumph for curricular reform and changed significantly the representation and standing of jazz music in the academy. Actively recruited for the first time during the 1960s, African American students at predominantly white schools outside the south employed the disruptive tactics of New Left campus movements to pursue their own liberation struggle. Radicalized by urban unrest and Dr. King's assassination, black student unions made their presence felt once African American enrollment reached a critical mass. Student concerns centered around a belief that existing courses either excluded or distorted black history and culture, making academics irrelevant to their experiences and needs. They demanded a voice in revising the curriculum, hiring faculty, and determining admissions policies for Black Studies programs. The degree of autonomy students sought reflected competing pluralist, nationalist, and separatist visions for the emerging discipline. Activists at San Francisco State College and Cornell University employed strikes and building occupations to further the cause of self-government for, and the exclusion of white students from, Black Studies programs. By contrast, Yale's Black Students Alliance accepted an integrated faculty and student body to secure the first degree-granting Afro-American Studies program at an Ivy League university.[18]

While they rarely achieved the administrative independence they sought, African American students transformed higher education with remarkable speed. San Francisco State College established the first Black Studies program in 1967. By 1970, approximately two-thirds of all four-year colleges offered similar courses, while African American enrollment more than doubled. As administrators hurried to forestall further protests, they launched far-reaching searches for candidates who might prove acceptable to newly-empowered students. Most of these activists considered the black arts a key topic, reflecting some of the most unique and self-defined contributions of African Americans to the country's culture and identity. Nathan Hare, the first coordinator of Black Studies at San Francisco State, proposed "The Music of Blackness" as a core course in the cultural concentration.[19] Almost single handed, Amiri Baraka, Larry Neal, A. B. Spellman, and the Black Arts Movement had established music at the center of a black aesthetic and jazz, especially the more esoteric variations, as its highest expression. The widespread use of two anthologies in Black Studies programs illustrated this connection best. Edited by Baraka and Neal, *Black Fire* (1968) drew upon critics, poets, and playwrights such as Spellman, Harold Cruse, and Sonia Sanchez to demonstrate, celebrate, and explicate the values of the new black art. Like *The Black Aesthetic* (1971), edited by Black Studies pioneer Addison Gayle, Jr., its essays repeatedly pointed to experimental black music as the standard and inspiration for contemporary African American creative expression.[20]

The Black Arts Movement's legitimation of free improvisation made experimental musicians attractive candidates for teaching positions in the emerging Black Studies programs. Free form instrumentalists pioneered an expanded role for jazz in colleges and universities that reinforced its suitability for academic rather than merely vocational study. When the State University of New York (SUNY) at Buffalo began recruiting faculty for its new Black Studies program in 1968, Roswell Rudd's cousin—who worked in the SUNY system—called his relative for suggestions. Rudd, a prominent white free improviser, nominated his longtime collaborator Archie Shepp. After four years at Buffalo, Shepp accepted a tenured position at the W. E. B. Du Bois Center of Afro-American Studies at the University of Massachusetts-Amherst, where he joined another "militant black artist," Max Roach. Shepp taught two music workshops and a lecture course entitled "Revolutionary Concepts in African-American Music" each semester, while spending the remaining four months of the year on the road with his band.[21]

Shepp's duties at Buffalo illustrated the diverse functions served by the new hires. Faced with criticism that they courted ill-prepared African American students and drew radical minorities to campus in a misguided attempt to relieve urban unrest, university officials expected Black Studies faculty to act as recruiters, counselors, and community liaisons in addition to teachers. As a mentor for African American students, Shepp spent much of his time attracting underclassmen and negotiating their administrative problems with the institution. Jackie McLean, who had fused free improvisation with traditional bebop structures in the mid-1960s, joined the Julius Hartt School of Music in Hartford, Connecticut, in 1970 and founded its Department of Afro-American Music. He worked also as a consultant for the Hartford Commission on the Arts and in this capacity founded the Arts Collective, which presented jazz and other creative performances to inner-city children. The high demand for suitable minority candidates meant that some musicians accepted more than one appointment and acquired traditional qualifications while they worked. Marion Brown, who had played saxophone with John Coltrane, Archie Shepp, Sun Ra, and Pharoah Sanders, taught at Bowdoin College and Brandeis University from 1971 to 1974 and at Wesleyan University from 1974 to 1976. Simultaneously, he completed a bachelor's degree in music education at Bowdoin in 1974, and a master's in ethnomusicology at Wesleyan in 1976.[22]

Not all free improvisers lacked academic credentials or gravitated to Black Studies programs. Bill Dixon, one of the first experimental musicians to accept a permanent university position, had taught art history and private music lessons for many years. His career provides an important reminder that changes in the music, and its compatibility with modernist imperatives in other contemporary arts, made an important contribution to the acceptance of jazz on campus. Dixon's appointment to the Bennington College faculty in 1968 resulted from his professional relationship with dancer Judith Dunn. After five years with the Merce Cunningham Dance Company, Dunn helped found the cooperative Judson Dance Theater in 1962. Just as free improvisers sought to liberate jazz from inflexible rules, the Judson performers pursued an abstract approach to dance by deliberately avoiding structural constraints. At a time when dance instructors taught premeditated movement along a diagonal line, Dunn staged her first solo concert entirely in-the-round and incorporated randomly calculated maneuvers into another. Introduced to Dixon's music in 1965, shortly after the disintegration of the Jazz Composers Guild, Dunn asked the trumpeter to participate in a dance workshop. Their partnership continued for eight years. Dixon accompanied Dunn's performances and the two artists taught collaboration between musicians, dancers, composers, and choreographers at various schools including Bennington, where Dixon accepted a joint appointment in music and dance before receiving tenure in the music department during the early 1970s.[23]

While Dixon and Shepp moved into academia during the late 1960s and remained for several decades, other musicians took a shorter break from the commercial world. Temporary appointments provided relief from competitive pressures and a chance for performers to fortify their credentials before pursuing outside opportunities. The University of Wisconsin at Madison hired Cecil Taylor in 1970, following a student strike that brought 2,100 National Guard troops armed with machine guns and tear gas to campus. Retained to teach the principles of black aesthetics based on black music, Taylor spent the next five years at Madison and Antioch College. Like Sun Ra, who taught briefly at Berkeley and San Francisco State, Taylor affiliated with Black Studies departments or special music programs that owed their existence to insistent student demands. The initial proposal for Taylor's collaborative workshop between musicians, poets, and dancers at Antioch, for example, emerged from a dialogue between the college president and student representatives of the Afro-American Studies Institute.[24] Experimental musicians benefited also from a growing number of artist-in-residence appointments. During the 1970s, Dixon brought Jimmy Lyons, Jimmy Garrison, Alan Shorter, and Alan Silva to Bennington College, which also retained Milford Graves in 1973. Antioch College offered two-year residencies to Lyons and drummer Andrew Cyrille, in effect securing the services of Cecil Taylor's trio.[25]

Experimental performers helped validate jazz as a subject for serious study in part by drawing attention to the aesthetic compatibility between free improvisation and other creative disciplines (European and African American). Not surprisingly, perhaps, free jazz exerted less influence over vocationally oriented college music programs. Throughout the 1970s, jazz pedagogy emphasized mainstream styles, some form of chord- or scale-based theory, and individualistic solos to the detriment of freer sounds and collective interaction. The expansion of jazz education precipitated an influx of college jazz instructors with relatively little professional experience. In its place, they often depended upon codified and standardized teaching methods—precisely the opposite of the expansive, interdisciplinary programs created by Taylor, Dixon, Shepp, and other experienced, innovative performers. Popular texts such as Jerry Coker's *Improvising Jazz* (1964), Jamey Aebersold's *A New Approach to Improvisation* series (beginning 1967), and David Baker's *Jazz Improvisation* (1969) emphasized disciplined harmony and meter, an approach that lent itself to the teaching, demonstration, and evaluation of quantifiable technical skills. By contrast, collective improvisation, indistinct tonality, free meter, and overblown effects proved least compatible with the conservatory training of many jazz instructors, and indeed challenged the primacy of both the teacher and the tradition of virtuoso jazz soloists. Thus, as David Ake has demonstrated, even jazz educators who introduced material by experimental musicians such as John Coltrane emphasized his pattern-based approach to chords and scales (such as "Giant Steps" and "Impressions") rather than his "outside" work (on the albums *Ascension* and *Meditations*, for example).[26]

Yet the emphasis on chord-based improvising that dominated jazz education in the 1970s did not impede a minority of adventurous students and teachers from exploring alternative methods and goals. Free improvisation afforded musicians a choice whether to play inside or outside traditional structural constraints. Even sympathetic educators

Figure 20. Cecil Taylor circa 1972. Courtesy Institute of Jazz Studies, Rutgers University.

argued that student musicians ought to learn the vocabulary and grammar of traditional styles before moving on to advanced experimentation. Catering to large numbers of students with diverse abilities, not to mention the instructor's personal tastes, many music departments understandably shunned free jazz. Nevertheless, the large and prestigious programs often accommodated their students' interest in experimental forms. In his influential *Jazz Pedagogy* (1979), for example, David Baker recommended that students learn to improvise within a variety of structures, including free forms, and provided examples of student recitals at Indiana University featuring works by Ornette Coleman. Meanwhile, jazz educators across the country gradually incorporated "outside" musicians into their jazz history syllabi.[27]

Free improvisers exploited new sources of prestige and income for jazz musicians in the higher education sector. Six years after the demise of the Jazz Composers Guild, all four African American founders held academic employment. By the 1990s, name musicians from the 1960s who had not benefited from teaching positions, artist-in-residence opportunities, or visiting lectureships represented the exception rather than the rule. White university administrators became important custodians of an artistic style largely rejected by African American listeners, yet this irony should not obscure the Black Arts Movement's role in radicalizing African American intellectuals and students. Political pressure exerted by the student movement, together with developments in the music itself, fortified the position of jazz in the colleges and universities. During the 1960s and 1970s, the transformation of the nonprofit grants economy provided jazz performers with further access to institutional endorsements and revenue streams previously reserved for musicians in the classical European tradition. Despite the continued marginality of free improvisation within the evolving jazz canon, experimental musicians once again led the way owing to economic necessity, their music's aesthetic compatibility with modernist developments in other genres, and the shifting nature of identity politics.

During the twentieth century, and particularly since World War II, nonprofit organizations have become the major suppliers of the performing and visual arts. Nearly all symphony orchestras, resident theaters, dance troupes, opera companies, and two-thirds of art museums operate on a not-for-profit basis. Allowing for variations among the genres, these bodies depend upon philanthropic support and earned income in approximately equal proportions.[28] Paul DiMaggio's study of cultural entrepreneurship in nineteenth-century Boston suggested that the foundation of nonprofit corporations such as the Museum of Fine Arts and the Boston Symphony Orchestra by the city's social elite helped to define and institutionalize the differences between high culture and the emerging entertainment industry. Boston's Brahmins pioneered an organizational form that perpetuated their control, insulated their tastes from the demands of the masses, yet offered the flexibility to educate— and generate revenue from—the growing middle classes. DiMaggio argued not only that the lines between highbrow and lowbrow forms have changed over time, anticipating the work of Lawrence Levine, but also that divisions between nonprofit and proprietary cultural ventures have fluctuated considerably. Changing boundaries between art and popular culture—the separation of Shakespeare, Italian opera, and painting from competition with contortionists, pop songs, and bearded ladies—owed a great deal to the fluid relationship between performers and their sponsors.[29]

Since the late 1960s, jazz musicians have exploited new sources of financial support outside the marketplace both directly and via non-profit presenting organizations. Those grant-making agencies most susceptible to political pressure made the greatest effort to broaden their recipient base, as the era's first major controversy over government sponsorship of the arts revealed. Before the 1960s federal subsidy occurred largely through indirect means. The Smithsonian Institution housed individual bequests to the United States, several New Deal agencies provided work relief for artists, and nonprofit organizations and gifts enjoyed exemption from taxation. President John F. Kennedy significantly expanded the government's role by establishing a Federal Advisory Council on the Arts by Executive Order in June 1963. Kennedy proposed a partnership between government, private institutions, and business with the goals of fostering excellence and saving existing cultural institutions threatened by financial crisis. He died before making any appointments to the Council, but in the next twenty-two months President Lyndon Johnson supported legislation creating the National Endowment for the Arts (NEA) and the National Endowment for the Humanities (NEH) in September 1965. In October, Johnson authorized an initial appropriation for the NEA of $2.5 million for Fiscal Year (FY) 1966.[30]

President Johnson retained Kennedy's understanding that the federal government should stimulate rather than supplant private and local initiatives. A statutory requirement that the government could not provide more than 50 percent of the costs of any project attempted to elicit matching awards from private donors. Although the NEA provided non-matching fellowships to individual artists and performers, the principle assured that programs directed most monies to nonprofit organizations. In addition, the NEA distributed a significant proportion of federal dollars to the states, also in the form of challenge grants. These block allocations accounted for one-third of the NEA's budget during the 1960s, and 20 percent from the early 1970s to 1990. Federal disbursement encouraged the rapid growth of state art agencies, which increased from a handful before 1965 to every state and six special jurisdictions by the mid-1970s. They made numerous grants, in turn, to local or regional arts organizations.[31]

Lyndon Johnson significantly altered national policy, however, by incorporating support of the arts into the educational agenda of the

Great Society. As Margaret Wyszomirski has demonstrated, Johnson attempted to change the pattern of public benefits from arts subsidies. Thus, from the beginning, a federal commitment to cultural pluralism matched the NEA's dedication to excellence. Officers had few resources to complete their mission at first, as appropriations remained anchored around $7 million until FY 1970. The NEA suffered a fate similar to many Great Society agencies in the later years of the Johnson presidency. Increasingly consumed with the Vietnam War, Johnson lost the ability to carry through much of his domestic program. Facing demands for cost-saving cuts, congressional supporters could do little more than maintain a nominal federal commitment to the arts.[32]

The NEA's budget soared under its second Chairperson, Nancy Hanks (1969–77). Hanks's organization of arts advocacy groups, and regular visits with congressional members, proved especially useful in convincing legislators and President Richard Nixon that the NEA enjoyed widespread support from arts benefactors, trustees, and other important community leaders across the country. According to White House special assistant Leonard Garment, with whom Hanks worked closely, Nixon "wanted for his own an issue that would not automatically divide his audience into sympathetic hawks and hostile doves."[33] Hanks's efforts persuaded him that the arts offered such an opportunity, and under her tenure the NEA budget rose from $8.2 million in FY 1970 to $123.5 million in FY 1978. As a result, annual grants to state arts agencies increased from $36,000 each in 1970 to $215,000 each in 1976.[34]

In 1968 the NEA established its first jazz panel, which included musicians Jaki Byard, Dizzy Gillespie, and Gunther Schuller, radio announcer Willis Conover, critic Dan Morgenstern, and author Russell Sanjek. During the 1970s, its rotating membership embraced educators, museum curators, a priest, and many other jazz specialists selected by the NEA Chairperson for their expertise and diversity. The panel made its first award to George Russell in 1969 (a fellowship of $5,500) and initiated a series of annual grants in FY 1970.[35] Out of a music budget of $2.5 million, it dispersed thirty grants totaling $20,050 in four categories. Jazz composers and arrangers received the largest number of awards as commissions, reflecting a residual European-derived value scale that gave preference to music writers rather than improvisers. The NEA also made grants to colleges and universities for jazz residencies, clinics, and workshops, to elementary and secondary schools for staging jazz concerts, and to individual musicians and students for travel or study.

The decision to sponsor jazz resulted in part from the music's diminishing commercial prospects, a circumstance illustrated amply by free improvisers. The agency's statement announcing the first jazz panel made this rationale clear. "Jazz has been one of the most important of

TABLE 1. NATIONAL ENDOWMENT FOR THE ARTS DISBURSEMENTS. TOTAL
AMOUNTS AWARDED IN THE FOUR JAZZ CATEGORIES, AND THE MUSIC PROGRAM'S
OVERALL BUDGET, BETWEEN 1969 AND 1980

Year	Jazz Program	Music Program
1969	$ 5,500	$ 861,620
1970	20,050	2,525,195
1971	50,325	5,188,383
1972	244,925	9,745,797
1973	227,238	10,382,210
1974	419,298[a]	16,116,310
1975	671,208[a]	14,894,833
1976	1,059,864[a]	17,249,296
1977	843,092[a]	17,332,202
1978	695,573	19,457,000
1979	1,063,900	16,375,408
1980	1,363,329	13,572,300

[a]From 1974 to 1977 the NEA included other indigenous music forms in an expanded Jazz/
Folk/Ethnic Program, although the overwhelming majority of funds went to jazz
composers, performers, and organizations.

our art forms, providing enrichment for Americans and for all the peoples of the world. Despite its continuing vitality, jazz is not sharing in the prosperity of other forms of music. For this reason, the Endowment established, in Fiscal 1970, a pilot program in support of jazz."[36] Jazz funding increased during the 1970s as NEA budgets grew, although it remained a junior partner to established highbrow genres. By 1975 the jazz allocation had risen to $671,000, and in 1976 jazz spending through the music program reached $1 million. The 1976 appropriation reflected the cost of several special projects to celebrate the nation's bicentennial, and jazz awards dipped over the next two years, but in 1979 funding once again topped $1 million (out of a $16.9-million music budget). Despite the fate of free improvisation in the trade press, the recipients included many experimental musicians. Muhal Richard Abrams, Carla Bley, Marion Brown, Henry Threadgill, and over 20 other free players received fellowships of up to $2,000 in the first five years.[37] The jazz panel also funded special initiatives during the 1970s, such as an oral history project, and additional money reached experimental performers through other music categories and interdisciplinary programs.[38]

As arts funding expanded dramatically during the 1970s, resentment increased among some endowment staffers and arts professionals, who believed that a fundamental contradiction existed between the goals of excellence and pluralism. The rebellions of the 1960s had made funding allocation a sensitive issue although, as Edward Arian has demonstrated, the NEA continued to prioritize symphony orchestras and art museums above other recipient organizations.[39] The discomfort of many policy-makers gained national attention in 1976, when Senator Claiborne Pell's oversight committee blocked the reappointment of NEH Chair Ronald Berman and in 1977, when President Jimmy Carter nominated former Pell staffer and avowed populist Livingston Biddle to head the NEA. Public debate over these appointments underscored the extent to which the NEA had defined the function of art as "quintessentially socially useful." To support this contention, Berman cited the agency's 1973 reauthorization hearings, at which advocates lauded the role of publicly funded art in counteracting adolescent violence and anomie, offering alternatives to drug addiction, discouraging crime, and relieving inner-city tensions.[40] Berman gained support from NEA Deputy Chairman Michael Straight, who charged "pressure groups" and "vested interests" (including African Americans and women) with imposing virtual representation and funding quotas upon the endowments. This view of distributing federal money as a means of affirmative action received encouragement in 1977 from the vice-president's wife, Joan Mondale, who acted as an unofficial administration spokesperson for the arts. "You've got to remember that most dancers and actors and musicians are white, educated, middle class people," she told the *New York Times*. "And you can't help them when there's this big social problem to be solved with the blacks and other minority groups."[41] Critics charged that arts policy had become a means of assuaging militant activists seeking a higher profile for their causes and resulted in funding for projects of dubious merit.[42]

The NEA's mission to increase access to and representation among the arts coincided with the rising visibility of the Black Arts Movement's agenda and provided a further rationale for funding jazz. Amiri Baraka, Larry Neal, A. B. Spellman, and others provided an intellectual basis for viewing jazz as a uniquely African American form, and their emphasis on the music's racial distinctiveness appealed to top-level policy-makers. As Nancy Hanks wrote in the mid-1970s:

The idea of an "American melting pot" went out of fashion with an awareness that the nation's mettle is strong because its elements are diverse, not homogeneous. Nowhere is this clearer than in the cultural realm. Our cultural heritage includes the traditions of countless immigrant and native peoples; the living traditions are as varied as George Ballanchine's ballets and Aleut carvings . . . jazz, steel beam architecture, modern dance and movies, to name just a few.[43]

Soon after Hanks issued this statement, the NEA recruited A. B. Spellman as a policy study consultant. In 1978 he joined the Expansion Arts

Program, which had directed resources to urban neighborhoods, rural communities, and other culturally undercapitalized areas since 1971. Other prominent theoreticians of black aesthetics found a home in government agencies too. Between 1976 and 1979 Larry Neal served as executive director of the D.C. Commission on the Arts and Humanities, an NEA and District of Columbia-funded special jurisdiction equivalent to a state arts council. During a period of intense competition for public resources between established Washington arts organizations and emerging cultural institutions in the African American community, Neal battled political interference and limited budgets to maximize opportunities for all local constituents.[44] Like Hanks, Neal and Spellman recognized jazz music's potential to draw minorities into the arts audience, educate African Americans about their cultural inheritance, and strengthen the bond between arts professionals and students. The 1971 NEA annual report affirmed these goals in reporting a successful grant from the previous fiscal year: "A young jazz musician who taught drums at no salary in a free clinic to 35 teenagers in a disadvantaged New York community reported an average attendance of 92 percent. He added an additional group of 17 students, assuming the extra expense himself and called the experience a 'Divine Blessing.' "[45]

The NEA offered a number of opportunities for jazz musicians during the 1970s. Fellowships provided a source of income for a small but growing number of individual musicians, including free improvisers. In addition, these grants carried a new level of prestige, a "good housekeeping seal of approval" according to Margaret Wyszomirski and Kevin Mulcahy.[46] Most significantly, the endowment encouraged a fundamental transformation of the jazz business. NEA support began at such a low level compared to other art forms in part because the music lacked a widespread network of nonprofit organizations. As musicians and promoters learned how the grants economy operated, however, they formed presenting organizations that supplemented income from ticket sales with public subsidy. Pioneer nonprofits such as the AACM, which began to receive municipal, state, and national awards after initial reluctance and rejection, inspired numerous other bodies, often run by the musicians themselves. Carla Bley, Mike Mantler, and other members of the Jazz Composers Guild founded an orchestra in 1964, which played at the series "Four Days in December" and subsequent Guild concerts at the Contemporary Center. After the collective's demise, Bley and Mantler incorporated the Jazz Composers Orchestra Association as a nonprofit enterprise to produce the group's concerts and recordings. It won NEA grants in 1970, 1971, 1972, 1975, and 1976.[47] In 1969, Reggie Workman—former bassist with John Coltrane, Art Blakey, and Yusef Lateef—met with several New York-based musicians to address the economic, social, and educational shortcomings of the jazz industry. As a result, Workman and trumpeter Jimmy Owens incorporated the Collective Black Artists (CBA), a charitable body that sponsored concerts and lecture courses on music technique, history, and business for musicians and community organizations. Government grants provided the CBA's largest and most consistent source of income during the 1970s, including notable contributions of $52,750 from the New York State Council on the Arts in 1974 and $28,500 from the NEA ("Jazz" and "Expansion Arts" categories) in 1979.[48] By then the Endowment had became the largest single patron of the arts in the United States.

The willingness of private grant-making foundations to sponsor jazz activities since the late 1960s has further expanded support sources for name musicians and presenting organizations, gained a degree of status for the music through association with awards conferred in the field of high culture, and increased the diversity of musical expression sanctioned by elite patronage programs. Jazz projects received considerably less support from these giving organizations than from government during the 1970s, probably because—as DiMaggio has pointed out—foundations and corporations face institutional constraints that favor gifts to large, established organizations and discourage support of innovative or minority arts. Trustees of local or regional foundations are integrated into networks of reciprocity that reinforce aesthetic conservatism and the diversion of funds to powerful, traditional institutions. National foundations, on the other hand, control the high cost of obtaining reliable information about applicants by favoring nonprofit organizations with an established record.[49] Although foundations did not isolate jazz activities from the commercial sector, they offered a diverse array of funding supplements for artists and arts providers to explore.

During the early twentieth century, income and inheritance tax legislation encouraged the growth and professionalization of private philanthropic foundations. By World War II, the Rockefeller, Carnegie, and Mellon organizations employed large staffs of administrators in place of the individual lawyers or accountants who typically advised nineteenth-century donors. Foundations represent the oldest source of institutional support for the arts, although funding levels remained low until the 1950s. In FY 1930, for example, foundations contributed around half a million dollars to "aesthetics," 82 percent of which came from the Carnegie Corporation. In 1957 the young Ford Foundation made the arts a national priority, donating $249.8 million to the field between 1957 and 1973. Ford's giving to orchestras, residential theaters, ballet, and opera companies encouraged greater contributions to the arts from the Rockefeller Foundation and, by the 1970s and 1980s, the Mellon and Getty

Figure 21. Carla Bley performing at the Hearst Auditorium, San Francisco, 1978. Photograph by Lee Tanner/The Jazz Image.

Foundations (which specialized in the visual arts), Kresge, Hewlett, the Mabel Pew Myrin Trust, the Ahmanson Foundation, and others.[50] By the early 1970s, foundations accounted for approximately 15 percent of total contributions to the arts and humanities.[51] With a few notable exceptions, such as the Guggenheim and (since 1978) MacArthur Foundations, these donations underscored a commitment to established non-profit organizations facing spiraling costs rather than to individual creative artists.

Foundations' initial reluctance to fund jazz reflected the paucity of eligible institutions and a perception that musicians enjoyed widespread opportunities in the marketplace. Ford Foundation vice-president W. McNeil Lowry confirmed this position in 1966, when he specifically addressed calls from free improvisers and their champions for greater attention. "We have nothing under consideration at this time for the new jazz," Lowry noted. "We consider it a legitimate part of the arts but nobody has come forward with a proposal about what we might do for this handful of musicians. We've always felt that jazz offers a much easier commercial place for the artist than a lot of the other arts."[52] Thus Ford's contribution to jazz during the 1960s and the early 1970s comprised three grants totaling $156,000 to the jazz archives of Tulane University and $140,000 (over three years) to the New York Jazz Museum for performances and educational programs. Although jazz musicians did not confront the same overheads as traditional highbrow ventures, Ford's $40,000 installment of the Jazz Museum gift in 1973 paled in comparison to a $1-million appropriation for the San Francisco Opera Association or a $500,000 grant to the New York City Opera.[53]

Yet free improvisers did a lot to dispel the notion that jazz musicians plied a lucrative trade. The Ford grant of 1973 signaled the way non-profits would serve increasingly as conduits for philanthropic as well as government funding to reach jazz musicians. The evolving grants economy provided opportunities for nonprofit jazz presenting organizations to benefit from several sources of support. The New York Jazz Museum, for example, received a smaller grant of $4,000 from the Andrew W. Mellon Foundation in the same year. Although the gift represented Mellon's only apparent donation to jazz in 1973—out of a $2-million budget for the performing arts—such small contributions set a precedent for future funding by a select number of institutions.[54] Their example exercised greatest influence over regional and community foundations, which had multiplied rapidly between 1920 and 1960 on account of the rise of new regional elites and the cost advantages of contributing to existing philanthropic concerns. A growing number of government-funded jazz service organizations, such as the Consortium of Jazz Organizations and Artists, the National Jazz Service Organization, and the National Jazz Presenting Network, provided referrals and technical assistance to emerging nonprofit enterprises seeking local funding for jazz performances and educational workshops. By the 1990s, jazz presenting organizations competed for arts funding in large and small urban markets across the country. Between 1993 and 1997, for example, San Francisco's Jazz in the City received $100,000 from the James Irvine Foundation of California, $140,000 from the William and Flora Hewlett Foundation of California, and $25,000 from the San Francisco Foundation. During the same period, the Jazz Arts Group of Columbus, Ohio, garnered $80,600 from the Columbus Foundation and Affiliated Organizations, and $15,000 from the Nationwide Insurance Enterprise Foundation of Ohio.[55]

Grants to individual musicians provide the most compelling evidence of the links between experimental jazz, its incompatibility with music industry mechanisms, and increased foundation support. The John Simon Guggenheim Memorial Foundation has awarded fellowships to creative artists since the 1920s. In 1967 Ornette Coleman received the first Guggenheim award in the field of jazz composition, a sum probably in the region of $10,000. Significantly, the fellowship supported Coleman's completion of *Inventions of Symphonic Poems*, a work for symphony orchestra with jazz soloist reminiscent of his Third Stream collaborations with Gunther Schuller. Subsequent disbursements appeared to confirm that Coleman's commitment to an aesthetic modernism compatible with the classical tradition helped him secure the honor. Between 1968 and 1971, the Guggenheim Foundation made five awards in jazz composition, each to a musician known also for working in European music or using complex experimental orchestrations: Gil Evans, Jimmy Giuffre, George Russell, Charlie Haden, and Charles Mingus.[56] Ten years later the John D. and Catherine T. MacArthur Foundation began a unique program to support creative artists. By the late 1990s its signature "genius grant" provided five years' support of up to $75,000 per year, depending on age. Fellowships in the field of jazz have strongly favored free improvisers and other experimental musicians, including Cecil Taylor (who also won a Guggenheim in 1973), George Russell (who won a second Guggenheim in 1972), Ornette Coleman (who won a second Guggenheim in 1974), Steve Lacy, Anthony Braxton, and Ken Vandermark.[57]

Discussions within the Rockefeller Foundation surrounding Cecil Taylor's proposed Antioch residency illustrate how its directors came to view free jazz as an art form worthy of their support. As late as December 1963, Assistant Director Gerald Freund had refused a grant request by Johan Kunst, Jr., of Jazz Workshop, Inc. on behalf of Charles Mingus. Freund cited an ongoing review of the music program's activities and concluded "it seems unlikely that we will be able to assist professional musicians in the jazz field." By 1968, however, Arts Director Norman Lloyd and Assistant Director Howard Klein had begun looking for the opportunity to sponsor a "serious" jazz performer. Internal memos written by Klein during late 1968 and early 1969 identified Taylor's music as an art form in direct contrast to "the cabaret jazz of a decade ago" and other "cultural commodities." For Klein, the critical factors in determining the artistic character of free jazz included its sophisticated and avant-garde musical techniques, which "for the most part could not be distinguished from 'classical' music," and its economic difficulties in the entertainment milieu. Klein cited also the support and recognition afforded jazz by European composers such as Ravel, Milhaud, and Stravinsky, and serious European critics.[58]

Political pressure to increase minority representation also may have encouraged the foundations to include jazz musicians in their plans. In March 1971 Archie Shepp led an informal group known as Black Artists for Community Action in a "play-in" at the Guggenheim's New York offices. Beaver Harris, Rahsaan Roland Kirk, Roswell Rudd, and other activists protested the perceived exclusion of artists representing the African American cultural experience and an alleged policy of tokenism toward minorities. The demonstration, which received considerable exposure in the jazz press, resulted from the Guggenheim's refusal to consider a petition from Shepp's organization demanding a $1-million dollar fund for African American writers and performers and honorary awards for elder statesmen of the black arts. Although the foundation denied that militant pressure influenced funding decisions in any way, and some of the elder statesmen Shepp mentioned had actually received Guggenheim fellowships in the past, the music panel made four awards to jazz musicians in 1972—considerably more than in previous years—and invited former recipient Ornette Coleman to join the music jury shortly after.[59] Reports by Rockefeller Foundation officers confirm that the appeal of Cecil Taylor's music to black students at Antioch, and the possibility of drawing support from urban African American communities in nearby cities, enhanced the attractiveness of funding an experimental jazz workshop.[60]

Business philanthropy expanded rapidly from the late 1950s also, as courts lifted restrictions on the range of donations allowed under corporate charters. Gifts to the arts remained a low priority, however. According to the Business Committee for the Arts, an advocacy group founded by Chase Manhattan President David Rockefeller in 1966, corporations contributed approximately $80 million to the arts in 1973, plus an estimated $75 million in written-off expenses. At the time, business philanthropy equaled approximately $1 billion per year.[61] Although policy analysts debate the economic, political, and social motives behind these gifts, surveys indicate that consumer product manufacturers tend to support cultural events in their region or city of operation and that corporations with significant public image challenges (such as oil and tobacco companies) favor high-profile projects in the arts.[62] Thus corporations

Figure 22. Archie Shepp (center) reading a list of demands to an official at the John Simon Guggenheim Memorial Foundation, New York City, during a March 1971 "play-in." Shepp is supported by (from right) Rahsaan Roland Kirk and Beaver Harris. Photograph by Irene Fertik. Courtesy Institute of Jazz Studies, Rutgers University.

have provided another door for jazz musicians and festival planners to knock on.

The combination of federal, state, and local agencies, private foundations, corporate donors, and even individual gifts has provided a significant source of income and prestige for leading jazz musicians, in particular experimental performers. The acknowledgements on Cecil Taylor's album *Three Phasis* (1978), for example, required almost as much space as the musical credits: "This disc was made possible by grants from American Broadcast Companies; Armco, Inc.; Capital Cities Communication; Dow Jones; Mr. Francis Goelet; Gilman Foundation, Inc.; Occidental Petroleum Corporation; the Rockefeller Foundation; Sony Corporation; Union Pacific Corporation; and the National Endowment for the Arts."[63] Nonprofit jazz organizations such as Collective Black Artists drew income from an equally diverse array of benefactors. In addition to repeated grants from the NEA and the New York State Council on the Arts, CBA received legal aid from Volunteer Lawyers for

Figure 23. (Left to right, foreground) Rahsaan Roland Kirk and Roswell Rudd leading the "play-in" at the John Simon Guggenheim Memorial Foundation, New York City, March 1971. Photograph by Irene Fertik.

the Arts, office space for a nominal fee from the charitable group New York New Careers, and financial contributions from the New York Department of Cultural Affairs, the Congress of Racial Justice, the New York Board of Education, the Coordinating Council of Little Magazines, individual donors, and ticket sales.[64] Although government subsidies and private philanthropy provided little more long-term stability than the commercial world, they offered a new fount of prestige and revenue unavailable in the past. While individual fellowships benefited a few name performers, the emergence of a grants economy channeled money to large numbers of jazz professionals through nonprofit presenting organizations.

The beginning of public and private funding for jazz played an important role in transforming the music's place in American culture. As jazz has taken on some of the stature of its sponsors, many of which also fund the traditional high arts, the role of experimental performers in this process is often overlooked. It is easy to assume that because visible authorities have marginalized free improvisation within the jazz canon, the main contribution of Ornette Coleman, Cecil Taylor, and others to the music's rising status has occurred as a result of their exclusion. By deviating from strict definitions of jazz and often dissociating themselves from what they considered a limiting category, "outside" performers cast into relief the music's core values.

This conclusion underestimates the extent to which, at a critical juncture during the late 1960s and early 1970s, experimental musicians explored new contexts for the production and presentation of African American art. Free improvisers were not the only jazz musicians to receive financial support from colleges and universities, government agencies, private foundations, and business corporations at this time. Musicians as diverse as Lee Konitz, Chuck Mangione, and Cedar Walton received NEA grants during the early 1970s, for example. But the key facilitating factors in jazz music's ascendancy within the nonprofit arena—its compatibility with contemporary European concert techniques, the push for greater diversity at grant-making institutions, and its lack of commercial appeal—made free improvisers especially attractive candidates for sponsorship. Their development of challenging forms, championship by outspoken black nationalists, and difficulties in the marketplace help account for the pioneering role of Ornette Coleman at the Guggenheim Foundation, Cecil Taylor at the Rockefeller Foundation, George Russell at the NEA, Bill Dixon in higher education, and the continued over-representation of "outside" performers in the award of grants and appointments to academic (rather than vocational) music programs into the 1970s. "The institutionalization of jazz," Krin Gabbard has written, "is consistent with current demystifications of the distinctions between high and low culture, with the growing trend toward multiculturalism in university curricula, and with the postmodern cachet now enjoyed by marginal arts and artists."[65] To the extent that Gabbard is right—that jazz has subverted the stratification of American culture—free improvisers and their radical champions deserve more credit than today's guardians of the canon have given them. Forced to confront the economic implications of shrinking audiences and declining business before more accessible stylists, experimental musicians took advantage of the controversy over jazz music's identity by forging new opportunities in the evolving cultural landscape.

Yet Gabbard admitted only reluctantly the possibility that jazz has not so much transformed Americans' understanding of what art is, as it has expanded the definition of what is art. Although Levine's turn-of-the-century highbrows had little time for nontraditional, nonwestern, nonwhite forms, the history of free improvisation suggests that jazz music's status in the 1960s depended upon many of the same variables that mattered to them: esoteric performance styles, appropriate venues and audience behavior, European sanction, professional criticism, academic endorsement, and nonprofit sponsorship. Indeed, institutions of learning and culture hardly provided the welcome that some observers hoped, suggesting that remnants of the old hierarchical order persisted. Despite the opening of colleges, endowments, and foundations to African American performers and artistic forms, jazz has not matched the representation or funding of traditional highbrow genres. *Down Beat* publisher Charles Suber, an expert on jazz education, estimated in the late 1970s that only 15 percent of the 500 or more colleges offering an ensemble or accredited course granted degrees in jazz. Furthermore, a 1980 survey revealed that only 37 percent of jazz programs—which study a field dominated by African Americans—employed even one black instructor (full- or part-time). Only 63 percent of schools offering jazz instruction had ever hired an African American faculty member to teach the subject. Survey administrator J. F. Gould concluded that college officials perceived the African American musician "as essentially a creative performer who finds the traditional European-oriented academic approach to music to be an alien and stifling environment."[66] Clearly traditional biases against jazz—and black musicians in particular—remained.

In recent years, cultural historians and reception theorists have celebrated a greater diversity among officially sanctioned art and a popularization of some forms in the marketplace as evidence that the highbrow/lowbrow dichotomy has finally disintegrated. Rejecting critical theory and organizational models that conceded the power of media brokers to impose their priorities and values on a mass audience, adherents of the new media studies such as Horace Newcomb, John Fiske, and Linda Steiner have successfully demonstrated the ability of audiences to derive multiple meanings from newspapers, magazines, and television shows. The possibility of choice does not, however, equate to complete autonomy as these writers sometimes imply, and should encourage scholars to examine further the social, economic, aesthetic, and political structures that frame decisions about cultural meaning and value.[67] For although free improvisers and their supporters vigorously challenged the construction of jazz as "America's art form," their subsequent—if ambivalent—embrace by sectors of the high arts establishment suggests the difficulty of resisting ongoing attempts to sustain the stratification and sacrilization of American culture.

Epilogue

A cursory examination of reader letters published in *Down Beat* during the mid-1960s reveals the disruption and division caused by free improvisation among fans, musicians, businessmen, educators, and critics. While one writer praised the "originality and creativity" of John Coltrane's "abstract" style, another described a recent "outside" performance as "a great mass of cold, crude sounds lacking in every aspect of harmonic and rhythmic unity."[1] By experimenting with the boundaries of orthodox chords, bars, pitches, and tempos, Ornette Coleman, Cecil Taylor, John Coltrane, and their followers displaced aesthetic and ideological reference points. Their collective and expressive approach to the production of sound undermined the canonical values of the early Cold War era, challenged the establishment's commitment to continuous innovation based upon an extension of modernist freedom, and accelerated stylistic fragmentation. Jazz-rock fusion further disrupted the music's fragile paradigm in the 1970s. Although it helped dissociate experimental music from black nationalism, and reconciled jazz to the marketplace, fusion invited charges of blatant commercialism and rhythmic stasis. Thus at a time African American instrumental music generated more revenue than at any point since World War II—Herbie Hancock recorded the genre's first million-selling album, *Headhunters*, in 1973—many critics bemoaned the death of jazz.[2]

In order to make sense of this musical eclecticism, prospective guardians employed a new conception of jazz as "America's classical music." The term reoccurred in the most significant post-free canonizing endeavors. In 1973, the Smithsonian Institution released the *Smithsonian Collection of Classic Jazz*, assembled by critic turned curator Martin Williams. An unprecedented attempt to bring jazz music's "masterpieces" from all eras and various record labels together in one place, the boxed, six-record set exerted enormous influence over the artistic pantheon. In addition to providing a soundtrack for Williams' critical tour de force, *The Jazz Tradition* (1970), the compilation helped set the agenda for two generations of jazz text books, many of which keyed their musical examples to the collection's unparalleled contents.[3]

The 1970s also witnessed the emergence of the first repertory orchestras, dedicated to preserving jazz music's essential performances and compositions. These units included the New York Jazz Repertory Company and the National Jazz Ensemble, both founded in 1974, the Smithsonian Jazz Repertory Ensemble (1980), and the American Jazz Orchestra (1985). A similar appeal to golden-age standards is evident in the title of Grover Sales' 1984 text book, *Jazz: America's Classical Music*, and in Billy Taylor's 1986 article of the same name. During the 1980s, a school of neoclassical musicians including Wynton Marsalis, Roy Hargrove, Terrence Blanchard, and Marcus Roberts rose to national attention. In addition to great poise and technique, each musician possessed a thorough familiarity with jazz music's past styles, especially bebop but also New Orleans, swing, and much of Duke Ellington's catalog. Marsalis first conducted a series of "Classic Jazz" concerts at New York's Lincoln Center for the Performing Arts in 1987, and when the institution established Jazz at Lincoln Center (JALC) as a permanent program in 1991 it hired the trumpeter as artistic director. With an initial annual budget of $1 million, Marsalis founded a permanent, touring orchestra, oversaw the transcription and rerecording of "classic" jazz works, and developed numerous educational activities—all with the expressed intent of creating and sustaining a jazz canon. In 1996, JALC assumed full constituent membership of Lincoln Center, on an equal footing with the Metropolitan Opera and New York Philharmonic, with an expanded budget and plans to amass a $10 million endowment. In 2004, the organization took possession of Frederick P. Rose Hall, a new $128 million, three-venue performing arts facility dedicated to jazz in New York's AOL-Time Warner Center. From its origins as an attempt to fill empty space in Lincoln Center's smallest hall during the cultural off-season, JALC reached the peak of institutional recognition by embracing a strategy of classicism.[4]

As Robert Walser has noted, the term "classical" represents "a cultural category that achieved prestige in part by obscuring diverse meanings and purposes."[5] Unsettled by both free improvisation and fusion, jazz classicists redefined the concept of freedom in a way that conveniently marginalized these troubling styles. Scott DeVeaux demonstrated that in place of a narrative of continuous musical innovation, which champions of "the new thing" had embraced, neoclassical performers and critics identified a "mainstream" musical current that preceded the controversial movements of the 1960s and early 1970s. The new tradition venerated the qualities of improvisation, swing, and blues, formal composition, and the musical language of bebop, each of which provided a point of departure for evaluating subsequent developments. In place of a discourse of inevitable musical progress, guardians of the canon recast counter-movements as "wrong turns" from the mainstream, both to the left (free jazz, with its angry license) and to the right (fusion, with its commercialism and reductionism).[6]

Writing in the *New York Times Magazine* in 1995, Frank Conroy demonstrated how the tradition acted as a rhetorical ploy to delegitimize radical exploration:

> For a long time, jazz fans and players have been obsessed with the idea of "progress." Because of the speed and abruptness of the be-bop revolution, people were looking for something quick, and what they got, mostly, were garden paths leading to no place in particular. Progress is a dubious concept in any art. . . . The idea is inappropriately linear, less useful than the model of a kind of pulsating spiral, moving out, moving in, but over time growing larger, covering more territory. . . . A distinction should be drawn between outdated notions of progress and modern attempts to trace and extend the organic evolution of jazz. . . . The way to strengthen one's ability to tell the difference between progress and evolution is to study the canon—that music which has had the longest and deepest influence—because the canon contains the evolutionary signposts and implies how jazz can spiral outward without losing its identity.[7]

Since the canon is a product of personal judgments, its keepers dismissed the parts of jazz history they found distasteful as "garden paths leading to no place in particular," while designating more favored—and generally less daring—movements as "organic evolution." The image of jazz music's development as a "pulsating spiral"—always moving, never ossified—suggested the music remained a vital, living art yet proved sufficiently vague for culture brokers to define true innovation as they saw fit.

The Smithsonian collection embodied the classical approach. Williams did not ignore free improvisation, but he limited his selections to largely conservative pieces and framed them in terms of canonical standards. Thus he paid tribute to Ornette Coleman's innovative approach to rhythm and composition through two late 1950s tracks and an excerpt from *Free Jazz*, and he acknowledged Cecil Taylor's debt to Ellington and Monk (two of the neoclassicists' favorite writers) with a single recording. He omitted the second wave of free improvisers, the AACM musicians, and barely recognized the enormous influence of John Coltrane's bands on later instrumentalists. By acknowledging the prominence of pianists as a sign of "retrenchment" in the aftermath of free jazz, Williams reinscribed the distance between experimental musicians operating on the parameters of the jazz tradition, and the music's core values. Fusion remained conspicuously absent from the original compilation and the 1987 reissue. Anticipating Conroy's language, Williams wrote during the 1980s that "although it may have produced some good music, the fusion effort seems to me largely over and was even something of a mistake. (Well, look, there can be some very handsome houses on a dead-end street.)"[8]

Like the Smithsonian compilation, Wynton Marsalis's programming at Lincoln Center sought to uplift the music through a process of codification and ultimately commodification. This objective entailed carefully observing the boundaries of "What Is—and Isn't—Jazz," to quote a typically strident early effort by Marsalis to strictly define the subject and facilitate its reproduction. Since he believed that maintaining the rules is essential to preserving jazz music's integrity, Marsalis rejected any efforts to muddy its purported purity or essence. As a result, he has faced criticism for slighting seasoned experimental performers such as Cecil Taylor and Muhal Richard Abrams, whom he accused of blurring the line between jazz and European avant-garde music. When Taylor spent $15,000 of his own money to hire Alice Tully Hall for a 1994 birthday concert, reasoning that Lincoln Center would never invite him to play the venue, he drew attention to the narrow-minded focus of rigid canon-building endeavors. Yet for Marsalis, Taylor's exclusion represented good taste and sound judgment. He did not swing, Marsalis argued, so he remained peripheral to the evolution of mainstream jazz. The trumpeter's belief that audiences did not identify with or want to listen to free jazz also explains his reluctance to showcase it. Although JALC's programming broadened considerably after the retention of artistic administrator Todd Barkan in 2001, including a concert tribute to Ornette Coleman after Marsalis had previously dismissed his music as "chaos," the continued emphasis on canonical traits kept free improvisers on the margins of its commissions, concerts, and educational agenda.[9]

The development of a jazz canon has helped solidify the music's legitimacy as an autonomous art by reconstructing its past in a way that curtailed open-ended experimentation. The pay-off for this approach is apparent in the opening credits of *Jazz*, Ken Burns's 19-hour documentary history that aired on the public television network PBS in 2001. Each of its ten episodes paid tribute to an A-list of corporate, foundation, government, and individual sponsors from General Motors to the Pew Charitable Trust, the Doris Duke Charitable Foundation, and both national endowments. Not surprisingly, in view of the on-screen prominence of senior creative consultant Wynton Marsalis, the narrative looked backward to the towering influence of Louis Armstrong and Duke Ellington in establishing the music's norms. Once again, however, the attempt to authenticate jazz as a self-contained art form led the director to marginalize or ignore musicians whose relationship to canonical practices may be deemed ambiguous. While most reviewers created a unique list of prominent jazz musicians slighted by the film-maker—from Erroll Garner to Art Pepper to Keith Jarrett—Burns undoubtedly gave free improvisation and subsequent experimentation the shortest shrift. His superficial summary of innovative music from the previous forty years in under one hour, and almost complete neglect of western swing, Latin jazz, and world music, speaks to a desire to promote jazz as a pure-bred art that can be judged according to apparently objective criteria. By eschewing the opportunity to define jazz according to a historical "family resemblance," or even as a dimension that affords music a greater or lesser degree of "jazzness," Burns established a seductive yet perhaps misleading rationale for ruling artists and recordings in or out of the music's pantheon.[10]

A fundamental problem with the neoclassical approach, as Ronald Radano stated in arguing for greater attention to the career of Anthony Braxton, lies in its simplification of the past. It relegates alternative paths to the background, and claims a legitimacy and primacy it may not deserve.[11] Furthermore, a prescribed tradition tends to emphasize an artist's work that most closely corresponds with a recognized stylistic movement, and ignores those performers and performances that defy categorization. Thus critics remember Braxton primarily for his early recordings with AACM musicians, while they struggle to negotiate his genre-crossing work since the early 1970s. Similarly, jazz writers applaud or abhor Ornette Coleman's formative influence on free improvisation, yet frequently ignore his symphonic or free-fusion experiments (the latter have dominated his repertoire since the mid-1970s). "The music industry is mainly interested in my past, never my future," Coleman told *Down Beat* in 1998. "People always want to talk about what I've done. I always hope I can do so much *more*." This commitment to ongoing innovation may well be jazz music's key inheritance from—and contribution to—the broader modernist tradition. Yet in their effort to fix the music's parameters, canonizers such as Marsalis and Burns both downplay the relationship between jazz and other artistic genres and constantly look back to a golden age rather than forward to a reconstituted future. Thus after the President of Blue Note records, Bruce Lundvall, heralded the signing of Wynton Marsalis to a recording contract in 2003, he inadvertently put the trumpeter on the defensive by claiming "that Wynton is on the cusp of an innovative new creative period musically." Marsalis reacted angrily to this marketing hyperbole on his behalf:

Cusp? No. Innovation? No. All my music comes from the same source. I don't go through periods. From my first album to *All Rise* [2002], my goal has always been to affirm jazz. Blues and swing. Written and improvised. I keep going in the same direction, exploring different music within the language of jazz. In no way is being at Blue Note a rebirth.[12]

Disagreements over the content of the Smithsonian collection, Jazz at Lincoln Center's programming, and Ken Burns's *Jazz* demonstrate that critics actively contested the musical choices of classical canonizers. Yet these debates took place within a fairly constricted ideological arena, echoing Cold War constructions of jazz as "America's art form." Billy Taylor spoke for many classicists when he identified jazz as a cultural symbol of key political values. Jazz, he wrote in the mid-1980s, is "a *national* music that expresses American ideals and attitudes to Americans and to people from other cultures all around the world." Taylor reconciled jazz music's African American origins with its ability to speak for the whole nation, by viewing its development as a yardstick for progressive integration. African American musicians, he believed, created "an authentic *American* music which articulated uniquely American feelings and thoughts, which eventually came to transcend ethnic boundaries. This classical music defines the national character and the national culture."[13] In 1987, both houses of Congress concurred that jazz "makes evident to the world an outstanding artistic model of individual expression and democratic cooperation within the creative process, thus fulfilling the highest ideals and aspirations of our republic." Intended by Michigan Representative John Conyers, Jr., as a belated tribute to jazz ambassadors such as Louis Armstrong and Dizzy Gillespie, Joint Congressional Resolution 57 urged cultural and educational institutions to document, preserve, and promulgate this "rare and valuable national American treasure."[14]

Beginning in the 1980s, Wynton Marsalis did more than any other contemporary musician or critic to articulate a holistic aesthetic and ideological identity for jazz. Sounding like a throwback to Willis Conover, Marsalis told an interviewer in 1990 that "in terms of illuminating the meaning of America, jazz is the primary art form, especially New Orleans jazz. Because when it is played properly it shows you how the individual can negotiate the greatest amount of personal freedom and put it humbly in the service of a group conception." This echo of Cold War American exceptionalism is hardly coincidental. Marsalis' intellectual mentors, Albert Murray and Stanley Crouch, both drew heavily upon the writings of American studies pioneers John Kouwenhoven and Ralph Ellison to position jazz as a black cultural achievement that draws African Americans into the center of American life and demonstrates the universal relevance of their experience. Marsalis's celebrated oratorio *Blood on the Fields*, which premiered in 1994 and charts the capture, transportation, enslavement, and finally acculturation in the United States of two African protagonists, embodies this goal. Its receipt of the Pulitzer Prize in 1997 affirmed the American cultural establishment's accommodation of jazz over thirty years after the board rejected its

music panel's recommendation of Duke Ellington for a lifetime achievement award. Similarly, Ken Burns's ability to gather so many blue chip
patrons for his PBS series hinged on his integration of jazz into the
broader development of American history, and ability to link both to the
sweeping themes of race and democracy in the United States. As Sherrie
Tucker has noted, however, Burns had to skim over the music since 1965
to avoid confronting the shortcomings of color-blind liberalism and critiques of the dominant jazz discourse provided by the black power and
radical feminist movements. By looking back to a tradition that peaked
in the late 1950s and early 1960s, before the "chaos" unleashed by free
jazz and black separatism, Burns and Marsalis invite viewers and listeners
to believe that overcoming cultural differences alone may prove sufficient to draw minority arts and populations into the American mainstream.[15]

The ideological dimension of the new tradition experienced little
resistance, in part because few organized voices provided a competition
of ideas. The Black Arts Movement had offered an alternative prism for
interpreting jazz during the 1960s and early 1970s by positioning it as
the embodiment of a black aesthetic. By identifying its most esoteric and
abstract style—free improvisation—as the apotheosis of a tradition
known primarily for its insistent beat and catchy hooks, cultural nationalists demonstrated a willingness to imaginatively challenge the stratification of American cultural values. By the mid-1970s, however, they
faced increasing criticism from a variety of African American intellectuals. This dissension arose not only from integrationists, who accused
radical artists of black chauvinism and poor artistic standards, but also
from revolutionary organizations such as the Black Panthers, which
denounced the "pork chop nationalism" of Amiri Baraka, Maulana Ron
Karenga, and others for threatening to dissipate the unrest of the
masses. In addition, African American feminists—whose establishment
of the National Black Feminist Organization in 1972 reflected their
growing cohesion—increasingly assailed gender discrimination among
militant movements in general. Dissatisfied with male attempts to limit
women to supporting roles in the fight for equality and self-realization,
and the undercurrent of macho posturing within nationalist discourse,
writers such as Frances Beal framed black sexism as both self-involved
and counter-revolutionary.[16]

Facing intense scrutiny, cultural nationalists often reverted to self-
criticism and introspection. During the late 1960s, Askia Touré—a co-
founder of BARTS—openly attacked Baraka and Karenga for advocating
a "reactionary Super-Blackism" and "dogmatic nihilism in Black literature as well as politics."[17] Touré's salvo resonated among a new generation of African American writers who emerged in the late 1960s and

1970s. Committed to a distinctively black approach to the arts and letters, they rejected the efforts of cultural nationalists to impose rigid political objectives for aesthetic projects. Stanley Crouch, known then as a poet rather than a critic, concluded in 1968 that "one of the major problems in Black writing today is that most of the people who pass themselves off as writers either cannot write, are capitalizing on something that has moved from true feeling to a name-calling fad masked as 'Revolutionary Black Nationalism,' or, *they have no respect for the craft.*"[18] Anticipating jazz classicists' appeal to musicians, young writers such as Crouch urged African American artists to prioritize structure, beauty, and discipline once more.

The leading figures of the Black Arts Movement subsequently reevaluated their objectives and strategies, although rarely in ways their critics predicted. In 1967, Baraka had returned to his hometown of Newark, building an arts network and embroiling himself in local politics. His activism helped elect the city's first African American mayor, but he soon appeared disillusioned with the insular black bureaucracy. In 1974 Baraka—who had assumed his name in 1968 under the influence of Karenga—publicly embraced Marxist-Leninism. In place of a black/white dichotomy, he urged unity among oppressed people of all races in opposition to "the yoke of capitalism." Although he remained committed to the revolutionary potential of art, Baraka's accommodation of leftist dogma—so soon after denouncing Eldridge Cleaver and the Panthers for advocating "some dead 1930s white ideology as a freedom suit"— diminished the prestige he had enjoyed as the foremost radical spokesman for the black arts.[19] With Archie Shepp and Marion Brown ensconced in academia, and Larry Neal and A. B. Spellman gravitating toward government arts bodies, revolutionary and cultural nationalists lacked the unity or focus to challenge effectively the emerging classical consensus in jazz.

Despite their conservative cultural politics, Lincoln Center's jazz authorities retained a deep commitment to the concern that inspired Baraka's music criticism in the first place: a desire for African Americans to take pride in an art that arose from their unique heritage and group experience. Indeed Wynton Marsalis has benefited more than he or the jazz establishment cares to admit from the efforts of black nationalists such as Baraka and free improvisers including Cecil Taylor and Ornette Coleman to disrupt traditional interpretations of jazz and its place in American culture. As Michael Eric Dyson and others have written, the rhetoric of black cultural unity has primarily served middle-class intellectuals, artists, and politicians seeking leverage with institutional power structures and privileged elites, and Marsalis and his cohorts at Lincoln Center are no exceptions. For Marsalis and Crouch, however, jazz provided an honorable alternative not to mainstream assimilation but to hip-hop, rap, and other supposedly vulgar forms of black popular expression. Thus Marsalis's attempt to elevate jazz music's status has led him into very public disagreements with Miles Davis (over fusion) and brother Branford Marsalis (over playing with pop icon Sting) because both compromised his vision of the jazz musician as artist. Yet the features Marsalis liked least about free improvisation—its obfuscation of aesthetic boundaries, its lack of appeal to a broad public, its appropriation by the Black Arts Movement—are most responsible for securing jazz music's foothold outside the marketplace. That Cecil Taylor has been the target of so much bad blood from the neoclassicists and their associates—snubbed by Lincoln Center, derided for his willful obscurity in *Jazz*—is more than a little paradoxical given his pioneering role in opening foundations, universities, and government agencies to jazz musicians and making a program like JALC conceivable to its original highbrow sponsors.[20]

Ironically, Wynton Marsalis's promotion of sympathetic black role models in the JALC Orchestra, and celebration of African American contributions to the nation by programming the music of black artists almost exclusively during his formative years as artistic director, drew charges of reverse racism reminiscent of the early 1960s furor over "Crow Jim." Gene Seymour of *Newsday*, the *New Yorker*'s Whitney Balliett, and *New York Times* critic Peter Watrous each questioned the exclusion of white artists in the early 1990s. After the 1991 summer season, for example, Balliett grumbled that "blacks invented jazz, but nobody owns it."[21] Yet the issue of ownership—and its implications for economic survival and identity politics—lay at the center of both controversies, and helps explain why jazz music's champions have so often clung to the symbols of high culture legitimacy. The fate of free improvisation demonstrated that when a popular music loses its popularity, the aura of art provides a critical route to financial safety. Disagreements over jazz programming at Lincoln Center reached such heated intensity on account of the scale of revenues and personal acclaim at stake, a situation exacerbated by the music's disadvantage in a cultural arena that too frequently equates "blackness" with passion, struggle, and spontaneity rather than contemplation, calculation, and composition.[22] Classicists embrace the trappings of legitimate culture in part because they learned from Cecil Taylor, Ornette Coleman, and their followers that official sanction offers the best means for jazz to overcome traditional biases against its class and racial origins. These free improvisers carved out a unique place in American public life, upsetting the ranked order of the national culture, yet their growing prestige depended in large part upon the same criteria that shaped late nineteenth-century attempts to solidify a cultural hierarchy. They both challenged and reconstituted the ongoing stratification and sanctification of American culture during the 1960s.

Notes

Introduction

1. Ornette Coleman Quartet, *This Is Our Music* (Atlantic 1353, 1960); Ornette Coleman Double Quartet, *Free Jazz* (Atlantic 1364, 1960).

2. Lawrence W. Levine, *Highbrow/Lowbrow: The Emergence of Cultural Hierarchy in America* (Cambridge, Mass.: Harvard University Press, 1988), 8.

3. Krin Gabbard, "The Jazz Canon and Its Consequences," in *Jazz Among the Discourses*, ed. Gabbard (Durham, N.C.: Duke University Press, 1995), 2–3.

4. Lawrence W. Levine, *The Opening of the American Mind: Canons, Culture, and History* (Boston: Beacon Press, 1996).

5. For an insight into debates over the jazz heritage, see Wynton Marsalis, "What Jazz Is—and Isn't," *New York Times* (July 31, 1988) Arts and Leisure: 21, 24; Stanley Crouch, "Cecil Taylor: Pitfalls of a Primitive," *Village Voice* (March 30, 1982): 50. For an analysis of these controversies, see Paul Erickson, "Black and White, Black and Blue: The Controversy Over the Jazz Series at Lincoln Center," *Jazz and American Culture* 2 (Summer 1997) [on-line journal, 5–6]; John Gennari, "Jazz Criticism: Its Development and Ideologies," *Black American Literature Forum* 25 (Fall 1991): 485–510; Larry Kart, "Provocative Opinion: The Death of Jazz?" *Black Music Research Journal* 10 (Spring 1990): 76–81.

6. For an overview of critical attempts to establish a jazz canon during the twentieth century, see Gennari, "Jazz Criticism," 449–523; Scott DeVeaux, "Constructing the Jazz Tradition: Jazz Historiography," *Black American Literature Forum* 25 (Fall 1991): 525–60; Gabbard, "The Jazz Canon and Its Consequences," 1–28.

7. For an extended examination of twentieth-century jazz criticism, see John Remo Gennari, "The Politics of Culture and Identity in American Jazz Criticism" (Ph.D. dissertation, University of Pennsylvania, 1993).

8. In addition to Levine's *Highbrow/Lowbrow*, see Paul J. DiMaggio, "Cultural Entrepreneurship in Nineteenth-Century Boston," in *Nonprofit Enterprise in the Arts: Studies in Mission and Constraint*, ed. DiMaggio (New York: Oxford University Press, 1986), 41–61.

9. David Hollinger, *In the American Province: Studies in the Historiography of Ideas* (Baltimore: Johns Hopkins University Press, 1985), 74–91; Matei Calinescu, *Five Faces of Modernity: Modernism, Avant-Garde, Decadence, Kitsch, Postmodernism*, rev. ed. (Durham, N.C.: Duke University Press, 1987); Peter Bürger, *Theory of the Avant-Garde*, trans. Michael Shaw (Minneapolis: University of Minnesota Press, 1984); Pierre Bourdieu, *Distinction: A Social Critique of the Judgement of Taste*, trans. Richard Nice (Cambridge, Mass.: Harvard University Press, 1984); Andrew Ross, *No Respect: Intellectuals and Popular Culture* (New York: Routledge, 1989); Joan Shelley Rubin, *The Making of Middlebrow Culture* (Chapel Hill: University of North Carolina Press, 1992).

10. Lawrence W. Levine, "Jazz and American Culture," *Journal of American Folklore* 102 (January–March 1989): 6–22.

11. For a summary overview of jazz music's evolving place in American culture, see Burton W. Peretti, *Jazz in American Culture* (Chicago: Ivan Dee, 1997).

Chapter 1. The Resurgence of Jazz in the 1950s

1. Gilbert Millstein, "Jazz Makes It Up the River," *New York Times Magazine* (August 24, 1958): 14, 50–54; Leonard Feather, "Jazz Achieves Social Prestige," *Down Beat* 22 (September 21, 1955): 11; Eliot Elisofon, "New Life for U.S. Jazz," *Life* 38 (January 17, 1955): 42–49; "The Golden Age of Jazz," *Esquire* 51 (January 1959): 98–118; George Frazier, "Blue Notes and Blue Stockings: Impresario Wein and the Newport Jazz Festival," *Esquire* 44 (August 1955): 55–58; Elaine Guthrie Lorillard with Richard Gehman, "Hot Time in Old Newport," *Collier's* 138 (July 20, 1956): 50–52; Nat Hentoff, "Jazz in Mid-Passage," *High Fidelity* 4 (September 1954): 44–46, 118.

2. On the origins of bebop, see Scott DeVeaux, *The Birth of Bebop: A Social and Musical History* (Berkeley: University of California Press, 1997). For an extended discussion of bebop's militant stance see Eric Lott, "Double V, Double Time: Bebop's Politics of Style," *in Jazz Among the Discourses*, ed. Krin Gabbard (Durham, N.C.: Duke University Press, 1995), 243–55. Ingrid Monson explores white assumptions about bebop's transgressive identity and its place in African American life in "The Problem with White Hipness: Race, Gender, and Cultural Conceptions in Jazz Historical Discourse," *Journal of the American Musicological Society* 48 (Fall 1995): 409–20.

3. Charles A. Thomson and Walter H. C. Laves, *Cultural Relations and U.S. Foreign Policy* (Bloomington: Indiana University Press, 1963), 79.

4. W. T. Lhamon, Jr., *Deliberate Speed: The Origins of a Cultural Style in the American 1950s* (Washington, D.C.: Smithsonian Institution, 1990), 99, 101. Lhamon makes a convincing case for the interpenetration of high and vernacular cultures during the 1950s although, as the next chapter argues, I believe that his use of Ornette Coleman to illustrate the new "congeniality" of "poplore" is misplaced. For an account of the Book-of-the-Month Club's role in sustaining a middlebrow audience for literary "classics," see Joan Shelley Rubin, *The Making of Middlebrow Culture* (Chapel Hill: University of North Carolina Press, 1992), 93–147.

5. Jacques Barzun, "America's Passion for Culture," *Harper's Magazine* 208 (March 1954): 40–47. Lynn Spigel uses the term "modern vernacular" to describe the new style of the 1950s much as Lhamon uses the term "poplore." Both look ahead to 1960s pop art as the logical extension of these styles. Lynn Spigel, "High Art in Low Places: Television and Modern Art, 1950–1970," in *Disciplinarity and Dissent in American Cultural Studies*, ed. Cary Nelson and Dilip Parameshwar Gaonkar (New York: Routledge, 1996), 318–23; Lhamon, *Deliberate Speed*, 98.

6. Spigel, "High Culture in Low Places," 317–18, 326–27. On the commodification and marketing of modern art, see also Stuart D. Hobbs, *The End of the American Avant-Garde* (New York: New York University Press, 1997), 139–68. For similar trends in other genres see Harold C. Schonberg, "What Bernstein Is Doing to the Philharmonic," *Harper's Magazine* 218 (May 1959): 43–44; Katie Gunther Kodat, "Making the World Safe for Ballet: The Case of *The Nutcracker*," paper presented at the Great Lakes American Studies Association, Toledo, Ohio,

April 1996, 2–5; Leonard Feather, "Jazz U.S.A.," in *The New Yearbook of Jazz* (New York: Horizon, 1958), 26–27; Paul A. Carter, *Another Part of the Fifties* (New York: Columbia University Press, 1983), 155–57.

7. Harry S. Truman, "Going Forward with a Campaign of Truth," *Department of State Bulletin* 22 (May 1, 1950): 669, 672. Historians continue to disagree strongly over the origins of the Cold War, specifically the issue of blame. For an overview of the debate, see Thomas T. Hammond, "Introduction: The Great Debate Over the Origins of the Cold War," in *Witnesses to the Origins of the Cold War* (Seattle: University of Washington Press, 1982), 3–26; Richard Crockett, *The Fifty Years War: The United States and the Soviet Union in World Politics, 1941–1991* (New York: Routledge, 1995), 64–88. On the same subject, see Allen Lynch, *The Cold War Is Over—Again* (Boulder, Colo.: Westview Press, 1992), 7–27; John Lewis Gaddis, *We Now Know: Rethinking Cold War History* (Oxford: Clarendon Press, 1997). A good source on the Truman Doctrine's "two worlds" premise is H. W. Brands, *The Devil We Knew: Americans and the Cold War* (New York: Oxford University Press, 1993), 17–30.

8. Brands, *The Devil We Knew,* 17–30. For an account of the Cold War's impact on American domestic politics and culture to 1965, see Stephen J. Whitfield, *The Culture of the Cold War,* 2nd ed. (Baltimore: Johns Hopkins University Press, 1996). For more on American perceptions of the atomic threat between 1945 and 1950, see Paul Boyer, *By the Bomb's Early Light: American Thought and Culture at the Dawn of the Atomic Age* (New York: Pantheon, 1985).

9. Frances Stonor Saunders, *The Cultural Cold War: The CIA and the World of Arts and Letters* (New York: New Press, 1999), 16–31; J. D. Parks, *Culture, Conflict, and Coexistence: American-Soviet Cultural Relations, 1917–1958* (Jefferson, N.C.: McFarland, 1983), 124–26; Thomson and Laves, *Cultural Relations,* 63–72, 78–88.

10. Saunders, *The Cultural Cold War,* 1–6; Parks, *Culture, Conflict, and Coexistence,* 124–26; Thomson and Laves, *Cultural Relations,* 63–72, 78–88; Brands, *The Devil We Knew,* 61–62. On the Voice of America see Center for Strategic and International Studies, *International Information Educational and Cultural Relations: Recommendations for the Future* (Washington, D.C.: Center for Strategic and International Studies, 1975), chapter 5.

11. In March 1950, Senator William Benton listed the five key themes of Soviet propaganda attacks against the United States, including "Fifth: Our character is bad—we are culturally barbarous, money-mad, lawless, crime-ridden, and effete." Thomson and Laves, *Cultural Relations,* 79.

12. Whitfield, *The Culture of the Cold War,* 53–76; Thomson and Laves, *Cultural Relations,* 79, 122–26; Gary O. Larson, *The Reluctant Patron: The United States Government and the Arts* (Philadelphia: University of Pennsylvania Press, 1983), 102; Don DeMicheal, "Jazz in Government [part I]," *Down Beat* 30 (January 17, 1963): 15; Wilson P. Dizard, *The Strategy of Truth: The Story of the United States Information Service* (Washington, D.C.: Public Affairs Press, 1963), 179–81; W. McNeil Lowry and Gertrude S. Hooker, "The Role of the Arts and Humanities," in *Cultural Affairs and Foreign Relations,* ed. Paul J. Braisted (Washington, D.C.: Columbia, 1968), 52–57.

13. Saunders, *The Cultural Cold War,* 21.

14. "Alter-Proof Order for Drugs Sought," *New York Times* (April 26, 1955): 17.

15. Paul Oliver, "Jazz Is Where you Find it: The European Experience of Jazz," in *Superculture: American Popular Culture and Europe,* ed. C. W. E. Bigsby

(London: Paul Elek, 1975), 140–44; Bill Moody, *The Jazz Exiles: American Musicians Abroad* (Reno: University of Nevada Press, 1993), 12–17; S. Frederick Starr, *Red and Hot: The Fate of Jazz in the Soviet Union, 1917–1980* (New York: Oxford University Press, 1983), 37–38; James Lincoln Collier, *The Making of Jazz: A Comprehensive History* (Boston: Houghton Mifflin, 1978), 313.

16. Allen F. Davis, "Introduction: The American Impact on the World," in *For Better or Worse: The American Influence in the World* (Westport, Conn.: Greenwood, 1981), 12.

17. A. David Franklin, "A Preliminary Study of the Acceptance of Jazz by French Music Critics in the 1920s and Early 1930s," in *Jazz Research Papers 1984*, ed. National Association of Jazz Educators (Manhattan, Kan.: NAJE Publications, 1984), 63.

18. James Lincoln Collier, *The Reception of Jazz in America: A New View* (New York: Institute for Studies in American Music, 1988); Ted Gioia, *The Imperfect Art: Reflections on Jazz and Modern Culture* (New York: Oxford University Press, 1988), 24–26.

19. Marc H. Miller, "Louis Armstrong: A Cultural Legacy," in *Louis Armstrong: A Cultural Legacy* (Seattle: University of Washington Press, 1994), 59; "Delaunay [sic] on 1st Visit to America," *Down Beat* 13 (August 26, 1946): 4. After the war, stories continued to circulate about the military use of jazz by the French resistance. In one account, agents used jive talk as code for their secret communications; in another, the serial numbers of "hot" records comprised the code. Strung together, the song titles represented by the numbers read as messages. John S. Wilson, *Jazz: The Transition Years, 1940–1960* (New York: Appleton-Century-Crofts, 1966), 114; Dave Brubeck, "The Beat Heard Around the World," *New York Times Magazine* (June 15, 1958): 31.

20. Miller, "Louis Armstrong," 59–60; Gary Giddins, *Satchmo* (New York: Doubleday, 1988), 159–60; Wilson, *Jazz: The Transition Years*, 111–12; Marshall W. Stearns, *The Story of Jazz* (New York: Oxford University Press, 1956), 291.

21. "This Trumpet Madness," *Newsweek* 46 (December 19, 1955): 48; Felix Belair, "United States Has Secret Sonic Weapon—Jazz," *New York Times* (November 6, 1955): 1, 42.

22. For the impact of American occupation on the jazz scene in Austria, see Reinhold Wagnleitner, *Coca-Colonization and the Cold War: The Cultural Mission of the United States in Austria After the Second World War*, trans. Diana M. Wolf (Chapel Hill: University of North Carolina Press, 1994), 207–8.

23. Robert Alden, "Hands of U.S. Tied in Asia 'Cold War,'" *New York Times* (June 11, 1956): 11; Hal Davis, "Benny and the King of Siam," *Saturday Review* 40 (January 12, 1957): 64–65.

24. Leonard Feather, *The Jazz Years: Earwitness to an Era* (New York: Quartet, 1986), 198–99.

25. "Moscow Views the Zoot Suiter as Nothing But a Red Square," *New York Herald Tribune* (November 27, 1952), quoted in Stearns, *The Story of Jazz*, 286–87. As Stearns noted, the Russian writer probably meant "the divine Sarah," the stage name of bebop-influenced jazz singer Sarah Vaughan. On the "stiliagi," see Starr, *Red and Hot*, 236–43.

26. Starr, *Red and Hot*, 210, 243–44; "Big Jazz Behind the Iron Curtain," *Look* (November 20, 1962): 62; Lawrence Elliott, "The World's Favorite American," *Reader's Digest* (July 1985): 95.

27. "Jazz Around the World," *Time* 67 (June 25, 1956): 52; "Big Jazz Behind the Iron Curtain," 62; Dana Adams Schmidt, "U.S. Disk Jockey a Worldwide Hit:

'Voice' Broadcaster Ends a Visit to Some of His 30 Million Fans Abroad," *New York Times* (June 26, 1960): L9.

28. Edward L. Randal, "The Voice of American Jazz," *High Fidelity* 8 (August 1958): 31; Allen Hughes, "The Voice of America," *Musical America* 80 (April 1960): 9–10, 46.

29. Hughes, "The Voice of America," 9–10, 46; Thomson and Laves, *Cultural Relations*, 84–85.

30. "Remote Lands to Hear Old Democracy Boogie," *New York Times* (November 18, 1955): 16; "Gillespie Tour Starts Today," *New York Times* (March 23, 1956): 23; Marshall W. Stearns, "Is Jazz Good Propaganda?" *Saturday Review* 39 (July 14, 1956): 28–31.

31. Stearns, *The Story of Jazz*, 295; Leonard Feather, *Jazz: An Exciting Story of Jazz Today* (Los Angeles: Trend, 1958), 49.

32. Stearns, "Is Jazz Good Propaganda?" 29–30. The orchestra recorded two albums after returning from the Middle East, *Dizzy Gillespie: World Statesman* (Norgran MGN-1084, 1956) and *Dizzy in Greece* (Verve, MGV-8017, 1956) and another after touring South America, *Birks Works: Dizzy Gillespie Big Band* (Verve MGV-8222, 1957). Verve has reissued all three titles as a two-CD set, Dizzy Gillespie, *Birks Works: The Verve Big-Band Sessions* (Verve, 314527 900–2, 1995).

33. Stearns, "Is Jazz Good Propaganda?" 30; Dizzy Gillespie with Ralph Ginzburg, "Jazz Is Too Good for Americans," *Esquire* 47 (June 1957): 55.

34. Gene Lees, *Leader of the Band: The Life of Woody Herman* (New York: Oxford University Press, 1995), 219–20. For background on Nixon's trip, see Marvin R. Zahniser and W. Michael Weiss, "A Diplomatic Pearl Harbor? Richard Nixon's Goodwill Mission to Latin America in 1958," *Diplomatic History* 13 (Spring 1989): 163–90.

35. "Jazz Around the World," 12; Paul Hume, "Jazz Missing Beat Abroad, Senate Squares Say, But Nobody Was Looking at the Washing Machine," *Washington Post* (July 19, 1956), entered into record by Rep. Frank Thompson, Jr., *Congressional Record*, 84th Cong., 2nd sess. July 19, 1956: 13609; Don DeMicheal, "Jazz in Government [part I]," *Down Beat* 30 (January 17, 1963): 15.

36. Oren Stephens, *Facts to a Candid World* (Stanford, Calif.: Stanford University Press, 1955), 38, quoted in Thomson and Laves, *Cultural Relations*, 68.

37. Aaron H. Esman, "Jazz—A Study in Cultural Conflict," *American Imago* 8 (June 1951): 224, 225; Norman M. Margolis, "A Theory on the Psychology of Jazz," *American Imago* 11 (Fall 1954): 263–91. At the same time Esman and Margolis proposed and refined a theory of jazz music's appeal, Howard Becker and William Cameron—both of whom had worked in jazz and dance bands—developed a sociological profile of the jazz community. Becker and Cameron combined participant observation techniques with interviews to portray jazz musicians as disgruntled and conflicted professionals, isolated on the margins of the larger society by a process of self-segregation. At a time the world was displaying increasing interest in jazz, these portraits of the music and its practitioners disturbed Marshall Stearns, the leading jazz historian of the period. Stearns seized upon the psychiatrists' admission that listeners could take a mature interest in jazz to expand upon the positive nature of musical creation and appreciation. Howard S. Becker, "The Professional Dance Musician and his Audience," *American Journal of Sociology* (September 1951): 136–44; William Bruce Cameron, "Sociological Notes on the Jam Session," *Social Forces* 33 (December 1954): 177–82; Stearns, *The Story of Jazz*, 297–307. On the relationship between atomic anxieties and sexual containment during the Cold War, see

Elaine Tyler May, *Homeward Bound: American Families in the Cold War Era*, rev. ed. (New York: Basic Books, 1999), 80–97.

38. Gioia, *The Imperfect Art*, 30–31; Willie Ruff, "Jazz Mission to Moscow," *Down Beat* 27 (January 21, 1960): 16, 19. For more on Soviet attitudes to jazz, see Penny M. Von Eschen, *Satchmo Blows Up the World: Jazz Ambassadors Play the Cold War* (Cambridge, Mass.: Harvard University Press, 2004), 92–120.

39. Don DeMicheal, "Jazz in Government, Part II," *Down Beat* 30 (January 31, 1963): 19.

40. Randal, "The Voice of American Jazz," 30–31.

41. Belair, "United States Has Secret Sonic Weapon," 1; Von Eschen, *Satchmo Blows Up the World*, 18–20; Saunders, *The Cultural Cold War*, 1–6.

42. Wagnleitner, *Coca-Colonization*, 210.

43. Pete Welding, liner notes to *Birth of the Cool* (Capitol D-154138, 1989 reissue). For more on Kenton's music and cultivation of high school and college audiences, see Ted Gioia, *West Coast Jazz: Modern Jazz in California, 1945–1960* (New York: Oxford University Press, 1992), 143–51. André Hodeir analyzed the *Birth of the Cool* recordings in his landmark critical work *Jazz: Its Evolution and Essence*, trans. David Noakes (New York: Grove Press, 1956), 116–36.

44. Arnold Shaw, "West Coast Jazz," *Esquire* 46 (September 1956): 127. For more on Fantasy, see Robert Gordon, *Jazz West Coast: The Los Angeles Jazz Scene of the 1950s* (London: Quartet, 1986), 73–74; Gioia, *West Coast Jazz*, 62–65. On Pacific, see Gordon (73–76, 78–79, 136–38) and Gioia (111, 188). On Contemporary, see Gordon (87).

45. Kenton formed his big band in 1940 and soon developed a reputation for dramatic high art pretension. The band's instrumentation (at one point augmented with a forty-piece string section), use of classical forms such as suites and symphonies, and ambitious arrangements helped substantiate these charges. Like other orchestra leaders of his day, Kenton made use of concert halls such as Carnegie Hall and the Chicago Civic Opera. He retained a large and loyal fan base, topping *Down Beat* and *Metronome* readers' polls in the late 1940s at a time when many critics displayed open skepticism about the aesthetic value of his music. Gioia, *West Coast Jazz*, 143–64.

46. "The Man on Cloud No. 7," *Time* 64 (November 8, 1954): 74; "Counterpoint Jazz," *Time* 61 (February 2, 1953): 36; "Mulligan in Stew: Tries to Hush Noisy Patrons," *Down Beat* 20 (May 20, 1953): 4.

47. Gunther Schuller, "Jazz and Classical Music," in *The Encyclopedia of Jazz* by Leonard Feather (New York: Horizon Press, 1960), 498. Gunther Schuller, "And Perhaps the Twain Shall Meet," *New York Times* (November 15, 1959), II: 1.

48. Bill Cole, *Miles Davis: A Musical Biography* (New York: William Morrow, 1974), 70–74; George Avakian, "1956–1996: A Fond Reminiscence," from CD liner notes to *The Birth of the Third Stream* (Columbia/Legacy CK 64929, 1996): 18.

49. Cole, *Miles Davis*, 70; Jack Chambers, *Milestones I: The music and times of Miles Davis to 1960* (Toronto: University of Toronto Press, 1983), 258; Ian Carr, *Miles Davis: A Critical Biography* (New York: Quartet, 1982), 80–83.

50. Gioia, *West Coast Jazz*, 195–96; Graham Marsh and Glyn Callingham, eds., *New York Hot: East Coast Jazz of the 50s and 60s: The Album Cover Art* (San Francisco: Chronicle, 1993); Graham Marsh and Glyn Callingham, eds., *California Cool: West Coast Jazz of the 50s and 60s: The Album Cover Art* (San Francisco: Chronicle, 1992).

51. Gordon, *Jazz West Coast*, 64.

52. Gioia, *West Coast Jazz*, 18; Fred M. Hall, *It's About Time: The Dave Brubeck Story* (Fayetteville: University of Arkansas Press, 1996), 46.

53. Hall, *It's About Time*, 50, 57–58, 83; Gioia, *West Coast Jazz*, 64, 96–97. Brubeck was especially proud of his quartet's appeal to African American jazz fans, as evidenced by its success in polls conducted by the *Pittsburgh Courier* among other newspapers. Von Eschen, *Satchmo Blows Up the World*, 283, n.85.

54. Walter Benjamin, "The Work of Art in the Age of Mechanical Reproduction," in *Illuminations*, ed. Hannah Arendt, trans. Harry Zohn (New York: Harcourt, Brace and World, 1958), 223.

55. Leonard Feather, "Jazz Millionaire," *Esquire* 47 (January 1957): 99–114; Frazier, "Blue Notes and Blue Stockings," 55–58; Wilson, *Jazz: The Transition Years*, 141–45.

56. Program of the Newport Jazz Festival 1954, 1, 8, 19, Newport Jazz Festival Manuscript Collection, Box 3, Institute of Jazz Studies, Rutgers University, Newark, N.J; Barry Kernfeld, "Festivals," in *The New Grove Dictionary of Jazz* (London: Macmillan, 1988), 1: 361; Whitney Balliett, "New Name Dropping at Jazzy Old Newport," *Saturday Review* 37 (July 31, 1954): 24; "Cats by the Sea," *Time* 64 (August 2, 1954): 43. For details of the festival's donations to the Institute of Jazz Studies, see "Minutes of the Regular Meeting of Board of Directors, The Jazz Festival of Newport, R.I., Inc., January 19, 1955," Newport Jazz Festival, Box 2; *Elaine G. Lorillard v. Newport Jazz Festival, Inc.*, civil action no. 2516, U.S. Dis Ct. R.I., deposition of Arnold London, April 6 and 21, 1960, 180–89, Newport Jazz Festival, Box 1. Letters between Stearns and Wein reveal a shared belief in the compatible missions of the Institute of Jazz Studies and the Newport Jazz Festival; see George Wein to Marshall Stearns, August 2, 1954; Marshall Stearns to George Wein, August 3, 1954, Newport Jazz Festival, Box 3.

57. Wilson, *Jazz: The Transition Years*, 147; Kernfeld, "Festivals," 360–61. For more on the financial arrangements of the Newport Jazz Festival, see Articles of Incorporation, Board Minutes 1954–56, Newport Jazz Festival, Box 2. See also depositions in *E. Lorillard v. Newport Jazz Festival* by George Wein (16–18, 35–45) and Arnold London (3–10). "Lorillard Reviews Growth of Jazz Event," *Providence Evening Bulletin* (February 19, 1959): 26; "Jazz Festival Progress Told," *Pawtucket, R.I. Evening Times* (February 19 1959), both in Newport Jazz Festival, Box 1.

58. John Corbett, "Fanfare for the Working Band, Part III: Rise and Fall of the Golden Era," *Down Beat* 64 (July 1997): 35–36; Wilson, *Jazz: The Transition Years*, 196–97; "Lorillard Reviews Growth of Jazz Event," 26.

59. Scott Saul, *Freedom Is, Freedom Ain't: Jazz and the Making of the Sixties* (Cambridge, Mass.: Harvard University Press, 2003), 99–122; Nat Hentoff, *The Jazz Life* (New York: Dial, 1961), 98–113, 104.

60. The Randall's Island Jazz Festival, originally held as a big band event in 1938, was revived in 1956 but did not match the profile of Newport or its west coast alternative, the Monterey Jazz Festival. *Playboy* magazine organized the largest festival of the period in summer 1959, a three day event at Chicago Stadium attracting 70,000 fans.

61. Lillian Ross, "You Dig it, Sir?" *New Yorker* 30 (August 14, 1954): 31–47, 46. For one critic's survey of the press coverage in 1954, see Frazier, "Blue Notes and Blue Stockings," 56.

62. Hentoff, "Jazz in Mid-Passage," 44–46, 118; "As the Editors See It: A Whisper to Cats," *High Fidelity* 8 (August 1958): 29; John Fischer, "The Editor's Easy Chair: Self Portrait of the Harper Reader," *Harper's Magazine* 217 (September 1958): 14–20.

63. Charles Suber, "The First Chorus," *Down Beat* 27 (September 15, 1960): 4. This interpretation of the *Down Beat* readership survey is forwarded in Saul, *Freedom Is, Freedom Ain't*, 34.

64. Andre Millard, *America on Record: A History of Recorded Sound* (Cambridge: Cambridge University Press, 1995), 208–9; Charles Graham, "Jazz and the Phonograph," in Leonard Feather, *The New Yearbook of Jazz* (New York: Horizon, 1958), 155–61; John Edward Hasse, *Beyond Category: The Life and Genius of Duke Ellington* (New York: Simon and Schuster, 1993), 311–12, 321, 324; Feather, "Jazz Millionaire," 99–114; Hentoff, "Jazz in Mid-Passage," 45; Leonard Feather, "The Biggest Year in Jazz," *New York Journal American* (December 7, 1957): 60.

65. Henry Schipper, *Broken Record: The Inside Story of the Grammy Awards* (New York: Birch, 1992), 1–6, 15, 19–25; Leonard Feather, "Jazz U.S.A.," in *The New Yearbook of Jazz*, 26–27; Klaus Stratemann, *Duke Ellington: Day by Day and Film by Film* (Copenhagen: JazzMedia, 1992), 375–76, 381–83, 387–88, 395–97.

66. Krin Gabbard, *Jammin' at the Margins: Jazz and the American Cinema* (Chicago: University of Chicago Press, 1996), 107–29.

67. Michael J. Budds, *Jazz in the Sixties: The Expansion of Musical Resources and Techniques* (Iowa City: University of Iowa Press, 1990), 11; Lewis Porter and Michael Ullman with Ed Hazell, *Jazz: From Its Origins to the Present* (Englewood Cliffs, N.J.: Prentice-Hall, 1993), 257–71, 372–73; Ben Sidran, *Black Talk* (New York: Holt, Rinehart, Winston, 1971), 131. The east coast versus west coast polarization extended to the imagery record companies used to sell their product. Francis Wolff's dark, brooding, and intensely physical photographs on Blue Note covers, for example, diametrically opposed the sunny pastels and leisurely portraits of Contemporary sleeves.

68. John Remo Gennari, "The Politics of Culture and Identity in American Jazz Criticism" (Ph.D. dissertation, University of Pennsylvania, 1993), 193. For more on the prominence of abstract art as a Cold War weapon, see Serge Guilbaut, *How New York Stole the Idea of Modern Art: Abstract Expressionism, Freedom, and the Cold War,* trans. Arthur Goldhammer (Chicago: University of Chicago Press, 1983); Max Kozloff, "American Painting During the Cold War," *Artforum* 11 (May 1973): 43–54; Eva Cockcroft, "Abstract Expressionism, Weapon of the Cold War," *Artforum* 12 (June 1974): 39–41.

69. Philip Gleason, "World War II and the Development of American Studies," *American Quarterly* 36 (September 1984): 344; Robert F. Berkhofer, Jr., "A New Context for American Studies?" *American Quarterly* 41 (December 1989): 588–90; George Lipsitz, "Listening to Learn and Learning to Listen: Popular Culture, Cultural Theory, and American Studies," *American Quarterly* 42 (December 1990): 622; Lawrence W. Levine, *The Opening of the American Mind: Canons, Culture, and History* (Boston: Beacon Press, 1996), 88–89.

70. John A. Kouwenhoven, "What's 'American' About America," *Harper's Magazine* 213 (July 1956): 25–33.

71. John Kouwenhoven, *Made in America: The Arts in Modern Civilization* (Garden City, N.Y.: Doubleday, 1948), 264.

72. Berendt Ostendorf, "Ralph Waldo Ellison: Anthropology, Modernism, and Jazz," in *New Essays on Invisible Man*, ed. Robert O'Meally (Cambridge: Cambridge University Press, 1988), 115; Ralph Ellison, "The Charlie Christian Story," *Saturday Review* (May 17, 1958), reprinted in *Shadow and Act* (New York: Random House, 1964), 234.

73. For more on changing definitions of freedom during the Cold War see Eric Foner, *The Story of American Freedom* (New York: W.W. Norton, 1998), 249–73.

74. Gennari, "The Politics of Culture and Identity," 193, 201–9.

75. Stearns, *The Story of Jazz*, 282; Gennari, "The Politics of Culture and Identity," 211.

76. Bernard Gendron, "'Moldy Figs' and Modernists: Jazz at War (1942–1946)," in *Jazz Among the Discourses*, 31–56; Starr, *Red and Hot*, 99–100. As both Gendron and Starr acknowledge, jazz has always existed in the marketplace and hardly qualified as "folk music" by that or any other standard, even in its earliest days. Recognizing this fact, several left-liberal intellectuals dismissed jazz as the unwitting accomplice of capitalist mass culture. Waldo Frank and Theodor Adorno, for example, both viewed jazz as an escape from the rigors of urban-industrial life. It promised temporary release, they argued, while draining energies that might otherwise be employed to ameliorate social and economic hardship. On Frank, see Casey Nelson Blake, *Beloved Community: The Cultural Criticism of Randolph Bourne, Van Wyck Brooks, Waldo Frank, and Lewis Mumford* (Chapel Hill: University of North Carolina Press, 1990), 271–73. On Adorno, see Theodor W. Adorno, "Perennial Fashion–Jazz," in *Prisms*, trans. Samuel Weber and Shierry Weber (Cambridge, Mass.: MIT Press, 1981), 119–33. Statement on jazz attributed to the Union of Proletarian Musicians, 1929, quoted in Richard Hanser, "Okay, Comrades, Let's Jazz It Up: Russia Finds the Beat," *Saturday Review* 39 (June 16, 1956): 37.

77. DeMicheal, "Jazz in Government [part I]," 15; Paul Hume, "Jazz Missing Beat Abroad," 13609. Conover is quoted in DeMicheal, "Jazz in Government, Part II," 20.

78. Stearns, "Is Jazz Good Propaganda?" 28, 30; James M. Haswell, "Dizzy's Tour Costly to U.S.," *New York Journal American* [April 10, 1955], Marshall W. Stearns Manuscript Collection, Gillespie Tour—1956 folder, Institute of Jazz Studies.

79. Jane De Hart Matthews, "Art and Politics in Cold War America," *American Historical Review* 81 (October 1976): 762–87; Taylor D. Littleton and Maltby Sykes, *Advancing American Art: Painting, Politics, and Cultural Confrontation at Mid-Century* (Tuscaloosa: University of Alabama Press, 1989); Margaret Lynne Ausfeld, "Circus Girl Arrested: A History of the *Advancing American Art* Collection, 1946–1948," in Ausfeld and Virginia M. Mecklenburg, *Advancing American Art: Politics and Aesthetics in the State Department Exhibition, 1946–48* (Montgomery, Ala.: Montgomery Museum of Fine Arts, 1984), 11–32. The Hearst Press, traditionalist artists' organizations, and congressional critics also attacked *Advancing American Art* for its supposedly subversive social commentary, its expense, and the alleged Communist associations of some individual artists.

80. Quoted in Joseph N. Acinapura, "The Cultural Presentations Program of the United States" (master's thesis, University of Colorado, 1970), 73.

81. Senate Appropriations Report No. 2580, supplemental to H.R. 12138, quoted by Rep. Frank Thompson, Jr., *Congressional Record*, 84th Cong., 2nd sess., July 19, 1956: 13609; "Biceps and Choirs: Senate Group Backs Them to Promote U. S. Abroad," *New York Times* (July 18, 1956): L54.

82. Guilbaut, *How New York Stole the Idea of Modern Art*, 195–205; Kozloff, "American Painting During the Cold War," 43–49; Cockcroft, "Abstract Expressionism," 39–41.

83. Randall, "The Voice of American Jazz," 88–89. Conover repeated the same explanation many times. See, for example, Dizard, *The Strategy of Truth*, 76.

84. *Congressional Record* 96, March 22, 1950, 3764, quoted in Thomson and Laves, *Cultural Relations*, 79.

85. Mary L. Dudziak, "Desegregation as a Cold War Imperative," *Stanford Law Review* 41 (November 1988): 80–93.

86. Bert B. Lockwood, "The United Nations Charter and United States Civil Rights Litigation: 1946–1955," *Iowa Law Review* 69 (July 1984): 901–49; Dudziak, "Desegregation as a Cold War Imperative," 65–68, 103–13. Quotation from Brief for the United States as Amicus Curiae, *Brown v. Board of Education*, in Dudziak, 61.

87. For more on domestic anticommunism's threat to civil liberties, especially in the form of federal loyalty tests, see Athan Theoharis, "The Threat to Civil Liberties," in *Cold War Critics: Alternatives to American Foreign Policy in the Truman Years*, ed. Thomas G. Paterson (Chicago: Quadrangle, 1971), 266–98.

88. Dudziak, "Desegregation as a Cold War Imperative," 64, 119–20.

89. Penny M. Von Eschen, *Race Against Empire: Black Americans and Anticolonialism, 1937–1957* (Ithaca, N.Y.: Cornell University Press, 1997), 179. Armstrong is quoted in Gary Giddins, *Satchmo*, 159. Elliott Bratton, "The Sound of Freedom: Jazz and the Cold War," *Crisis* 105 (February–March 1998): 19.

90. Von Eschen, *Race Against Empire*, 179–81; Dizzy Gillespie with Ralph Ginzburg, "Jazz Is Too Good for Americans," 55.

91. Dizzy Gillespie with Al Fraser, *To Be or not . . . to Bop* (Garden City, N.Y.: Doubleday, 1979), 414; Giddins, *Satchmo*, 160–61.

92. Dave Brubeck et al., *The Real Ambassadors* (Columbia/Legacy CK 57663, 1994 reissue).

93. Brian Priestley, *Mingus: A Critical Biography* (New York: Quartet, 1982), 44; Leonard Feather, "Jazz in American Society," in *The Encyclopedia of Jazz* (New York: Da Capo, 1960), 84–85.

94. Leonard Feather, "Dear Stan . . . " *Down Beat* 23 (October 3, 1956): 17. For readers' letters in a similar vein, see "Chords and Discords" in the same issue, 4–6. The telegram appeared in "Chords and Discords," *Down Beat* 23 (September 5, 1956): 4. Leonard Feather, "The Jazzman as Critic: The Blindfold Test," in *The Encyclopedia of Jazz* (New York: Horizon Press, 1960), 477–78. Feather enlarged his comments on the issue of race in another essay from the encyclopedia, "Jazz in American Society," 79–88.

95. "The Thaw Exposed: Soviet Art Freezes Over," *Newsweek* (February 27, 1956): 88–93, 91; Richard Hanser, "Okay, Comrades," 36–38.

Chapter 2. Free Improvisation Challenges the Jazz Canon

1. For an in-depth analysis of the riot's causes and consequences, see Scott Saul, *Freedom Is, Freedom Ain't: Jazz and the Making of the Sixties* (Cambridge, Mass.: Harvard University Press, 2003), 99–122. See also Burt Korall, "Newport Tragedy: 'But jazz was not to blame,'" *Melody Maker* 35 (July 9, 1960): 2–3; Nat Hentoff, "Requiem for a Jazz Festival," *Commonweal* 72 (August 5, 1960): 393–96; Gene Lees, "Newport: The Trouble," *Down Beat* 27 (August 18, 1960): 20–23, 44.

2. Mingus is quoted in Saul, *Freedom Is, Freedom Ain't*, 103.

3. Saul addresses the rebels festival in *Freedom Is, Freedom Ain't*, 123–29. See also Whitney Balliett, "Jazz Concerts," *New Yorker* 36 (July 16, 1960): 84–88; Nat Hentoff, "Requiem for a Festival," 393–96.

4. Nat Hentoff, *The Jazz Life* (New York: Dial, 1961), 105.

5. Balliett, "Jazz Concerts," 88; John Litweiler, *Ornette Coleman: A Harmolodic Life* (New York: Da Capo, 1992), 82–83.

6. Litweiler, *Ornette Coleman*, 78–84; Lees, "Newport: The Trouble," 21–22.

7. Lawrence W. Levine, *Highbrow/Lowbrow: The Emergence of Cultural Hierarchy in America* (Cambridge, Mass.: Harvard University Press, 1988).

8. David Hyde, "The Paradox of Acting Reality: James A. Hearn and the Single Tax Movement," Katherine K. Preston, "Against the Aristocratic Grain: English-Language Opera Companies in Late Nineteenth-Century America," papers presented at the American Historical Association, Washington, D.C., January 1999; Andrew Ross, *No Respect: Intellectuals and Popular Culture* (New York: Routledge, 1989); Paul R. Gorman, *Left Intellectuals and Popular Culture in Twentieth Century America* (Chapel Hill: University of North Carolina Press, 1996).

9. Duchamp is quoted in Calvin Tomkins, *Marcel Duchamp: A Biography* (New York: Henry Holt, 1996), 185.

10. Peter Bürger, *Theory of the Avant-Garde*, trans. Michael Shaw (Minneapolis: University of Minnesota Press, 1984), 27, 49–54. For an overview of modernism's impact on the literary canon, see David Hollinger, *In the American Province: Studies in the Historiography of Ideas* (Baltimore: Johns Hopkins University Press, 1985), 74–91. For painting, see T. J. Clark, *The Painting of Modern Life: Paris in the Art of Manet and his Followers* (New York: Knopf, 1984). For music, see Martha Bayles, *Hole in Our Soul: The Loss of Beauty and Meaning in American Popular Music* (New York: Free Press, 1994).

11. Stuart D. Hobbs, *The End of the American Avant Garde* (New York: New York University Press, 1997); W. T. Lhamon, Jr., *Deliberate Speed: The Origins of a Cultural Style in the American 1950s* (Washington, D.C.: Smithsonian Institute Press, 1990). Cage is quoted in *John Cage: I Have Nothing to Say and I am Saying It*, dir. Allan Miller, 56 min., R. M. Arts, 1990, videocassette.

12. John Gennari, "Jazz Criticism: Its Development and Ideologies," *Black American Literature Forum* 25 (Fall 1991): 464–65.

13. Penny M. Von Eschen, *Satchmo Blows Up the World: Jazz Ambassadors Play the Cold War* (Cambridge, Mass.: Harvard University Press, 2004), 18–20.

14. John Remo Gennari, "The Politics of Culture and Identity in American Jazz Criticism" (Ph.D. dissertation, University of Pennsylvania, 1993), xiii–xiv, 80–82, 199–200, 246–57.

15. John Litweiler, *The Freedom Principle: Jazz After 1958* (New York: William Morrow, 1984), 110–11, 127–28; Eckhart Jost, *Free Jazz* (Graz: Universal Edition, 1974), 36, 39–43.

16. Joe Goldberg, *Jazz Masters of the Fifties* (New York: Macmillan, 1965), 213–20; Whitney Balliett, "Jazz: Cecil," *New Yorker* (May 5, 1986): 108–12.

17. Cecil Taylor, *Jazz Advance* (Blue Note CDP 7 844622, 1991), originally recorded by Transition, 1956; Ted White, "Cecil Taylor: The Danger of Style," *Metronome* 77 (September 1960): 36–37; A. B. Spellman, *Four Lives in the Bebop Business* (New York: Pantheon, 1966), 12–14; Whitney Balliett, "Jazz: Cecil," 111.

18. Whitney Balliett, *Dinosaurs in the Morning: 41 Pieces on Jazz* (London: Phoenix House, 1962), 27–29. Cecil Taylor is quoted in Goldberg, *Jazz Masters of the Fifties*, 218. Spellman, *Four Lives in the Bebop Business*, 29–30. Lawrence Kart argues that Taylor used dissonance primarily to enhance the force and direction with which he struck the keys, a perspective that supports the rhythmic importance of the pianist's work. See Lawrence Kart, "The Avant-Garde, 1949–1967," in *The Oxford Companion to Jazz*, ed. Bill Kirchner (New York: Oxford University Press, 2000), 454–55.

19. Whitney Balliett, *The Sound of Surprise: 46 Pieces on Jazz* (New York: Da Capo, 1978), 25; Martin Williams, *The Jazz Heritage* (New York: Oxford University

Press, 1985), 216; Goldberg, *Jazz Masters of the Fifties*, 220–21; Bill Coss, "Cecil Taylor's Struggle for Existence," *Down Beat* 28 (October 26, 1961): 21; Balliett, "Jazz: Cecil," 108.

20. Robert Levin, "Cecil Taylor," [*Jazz 'n' Pop* 1 (May 1957)]: 4, Cecil Taylor file, Institute of Jazz Studies, Rutgers University, Newark, N.J.; Joe Goldberg, "Cecil Taylor and the New Tradition," *Saturday Review* (February 9, 1963): 43; Robert Levin, "Cecil Taylor and the New Dynamism," *Village Voice* (May 2, 1963): 4–5; Frank Kofsky, "Cecil Taylor," *Down Beat* 28 (March 30, 1961): 40; Spellman, *Four Lives in the Bebop Business*, 6–27, 47–48; Leonard Feather, "The Blindfold Test: Billy Eckstine," *Down Beat* 28 (December 21, 1961): 45.

21. Williams, *The Jazz Heritage*, 217; Gary Giddins, *Riding on a Blue Note: Jazz and American Pop* (New York: Oxford University Press, 1981), 277–78; Harold L. Keith, "Cecil Taylor and the 'Mad' Monk: The Nonconformists of Jazzocracy," *Pittsburgh Courier* magazine section (March 23, 1957): A7. Taylor's comments on Giuffre and the Modern Jazz Quartet appear in Levin, "Cecil Taylor," 79. Gunther Schuller, "Reviews: Recordings," *Jazz Review* 2 (January 1959): 30–31. For Taylor's response to the critics, especially Schuller, see Spellman, *Four Lives in the Bebop Business*, 29–32.

22. The Cecil Taylor Quartet, *Looking Ahead!* (Contemporary S-7562, 1959); Cecil Taylor-Buell Neidlinger, *New York City R&B* (Candid 79017, n.d.), recorded 1961. For an overview of precedents for free improvisation in jazz see Kart, "The Avant-Garde, 1949–1967," 446–58. Taylor is quoted in Levin, "Cecil Taylor and the New Dynamism," 5.

23. Bayles, *Hole in Our Soul*, 15–16; Jeff Pressing, "Free Jazz and the Avant-Garde," in *The Cambridge Companion to Jazz*, ed. Mervyn Cooke and David Horn (Cambridge: Cambridge University Press, 2002), 206–9.

24. Susan Key and Larry Rothe, eds., *American Mavericks* (Berkeley: University of California Press, 2001); Bayles, *Hole in Our Soul*, 15–16.

25. Balliett, *The Sound of Surprise*, 26; Schuller, "Reviews: Recordings," 28–31. On Taylor's unconventional manipulation of the piano see Ekkehard Jost, "The Player Advances: Area and Plain," *Village Voice* (June 26, 1989): 19; Spellman, *Four Lives in the Bebop Business*, 36–37. Spellman quotes Taylor and his collaborators extensively in this chapter on the subject of John Cage and the Euro-American concert tradition.

26. Litweiler, *Ornette Coleman*, 21–33. Bradford is quoted in Barry McRae, *Ornette Coleman* (London: Apollo, 1988), 15–16. Martin Williams, liner notes for Ornette Coleman, *The Shape of Jazz to Come* (Atlantic 1317, 1959).

27. Litweiler, *Ornette Coleman*, 61–62.

28. Litweiler, *Ornette Coleman*, 55–76.

29. George Hoefer, "Caught in the Act: Ornette Coleman," draft concert review, Ornette Coleman file, Institute of Jazz Studies. The piece later appeared with revisions in *Down Beat* 27 (January 7, 1960): 40–41.

30. Williams, liner notes for Coleman, *The Shape of Jazz to Come*. John Lewis is quoted by Nat Hentoff in the liner notes for Ornette Coleman, *Tomorrow Is the Question!* (Contemporary M-3569, 1959).

31. Gennari, "The Politics of Culture and Identity," 1–64; Robert Walser, "'Out of Notes': Signification, Interpretation, and the Problem of Miles Davis," in *Jazz Among the Discourses*, ed. Krin Gabbard (Durham, N.C.: Duke University Press, 1995), 168–69.

32. Martin Williams, "'The New Thing' in Jazz," *Harper's* (October 1961): 73–75; Martin Williams, "Ornette Coleman: A New Kind of Jazz Improvising" *International Musician* (January 1962): 34.

33. Press Release, "Ornette Coleman 'Jazz Profiles' Concert on Mon., April 4 [1960]," Ornette Coleman file, Institute of Jazz Studies; Whitney Balliett, "Haymaker," *New Yorker* 36 (April 16, 1960): 170; Whitney Balliett, "Ornette Rides Again," *New Yorker* 40 (January 16, 1965): 118.

34. Whitney Balliett, "Abstract," *New Yorker* 37 (October 21, 1961): 168–72; Whitney Balliett, "Abstract (Continued)," *New Yorker* 37 (October 28, 1961): 164–68; Litweiler, *Ornette Coleman*, 93–95.

35. See, for example, Ralph J. Gleason, "Review: *The Shape of Jazz to Come / Tomorrow Is the Question!*" *HiFi/Stereo Review* 4 (February 1960): 93; Ralph J. Gleason, "Coleman Suffers From the Success Syndrome of the Jazz Artist," *San Francisco Chronicle* (September 18, 1960), Ornette Coleman file, Institute of Jazz Studies.

36. Jonathan Fineberg, *Art Since 1940: Strategies of Being*, 2nd ed. (New York: Harry N. Abrams, 2000), 20–115; Ann Eden Gibson, *Abstract Expressionism: Other Politics* (New Haven: Yale University Press, 1997), xix–xxvii; Michael Leja, "Jackson Pollock: Representing the Unconscious," in *Reading American Art*, ed. Marianne Doezema and Elizabeth Milroy (New Haven, Conn.: Yale University Press, 1998), 440–64.

37. Liner notes for Ornette Coleman, *Change of the Century* (Atlantic 1327, 1959); "Beyond the Cool," *Time* 75 (June 27, 1960): 56; Martin Williams, liner notes for Ornette Coleman Double Quartet, *Free Jazz* (Atlantic 1364, 1960); Bill, "Five Spot, N.Y." [December 1959], Ornette Coleman file, Institute of Jazz Studies; T. E. Martin, "The Plastic Muse, Part II," *Jazz Monthly* 10 (April 1964): 15; Don Heckman, "Ornette Coleman and the Quiet Revolution," *Saturday Review* 46 (January 12, 1963): 78; "The New Jazz," *Newsweek* 68 (December 12, 1966): 101.

38. Nat Hentoff, liner notes for Ornette Coleman, *Something Else! The Music of Ornette Coleman* (Contemporary C-3531, 1958); Nat Hentoff, "Ornette Coleman's Free Jazz: Liberation or Anarchy?" *HiFi/Stereo Review* 8 (February 1962): 88.

39. "Ornette Still Struggling," press clipping [November 14, 1961], Ornette Coleman file, Institute of Jazz Studies; Philip Larkin, *All What Jazz: A Record Diary, 1961–1971* (New York: Farrar-Straus-Giroux, 1985), 180.

40. Peter J. Welding, "Review: *This Is Our Music*," *HiFi/Stereo Review* 7 (July 1961): 78.

41. Don DeMicheal, "Spotlight Review," *Down Beat* 28 (May 11, 1961): 25; Tom Scanlon, "Tomorrow Is Not the Question" [1959, probably *Army Times*], Ornette Coleman file, Institute of Jazz Studies.

42. Dorothy Seiberling, "Baffling U.S. Art: What It Is About," *Life* 47 (November 9, 1959): 68–80. Mehegan's comments appeared in "Chords and Discords," *Down Beat* 26 (December 24, 1959): 6. Scanlon, "Tomorrow Is Not The Question"; Leonard Feather, "André Previn: Blindfold Test, Part Two," *Down Beat* 28 (November 9, 1961): 37; Leonard Feather, "Hierarchy of the Jazz Anarchy," *Esquire* (September 1965): 123.

43. Leonard Feather, "Ruby Braff: The Blindfold Test," *Down Beat* 27 (January 21, 1960): 37; Leonard Feather, "Quincy Jones: The Blindfold Test," *Down Beat* 28 (March 2, 1961): 43.

44. Lewis Porter, *John Coltrane: His Life and Music* (Ann Arbor: University of Michigan Press, 1998), 1–34; Eric Nisenson, *Ascension: John Coltrane and his Quest* (New York: Da Capo, 1993), 3–5.

45. Porter, *John Coltrane*, 35–170.

46. The title track of Coltrane's *Giant Steps* (Atlantic 1311–2, 1959) provided a good example of vertical or chord-stacking improvisation. "Naima" displayed the harmonically-simple horizontal approach. Coltrane recorded *The Avant-Garde* (Atlantic 90041, 1966) with the Ornette Coleman Quartet, minus its leader, in 1960. Atlantic released the album in 1966. Coltrane had previously recorded as a sideman on Cecil Taylor's *Hard Driving Jazz* (United Artists UAL 4014, 1958) under the pseudonym Blue Train.

47. John Fraim, *Spirit Catcher: The Life and Art of John Coltrane* (West Liberty, Ohio: Great House, 1996), 102–3; Porter, *John Coltrane*, 177–79.

48. Porter, *John Coltrane*, 216–17.

49. Martin Williams, "Reviews," *Down Beat* 29 (January 18, 1962): 29, 32; Whitney Balliett, "Check List" [1959–60], John Coltrane file, Institute of Jazz Studies; Peter Welding, "Reviews," *Down Beat* 28 (June 22, 1961): 30, 32; Peter Welding, "Double View of Coltrane 'Live'" *Down Beat* 29 (April 26, 1962): 29; Ralph J. Gleason, "Weinstock vs. Gleason on Coltrane," *Los Angeles Mirror News* (March 28, 1960), John Coltrane file, Institute of Jazz Studies.

50. John S. Wilson, "One Man's Way," *New York Times* (December 10, 1961), 2: 28; John S. Wilson, "New Jazz Series Begins at Y.M.H.A.," *New York Times* (February 26, 1962): L30. For Feather's comments on Coltrane, see Nisenson, *Ascension*, 74–75; Leonard Feather, "André Previn: Blindfold Test," *Down Beat* 30 (May 9, 1963): 33; Tynan, "Caught in the Act," *Down Beat* 26 (August 6, 1959): 32.

51. John Tynan, "Take Five," *Down Beat* 28 (November 23, 1961): 40; Don DeMicheal, "John Coltrane and Eric Dolphy Answer the Jazz Critics," *Down Beat* 29 (April 12, 1962): 21; "Chords and Discords," *Down Beat* 29 (January 4, 1962): 6; "Chords and Discords," *Down Beat* 29 (February 1, 1962): 9.

52. For Tynan's change of heart, compare John Tynan, "Ornette: The First Beginning," *Down Beat* 27 (July 21, 1960): 32–33, 58; John Tynan, "Double View of a Double Quartet," *Down Beat* 29 (January 18, 1962): 28. For Gitler's early encouragement of Coltrane, see Ira Gitler, "'Trane on the Track," *Down Beat* 25 (October 16, 1958): 16–17. For his response to the John Coltrane Quartet with Eric Dolphy, see Ira Gitler, "Double View of Coltrane 'Live,'" *Down Beat* 29 (April 26, 1962): 29.

53. Leonard Feather, "Jazz: Going Nowhere," *Show* (January 1962): 12–14; Leonard Feather, "Feather's Nest," *Down Beat* 29 (February 15, 1962): 40.

54. Sonny Rollins used Coleman's approach and, like Coltrane, some of his sidemen on the albums *On The Outside* (Bluebird 2179–2, 1962) and *Our Man in Jazz* (RCA 2612, 1962). Jackie McLean produced a series of records during the early 1960s that betrayed Coleman's influence, including *Let Freedom Ring* (Blue Note 46527, 1962), *One Step Beyond* (Blue Note 46821, 1963), and *Destination Out* (Blue Note 4165, 1963). For Coltrane's influence on other mainstream musicians, see Nisenson, *Ascension*, 159–61.

55. Hobsbawm is quoted in Nat Hentoff, "Jazz in Print," *Jazz Review* 3 (November 1960): 34.

56. Interviews with Chicago jazz promoter Joe Segal and musician Donald Rafael Garrett suggest that some of the most adventurous musicians in town were either unmoved by or actively opposed to Coleman's music in 1960. See "Joe Segal-interviewed by J. B. Figi" (August 22, 1990); "Rafael Garrett-interviewed by J. B. Figi" (December 7, 1981), Jazz Institute of Chicago Don De-Micheal Collection, Chicago Jazz Archive, University of Chicago Library. The report of John Coltrane's performance at Small's Paradise appears in Cuthbert

Ormond Simpkins, *Coltrane: A Biography* (New York: Herndon, 1975), 114. Coltrane's expectations about the effect of stylistic evolution on his audience are recorded in Nisenson, *Ascension*, 88. On Cecil Taylor's following and struggle for work see Spellman, *Four Lives in the Bebop Business*, 6–9.

57. John Clellon Holmes, "The Golden Age of Jazz: Time Present," *Esquire* 51 (January 1959): 100.

58. Ingrid Monson, *Saying Something: Jazz Improvisation and Interaction* (Chicago: University of Chicago Press, 1996), 199–203; Jon Panish, *The Color of Jazz: Race and Representation in Postwar American Culture* (Jackson: University Press of Mississippi, 1997), 3–15; Penny M. Von Eschen, *Race Against Empire: Black Americans and Anticolonialism, 1937–1957* (Ithaca, N.Y.: Cornell University Press, 1997), 153–59.

59. Eric Porter, *What Is This Thing Called Jazz? African American Musicians as Artists, Critics, and Activists* (Berkeley: University of California Press, 2002), 117–24; Steve Chapple and Reebee Garofalo, *Rock 'N' Roll Is Here to Pay: The History and Politics of the Music Industry* (Chicago: Nelson-Hall, 1977), 236–42; Arnold Shaw, "The Cool Generation," *Esquire* 41 (May 1954): 100–104; Arnold Shaw, "West Coast Jazz," *Esquire* 46 (September 1956): 79, 127–31.

60. Von Eschen, *Race Against Empire*, 177.

61. Alan Brinkley, *The Unfinished Nation: A Concise History of the American People*, vol. 2 (New York: McGraw-Hill, 1993), 789; Von Eschen, *Race Against Empire*, 179. Armstrong's statement during the Little Rock crisis, that "it's getting so bad a colored man hasn't got any country," contrasted starkly with his role as an unofficial ambassador of jazz music's universalism (180).

62. For more on the membership, programs, and internal disputes of the major civil rights organizations see Aldon D. Morris, *The Origins of the Civil Rights Movement: Black Communities Organizing for Change* (New York: Free Press, 1984); Adam Fairclough, *To Redeem the Soul of America: The Southern Christian Leadership Conference and Martin Luther King, Jr.* (Athens: University of Georgia Press, 1987); Clayborne Carson, *In Struggle: SNCC and the Black Awakening of the 1960s* (Cambridge, Mass.: Harvard University Press, 1981); August Meier and Elliott Rudwick, *CORE: A Study in the Civil Rights Movement 1942–1968* (New York: Oxford University Press, 1973). Oral history projects recover the voices of movement participants. See, for example, Howell Raines, *My Soul Is Rested: Movement Days in the Deep South Remembered* (New York: Penguin, 1983).

63. For more on "Crow Jim," see Paul Lopes, *The Rise of a Jazz Art World* (Cambridge: Cambridge University Press, 2002), 253–56; Charley Gerard, *Jazz in Black and White: Race, Culture, and Identity in the Jazz Community* (Westport, Conn.: Praeger, 1998), 8–9. Contemporary discussions of the issue appeared in Leonard Feather, "Jazz in American Society," in *The Encyclopedia of Jazz* (New York: Horizon, 1960), 83; Nat Hentoff, "The Pride of Black," *Nugget* (April 1962): 22; Leonard Feather, "Jazz and Race," *HiFi/Stereo Review* 10 (February 1963): 46. Feather also quoted Gleason on the subject of "Crow Jim." For an African American journalist's defense of frustrated black musicians, see George E. Pitts, "Are White Musicians Discrimination Victims?" *Pittsburgh Courier* (October 8, 1960): 23.

64. Figures taken from "Statement of Ownership, Management, and Circulation," *Down Beat* 30 (October 24, 1963): 42; *Down Beat* 34 (October 31, 1968): 40. A federal act of 1962 required annual publication of average circulation figures for journals receiving certain federal mailing privileges.

65. Dan Morgenstern, interview with the author, August 10, 1995. Leonard

Feather's survey of one thousand *Down Beat* readers in spring 1956, and a similar survey the following year, found that close to 60 percent of the magazine's subscribers were between the ages of thirteen and twenty-two years old. Leonard Feather, "The Jazz Fan," in *The Encyclopedia Yearbook of Jazz* (New York: Horizon, 1956), 27–32, 41–48; Leonard Feather, "The Biggest Year in Jazz," *New York Journal-American* (December 7 1957): 60.

66. Dan Morgenstern recalled that after ten years with the magazine (1964–1973), he remembered only one African American—assistant editor Bill Quinn—ever working in a full-time editorial position.

67. On the integration of San Francisco locals, for example, see *Down Beat* 26 (December 10, 1959): 14–15; *Down Beat* 27 (March 31, 1960): 16; "Racial Prejudice in Jazz, Part I," *Down Beat* 29 (March 15, 1962): 20–26; "Racial Prejudice in Jazz, Part II," *Down Beat* 29 (March 29, 1962): 22–25. All quotations, including Gitler's original review of *Straight Ahead*, taken from part I.

68. "The Need for Racial Unity in Jazz: A Panel Discussion," *Down Beat* 30 (April 11, 1963): 16, 18, 19. Lees is quoted in George E. Pitts, "Are White Musicians Discrimination Victims?" 23. "Chords and Discords," *Down Beat* 29 (May 10, 1962): 5–6.

69. Monson, *Saying Something*, 200–203. Taylor and Mingus are quoted in Hentoff, "The Pride of Black," 22.

70. Chapple and Garofalo, *Rock 'N' Roll Is Here to Pay*, 88.

71. Chapple and Garofalo, *Rock 'N' Roll Is Here to Pay*, 88, 259; Russell Sanjek and David Sanjek, *Pennies from Heaven: The American Popular Music Business in the Twentieth Century* (New York: Da Capo, 1996), 384.

72. Quoted in Samuel A. Floyd, Jr., *The Power of Black Music: Interpreting Its History from Africa to the United States* (New York: Oxford University Press, 1995), 179.

73. Chapple and Garofalo, *Rock 'N' Roll Is Here to Pay*, 27–47.

74. Chapple and Garofalo, *Rock 'N' Roll Is Here to Pay*, 24–25, 49–53, 57–60, 89–92.

75. LeRoi Jones [Amiri Baraka], "Loft Jazz," *Down Beat* 30 (May 9, 1963): 13, 42; Leonard Feather, "A View from the Bridge," 15–17; Herm Schoenfeld, "Jazz Mugged by 'New Thing': Latest Idiom Poison at B.O.," *Variety* (April 14, 1965): 49; Leonard Feather, "Feather's Nest," *Down Beat* 32 (August 26, 1965): 41; Arnold Shaw, "The Dilemma of Jazz," *Jazz* 4 (April 1965): 9.

76. Saul, *Freedom Is, Freedom Ain't*, 273–78; Leonard Feather, "A View from the Bridge," in *The Encyclopedia of Jazz in the Sixties* (New York: Da Capo, 1966), 14–15.

77. Nat Hentoff, "Paying the New Jazz Dues," *The Nation* (June 22, 1964): 635–38; Rob Backus, *Fire Music: A Political History of Jazz* (Chicago: Vanguard, 1976), 46–47.

78. Art DiLugoff, "'Experimentation' in Public: The Clubowner's Point of View," *Down Beat* 32 (April 8, 1965): 15; Nat Hentoff, "The New York Jazz Scene: The Establishment, the Clubs, and Those Who Wait," *New York Herald Tribune Sunday Magazine* (April 7, 1963): 9, 16, 26; Jones [Baraka], "Loft Jazz," 13, 42; Frank Kofsky, "The Jazz Scene," *Jazz* 6 (February 1967): 22.

79. LeRoi Jones [Amiri Baraka], "Voice From the Avant Garde: Archie Shepp," *Down Beat* 32 (January 14, 1965): 18–20, 36; Bill Quinn, "Marion Brown: Topside Underground," *Down Beat* 34 (February 9, 1967): 15–16, 38, 40; John F. Szwed, *Space Is the Place: The Lives and Times of Sun Ra* (New York: Pantheon, 1997), 180–81, 193–95; Elisabeth van der Mei, "Pharoah Sanders," *Coda*

8 (June 1967): 2–6; Martin Williams, "Pharoah's Tale," *Down Beat* 35 (May 16, 1968): 21–22; Nat Hentoff, "The Truth Is Marching In: An Interview with Albert & Don Ayler," *Down Beat* 33 (November 17, 1966): 16–18, 40; "Albert Ayler Dies," *Down Beat* 38 (January 7, 1971): 8.

80. Bill Dixon, interview with the author, August 9, 1995.

81. LeRoi Jones [Amiri Baraka], "Archie Shepp Live," *Jazz* 4 (January 1965): 8–9; Jones [Baraka], "Loft Jazz," 13, 42; Bill Dixon, interview with the author, August 9, 1995.

82. For more on Coltrane's contract with Impulse! see Nisenson, *Ascension*, 104; Fraim, *Spirit Catcher*, 191; J. C. Thomas, *Chasin' the Trane: The Music and Mystique of John Coltrane* (Garden City, N.Y.: Doubleday, 1975), 142–43, 179.

83. Dan Morgenstern, interview with the author, August 10, 1995. Circulation figures are taken from *Jazz* magazine's marketing pitch. See *Jazz* 5 (October 1966): 41. The monthly circulation quoted would have equaled approximately half of *Down Beat*'s average bi-weekly circulation of 63, 953 for 1966.

84. Bill Dixon, interview with the author, August 9, 1995.

85. Lopes, *The Rise of a Jazz Art World*, 93–98; Porter, *What Is This Thing Called Jazz?* 62–63; Scott DeVeaux, *The Birth of Bebop: A Social and Musical History* (Berkeley: University of California Press, 1997), 292–99.

86. Litweiler, *Ornette Coleman*, 103–6; Spellman, *Four Lives*, 139. On Ornette Coleman's challenge to prevalent models of masculinity, see David Ake, *Jazz Cultures* (Berkeley: University of California Press, 2002), 62–82. Charlie L. Russell, "Ornette Coleman Sounds Off," *Liberator* (July 1965): 13.

87. Bill Dixon, interview with the author, August 9, 1995; Archie Shepp, "An Artist Speaks Bluntly," *Down Beat* 32 (December 16, 1965): 11; Hentoff, "The New York Jazz Scene," 26; Spellman, *Four Lives*, 8, 46–49.

88. *Down Beat* 26 (June 25, 1959): 9–10; *Down Beat* 27 (November 24, 1960): 11.

89. Gene Lees, "Newport: The Trouble," 20–23; Dan Morgenstern, "Ornette Coleman: From the Heart," *Down Beat* 32 (April 8, 1965): 18.

90. Don DeMicheal, "On the Problem of Fork-Moving," *Down Beat* 28 (May 11, 1961): 13–14; "The Time for Action and Unity Is Now," *Down Beat* 29 (March 1, 1962): 13; "Music Men's Movement Would 'Bring Jazz Out of Its Narrow Shell,'" *Variety* (August 22, 1962): 43; Nat Hentoff, "Second Chorus," *Down Beat* 31 (April 9, 1964): 35.

91. "Editorial" [on jazz and narcotics], *Down Beat* 28 (February 2, 1961): 4; "The Other Side of the Jazz-Business Coin," *Down Beat* 29 (March 15, 1962): 16; Leonard Feather, "Feather's Nest," *Down Beat* 31 (April 23, 1964): 39.

92. Saul, *Freedom Is, Freedom Ain't*, 123–29.

Chapter 3. Free Jazz and Black Nationalism

1. Amiri Baraka, *The Autobiography of LeRoi Jones*, rev. ed. (Chicago: Lawrence Hill, 1997). For contrasting biographies see Komozi Woodard, *A Nation Within a Nation: Amiri Baraka (Leroi Jones) & Black Power Politics* (Chapel Hill: University of North Carolina Press, 1999) and Jerry Gafio Watts, *Amiri Baraka: The Politics and Art of a Black Intellectual* (New York: New York University Press, 2001).

2. Quotations appear in Baraka, *The Autobiography of LeRoi Jones*, 293. Woodard, *A Nation Within a Nation*, 63–66.

3. Woodard, *A Nation Within a Nation*, 63–66; Watts, *Amiri Baraka*, 156–58; LeRoi Jones [Amiri Baraka], "New Black Music: A Concert in Benefit of the

Black Arts Repertory Theater/School Live," in *Black Music* (New York: William Morrow, 1967), 172–76.

4. Matthew Countryman, *Up South* (Philadelphia: University of Pennsylvania Press, 2006), introduction; Robert O. Self, *American Babylon: Race and the Struggle for Postwar Oakland* (Princeton, N.J.: Princeton University Press, 2003), 1–20. For interpretations of black power as disruptive to the civil rights movement, see August Meier and Elliott Rudwick, *CORE: A Study in the Civil Rights Movement, 1942–1968* (Urbana: University of Illinois Press, 1973), 329–30, 374–75; Clayborne Carson, *In Struggle: SNCC and the Black Awakening of the 1960s* (Cambridge, Mass.: Harvard University Press, 1981), 287–88.

5. Timothy B. Tyson, *Radio Free Dixie: Robert F. Williams and the Roots of Black Power* (Chapel Hill: University of North Carolina Press, 1999); Self, *American Babylon*; Countryman, *Up South*, introduction.

6. William L. Van Deburg, *New Day in Babylon: The Black Power Movement in American Culture, 1965–1975* (Chicago: University of Chicago Press, 1992), 2, 22–26; Jack M. Bloom, *Class, Race, and the Civil Rights Movement* (Bloomington: Indiana University Press, 1987), 192–98; Stephen F. Lawson, *Running for Freedom: Civil Rights and Black Politics in America Since 1941*, 2nd ed. (New York: McGraw-Hill, 1997), 123–27.

7. Van Deburg, *New Day in Babylon*, 112–52. The National Economic Growth and Reconstruction Organization (NEGRO) offered one model for advancing urban development through black economic empowerment. This nonprofit corporation operated a hospital, chemical and textile factories, bus companies, a construction enterprise, and hundreds of housing units that served minority constituents in Watts, Harlem, and elsewhere.

8. Tyson, *Radio Free Dixie*, 291; Lawson, *Running for Freedom*, 129–30; Van Deburg, *New Day in Babylon*, 152–65.

9. Harold Cruse, "Revolutionary Nationalism and the Afro-American," in *Black Fire: An Anthology of Afro-American Writing*, ed. LeRoi Jones [Amiri Baraka] and Larry Neal (New York: William Morrow, 1968), 56; Malcolm X with Alex Haley, "From the Autobiography of Malcolm X," in *The Norton Anthology of African American Literature*, ed. Henry Louis Gates, Jr., and Nellie Y. McKay (New York: W. W. Norton, 1997), 1820–33.

10. Ronald Walters, "African-American Nationalism: A Unifying Ideology," *Black World* 22 (October 1973): 26, quoted in Van Deburg, *New Day in Babylon*, 26.

11. William L. Van Deburg, *New Day in Babylon*, 57–61, 171–73.

12. Addison Gayle, Jr., "Introduction," Hoyt W. Fuller, "Towards a Black Aesthetic," and Larry Neal, "The Black Arts Movement," in *The Black Aesthetic*, ed. Addison Gayle, Jr. (Garden City, N.Y.: Doubleday, 1971), xv–xxiv, 3–12, 272.

13. Henry Louis Gates, Jr., and Nellie Y. McKay, "The Black Arts Movement 1960–1970," in *The Norton Anthology of African American Literature*, 1796–1800; Van Deburg, *New Day in Babylon*, 182.

14. Nikki Giovanni, "Beautiful Black Men (With compliments and apologies to all not mentioned by name)," in *Black Feeling, Black Talk, Black Judgement* (New York: William Morrow, 1970), 77.

15. Harold Cruse, *The Crisis of the Negro Intellectual* (New York: William Morrow, 1967), 354–57; Henry Louis Gates, Jr., and Nellie Y. McKay, "Amiri Baraka," in *The Norton Anthology of African American Literature*, 1878.

16. Lorenzo Thomas, "Ascension: Music and the Black Arts Movement," in *Jazz Among the Discourses*, ed. Krin Gabbard (Durham, N.C.: Duke University

Press, 1995), 261–63; Sandra G. Shannon, "Amiri Baraka on Directing," in *Conversations with Amiri Baraka*, ed. Charlie Reilly (Jackson: University Press of Mississippi, 1994), 232–33, 238; Werner Sollors, *Amiri Baraka/LeRoi Jones: The Quest for a "Populist Modernism"* (New York: Columbia University Press, 1978), 217; David G. Such, *Avant-Garde Jazz Musicians: Performing "Out There"* (Iowa City: University of Iowa Press, 1993), 26; John F. Szwed, *Space Is the Place: The Lives and Times of Sun Ra* (New York: Pantheon, 1997), 209–12.

17. Baraka is quoted in Floyd Gaffney, "Amiri Baraka (LeRoi Jones)," in *African-American Writers After 1955: Dramatists and Prose Writers*, ed. Thadious M. Davis and Trudier Harris (Detroit: Gale, 1985), 24.

18. Baraka, *The Autobiography of LeRoi Jones*, 248–49; Cruse, *The Crisis of the Negro Intellectual*, 362–66; Watts, *Amiri Baraka*, 54–55, 85–87.

19. LeRoi Jones [Amiri Baraka] to Edward Dorn [September 1961, letter #1, 2], Dorn Manuscript Collection, courtesy Lilly Library, Indiana University. Ellipsis in the original.

20. A. B. Spellman, "Not Just Whistling Dixie," in *Black Fire*, 164–65.

21. LeRoi Jones [Amiri Baraka], "The Jazz Avant-Garde," *Metronome* 78 (September 1961): 9–11.

22. LeRoi Jones [Amiri Baraka], "Jazz and the White Critic," in *Black Music*, 14, 19; Leonard Feather, "Archie Shepp: Some of My Best Friends Are White," *Melody Maker* 41 (April 30, 1966): 6.

23. LeRoi Jones [Amiri Baraka], *Blues People: Negro Music in White America* (New York: William Morrow, 1963), 29.

24. James C. Hall, *Mercy, Mercy Me: African-American Culture and the American Sixties* (New York: Oxford University Press, 2001), 117–21; Kimberly W. Benston, *Baraka: The Renegade and the Mask* (New Haven, Conn.: Yale University Press, 1976), 73–84, 83.

25. James T. Stewart, "The Development of the Black Revolutionary Artist," in *Black Fire*, 3–5; Jimmy Stewart, "Introduction to Black Aesthetics in Music," in *The Black Aesthetic*, 82–85.

26. Melville Herskovits, *The Myth of the Negro Past* (Boston: Beacon, 1941); Jones [Baraka], *Blues People*, 7–10; Thomas, "Ascension," 262–63.

27. Jones [Baraka], *Blues People*, 147–48, 201–2; Jones [Baraka], "The Jazz Avant Garde," 9–12, 39.

28. LeRoi Jones [Amiri Baraka] to Edward Dorn, May 10, 1961 [2], Dorn Manuscript Collection, courtesy Lilly Library, Indiana University.

29. Jones [Baraka], *Blues People*, 230–36.

30. Nat Hentoff reviewed *Blues People* in *Book Week* (October 20, 1963): 5 and *The Commonweal* 81 (December 4, 1964): 358. See also Joe Goldberg, "Music, Metaphor, and Men," *Saturday Review* 47 (January 11, 1964): 69; Vance Rudolph, "The Roots Go Deep," *New York Times Book Review* (November 17, 1963): 22; George B. Murray in *Critic* 22 (February 1964): 88.

31. Ralph Ellison, "Blues People," in *Shadow and Act* (New York: Random House, 1964), 247–58; Albert Murray, *The Omni-Americans* (New York: Avon, 1971), 92.

32. Jones [Baraka], *Blues People*, 123–27; Hall, *Mercy, Mercy Me*, 119–21; David Ake, *Jazz Cultures* (Berkeley: University of California Press, 2001), 38–39.

33. Saunders Redding, "The Black Arts Movement in Negro Poetry," *American Scholar* 42 (Spring 1973): 330–34. Kiel is quoted in Kimberly W. Benston, *Baraka*, 89, n.15. See also Gates and McKay, "The Black Arts Movement," 1801; Ron Karenga, "Black Cultural Nationalism," in *The Black Aesthetic*, 33; Thomas, "Ascension," 256–58.

34. Larry Neal, "The Black Arts Movement," in *The Black Aesthetic*, 272; Larry Neal, "Black Art and Black Liberation," in *The Black Revolution: An Ebony Special Issue* (Chicago: Johnson Publishing Company, 1970), 31–41.

35. Jones [Baraka], *Blues People*, 231–32; Sollors, *Amiri Baraka/LeRoi Jones*, 173, 192. Hostile commentators increasingly taunted Baraka for the contradiction between lines such as "Rape the white girls . . . cut the mothers' throats" and his marriage to Hettie Cohen, a Jewish American woman. "When he is given his pistol and his signal, will he do his self-declared duty and begin the slaughter with his wife and children?" asked one reader of *Dissent* (Sollors, 173–74).

36. "Jazz and Revolutionary Black Nationalism: A Panel Discussion, Part 7," *Jazz* 5 (October 1966): 41; "Jazz and Revolutionary Black Nationalism: A Panel Discussion, Part 8," *Jazz* 5 (November 1966): 33.

37. Baraka, *The Autobiography of LeRoi Jones*, 295–328, 308. See also Watts, *Amiri Baraka*, 156–59; Woodard, *A Nation Within a Nation*, 64–66; Szwed, *Space Is the Place*, 209–11.

38. Baraka, *The Autobiography of LeRoi Jones*, 306–28; Watts, *Amiri Baraka*, 156–61; Woodard, *A Nation Within a Nation*, 66–68; Szwed, *Space Is the Place*, 210–12; James W. Sullivan, "The Negro 'National Consciousness' of LeRoi Jones," *New York Herald Tribune* (October 31, 1965), reprinted in *Jazz* 5 (January 1966): 10–11; Larry Neal, "The Social Background of the Black Arts Movement," *Black Scholar* 18 (January 1987): 18; Harold Cruse, *The Crisis of the Negro Intellectual*, 367–68; Gaffney, "Amiri Baraka," 30–31.

39. Joanne V. Gabbin, "Askia Muhammad Touré," in *Afro-American Poets Since 1955*, ed. Trudier Harris and Thadious M. Davis (Detroit: Gale, 1985), 330.

40. Nat Hentoff, liner notes for Ornette Coleman, *Something Else! The Music of Ornette Coleman* (Contemporary 3551, 1958); Martin Williams, liner notes for Ornette Coleman, *Free Jazz* (Atlantic 1364, 1960); Jones [Baraka], "The Jazz Avant Garde," 12; Jimmy Stewart, "Introduction to Black Aesthetics in Music," 87.

41. Alan Beckett, "The New Wave in Jazz," *New Left Review* 31 (May–June 1965): 92.

42. Ronald Milner, "Black Magic: Black Art," *Negro Digest* 16 (April 1967): 12; Lewis Porter, *John Coltrane: His Life and Music* (Ann Arbor: University of Michigan Press, 1998), 209–14. For more on African and Indian influences on jazz at this time, see Michael J. Budds, *Jazz in the Sixties: The Expansion of Musical Resources and Techniques* (Iowa City: University of Iowa Press, 1990), 15–23; Charley Gerard, *Jazz in Black and White: Race, Culture, and Identity in the Jazz Community* (Westport, Conn.: Praeger, 1998), 39–71. Norman Weinstein counted 18 Coltrane titles containing African themes in *A Night in Tunisia: Imaginings of Africa in Jazz* (Metuchen, N.J.: Scarecrow, 1992), 63.

43. Hentoff, liner notes for *Something Else!*; Jones [Baraka], "The Jazz Avant Garde," 12, 39; Jones [Baraka], *Blues People*, 227; Marion Brown, "Improvisation and the Aural Tradition in Afro-American Music," *Black World* 23 (November 1973): 14–19; Budds, *Jazz in the Sixties*, 18–19.

44. The John Coltrane Quartet, "Africa" [take 3], *The Complete Africa/Brass Sessions* (Impulse! IMPD-2-168, 1995), recorded June 1961.

45. Redding, "The Black Arts Movement in Negro Poetry," 334; Daniel Belgrad, *The Culture of Spontaneity: Improvisation and the Arts in Postwar America* (Chicago: University of Chicago Press, 1998), 1, 5.

46. Ronald M. Radano, *New Musical Figurations: Anthony Braxton's Cultural Critique* (Chicago: University of Chicago Press, 1993), 109–10.

47. Robert Ostermann, "The Moody Men Who Play the New Music," *National Observer* (June 7, 1965): 22; Budds, *Jazz in the Sixties,* 32–34.

48. John Cage, "The Future of Music: Credo," in *Silence: Lectures and Writings* (Cambridge, Mass.: MIT Press, 1961), 3. Although Cage dated the first delivery of "Credo" to 1937, Leta Miller has argued that clippings and programs of the Seattle Artists League, and a manuscript of the original lecture, indicate a more accurate date in 1940. Leta E. Miller, "The Art of Noise: John Cage, Lou Harrison, and the West Coast Percussion Ensemble," in *Perspectives on American Music, 1900–1950,* ed. Michael Saffle (New York: Garland, 2000), 230, 239.

49. Stockhausen is quoted in *"down beat* in review: 1960–69," *Down Beat* 43 (July 15, 1976): 21. Nat Hentoff, "The Truth Is Marching In," *Down Beat* 33 (November 17, 1966): 18.

50. Radano, *New Musical Figurations,* 111–12.

51. Baraka, *The Autobiography of LeRoi Jones,* 263; Jimmy Stewart, "Introduction to Black Aesthetics in Music" and Ron Welburn, "The Black Aesthetic Imperative," in *The Black Aesthetic,* 84–85, 141; James T. Stewart, "The Development of the Black Revolutionary Artist," in *Black Fire,* 5.

52. A. B. Spellman, "Revolution in Sound: Black Genius Creates a New Music in Western World," *Ebony* (August 1969): 86. For an example of Coltrane's reticence when pressed by an interviewer, see Frank Kofsky, *Black Nationalism and the Revolution in Music* (New York: Pathfinder, 1970), 224–30. See also Jimmy Stewart, "Introduction to Black Aesthetics in Music," in *The Black Aesthetic,* 95; Lindsay Barrett, "The Tide Inside, It Rages!" in *Black Fire,* 152.

53. Laurence [sic] P. Neal, [untitled] *Negro Digest* 17 (January 1968): 35, 81.

54. Scott Saul, *Freedom Is, Freedom Ain't: Jazz and the Making of the Sixties* (Cambridge, Mass.: Harvard University Press, 2003), 212–43, 260–68, 212.

55. Hall, *Mercy, Mercy Me,* 134–47. Coltrane is quoted in Lewis Porter, *John Coltrane,* 232.

56. Ronald M. Radano, "Jazzin' the Classics: The AACM's Challenge to Mainstream Aesthetics," *Black Music Research Journal* 12 (Spring 1992): 85, 87–90.

57. Szwed, *Space Is the Place,* 61–73, 79–87, 129–32, 142–47, 172–76.

58. A. B. Spellman, "Did John's Music Kill Him?" in *The Norton Anthology of African American Literature,* 1956; Lorenzo Thomas, "Ascension," 258; Jayne Cortez, "How Long Has Trane Been Gone," in *The Norton Anthology of African American Literature,* 1957–59. For tribute poems to free jazz musicians, see Stephen Henderson, *Understanding the New Black Poetry: Black Speech and Black Music as Poetic References* (New York: William Morrow, 1973); Jones [Baraka] and Neal, *Black Fire, Negro Digest* 17 (September–October 1968); Hall, *Mercy, Mercy Me,* 150.

59. Don DeMicheal, "Review: *Jazz in Silhouette,*" *Down Beat* 27 (April 14, 1960): 34; Bill Mathieu, "Review: *Other Planes of There* and *Sun Ra and His Solar Arkestra Visit Planet Earth,*" *Down Beat* 33 (June 16, 1966): 32–33; Martin Williams, "Some Kind of Advance Guard," in *Jazz Changes* (New York: Oxford University Press, 1992), 294–95; John S. Wilson, "'Space Age Jazz' Lacks Boosters," *New York Times* (February 19, 1962); John S. Wilson, "Sun Ra, Jazz Avant Savant, Digs Into Infinity," *New York Times* (February 11, 1967), Sun Ra file, Institute of Jazz Studies, Rutgers University, Newark, N.J. On Shepp, see Whitney Balliett, "Jazz," *New Yorker* 44 (April 6, 1968): 147–48; Philip Larkin, *All What Jazz: A Record Diary 1961–1971* (New York: Farrar-Straus-Giroux, 1985), 178–79.

60. Indeed, the exclusive nature of musical gatherings enhanced its listeners' elitism. "And we felt, I know I did, that we were linked to the music that Trane [John Coltrane] and Ornette [Coleman] and C.T. [Cecil Taylor], [Archie]

Shepp and [Eric] Dolphy and others, were making, so the old white arrogance and elitism of Europe was stupid on its face. We could saunter into a joint and be openly critical of whatever kind of show or program or party, because we knew, number one, it wasn't as hip as the music, and, number two, it wasn't as out as we were out, because now we began to realize or rationalize that we were on the fringe of the fringe. If the downtown Village/East Village society was a fringe of big-time America, then we were a fringe of that fringe, which put us way out indeed." Baraka, *The Autobiography of LeRoi Jones*, 267.

61. "Jazz and Revolutionary Black Nationalism: A Panel Discussion, Part 3," *Jazz* 5 (June 1966): 28.

62. LeRoi Jones [Amiri Baraka], "Voice from The Avant Garde: Archie Shepp," *Down Beat* 32 (January 14, 1965): 20, 36; "Chords & Discords," *Down Beat* 32 (February 25, 1965): 8, 10; "Chords & Discords," *Down Beat* 32 (July 1, 1965): 8.

Chapter 4. The Musicians and Their Audience

1. Dan Morgenstern and Martin Williams, "The October Revolution: Two Views of the Avant Garde in Action," *Down Beat* 31 (November 19, 1964): 15. For background on the "October Revolution" and subsequent attempts to organize musicians collectively in New York, see John Litweiler, *The Freedom Principle: Jazz After 1958* (New York: William Morrow, 1984), 138–39; Valerie Wilmer, *As Serious as Your Life: The Story of the New Jazz* (Westport, Conn.: Lawrence Hill, 1980), 213–15.

2. Morgenstern and Williams, "The October Revolution," 15, 33.

3. For summaries of the NEA jazz audience surveys, see Harold Horowitz, "The American Jazz Audience" in *New Perspectives on Jazz*, ed. David N. Baker (Washington, D.C.: Smithsonian Institution, 1990), 1–8; Scott DeVeaux, *Jazz in America: Who's Listening* (Carson, Calif.: National Endowment for the Arts/Seven Locks Press, 1995).

4. Horowitz, "The American Jazz Audience," 1; Robert Kenneth McMichael, "Consuming Jazz: Black Music and Whiteness" (Ph.D. dissertation, Brown, 1996), 18–19.

5. Ira Gitler, "The Columnist and the Club," *Down Beat* 31 (May 21, 1964): 13; Art D'Lugoff, "'Experimentation' in Public: The Clubowner's Viewpoint," *Down Beat* 32 (April 8, 1965): 14–15; "Americans in Europe: A Panel Discussion," *Down Beat* 30 (July 2, 1964): 64–73; Don DeMicheal, "On the Problem of Fork-Moving," *Down Beat* 28 (May 11, 1961): 13–14; Peter Loeb, "Jazz and the White Middle Class," *Jazz* 4 (1965): 23.

6. Joe Goldberg, "The Jazzman: Image and Reality," *HiFi/Stereo Review* 8 (January 1962): 58. Freddie Hubbard is quoted in "down beat in review: 1960–69," *Down Beat* 43 (July 15, 1976): 22.

7. Nat Hentoff, "Jazz In Print," *Jazz Review* 3 (November 1960): 34.

8. "Joe Segal-interviewed by J.B. Figi" (August 22, 1990), "Donald Rafael Garrett-interviewed by J. B. Figi" (December 7, 1981), Jazz Institute of Chicago Don DeMicheal Collection, Chicago Jazz Archive, University of Chicago Library. For information on the location of AACM-sponsored concerts, see the programs, ticket stubs, flyers, and AACM newsletters collected in the Jamil B. Figi Donation, Jazz Institute of Chicago Don DeMicheal Collection. See also John Litweiler, "Chicago's AACM," *Sounds & Fury* (August 1966): 45; Terry Martin, "The Chicago Avant-Garde," *Jazz Monthly* 157 (1968): 13–14. For commentary

on the audience and venues for Sun Ra's Arkestra, see John F. Szwed, *Space Is the Place: The Lives and Times of Sun Ra* (New York: Pantheon, 1997), 148–49, 154, 180–81, 190–95. For Hentoff's observations on the audience for free improvisation, see "Second Chorus," *Down Beat* 32 (July 1, 1965): 54; "The Jazz Revolution," *The Reporter* 32 (May 20, 1965): 42–45; "Phenomena: The New Jazz," *Vogue* 147 (February 1, 1966): 177, 197, 200–204.

9. On the variety of jazz venues and programming policies in Chicago see Ronald M. Radano, *New Musical Figurations: Anthony Braxton's Cultural Critique* (Chicago: University of Chicago Press, 1993), 77–83.

10. The idea that a black bohemian tradition informed the work of experimental musicians, especially members of the Art Ensemble of Chicago, is developed in Robin D. G. Kelley, "Dig They Freedom: Meditations on History and the Black Avant-Garde," *Lenox Avenue* 3 (1997): 13–27.

11. Amiri Baraka, *The Autobiography of LeRoi Jones*, rev. ed. (Chicago: Lawrence Hill, 1997), 308; Dan Morgenstern, interview with the author, August 10, 1995; Lawrence P. Neal, "A Conversation with Archie Shepp," *Liberator* 5 (November 1965): 24. See also A. B. Spellman, "Letter from Atlanta," *The Cricket* [4, n.d., 1969 or 1970]: 1–7; "Gossip," *The Cricket* [3] (1969): 41; "Gossip," *The Cricket* [4, n.d.]: 31, Schomburg Center for Research in Black Culture, New York.

12. Arthur Taylor, *Notes and Tones: Musician-to-Musician Interviews* (New York: Coward, McCann & Geoghegan, 1982), 278–79; Sherry Turner, "An Overview of the New Black Arts," *Freedomways* 9 (Spring 1969): 162.

13. Szwed, *Space Is the Place*, 59; Radano, *New Musical Figurations*, 79–80.

14. Dan Morgenstern, "Newport Report," *Down Beat* 32 (August 12, 1965): 24; Leonard Feather, "Feather's Nest," *Down Beat* 32 (September 23, 1965): 44; Herm Schoenfeld, "Jazz Mugged By 'New Thing': Latest Idiom Poison at B.O." *Variety* (April 14, 1965): 49.

15. Nat Hentoff, "The New York Jazz Scene," *New York Times Herald Tribune Sunday Magazine* (April 7, 1963): 9; Arnold Shaw, "The Dilemma of Jazz," *Jazz* 4 (April 1965): 11; Nat Hentoff, "Jazz Records Fall Outlook," *Down Beat* 31 (October 8, 1964): 14. Wexler is quoted in Brian Ward, *Just My Soul Responding: Rhythm and Blues, Black Consciousness, and Race Relations* (Berkeley: University of California Press, 1998), 143.

16. "Chords and Discords," *Down Beat* 30 (November 21, 1963): 6.

17. Sylvester is quoted in Gitler, "The Columnist and the Club," 13. This view of artists placing themselves above the marketplace appears in Henry Pleasants, *Serious Music—And All That Jazz* (New York: Simon and Schuster, 1969), 4–11, 132–45, 149–50; Martha Bayles, *Hole in Our Soul: The Loss of Beauty and Meaning in American Popular Music* (New York: Free Press, 1994), 12; Grover Sales, *Jazz: America's Classical Music* (Englewood Cliffs, N.J.: Prentice Hall, 1984), 127–30; Ward, *Just My Soul Responding*, 410–11. It is refuted best in Scott DeVeaux, *The Birth of Bebop: A Social and Musical History* (Berkeley: University of California Press, 1997), 8–17.

18. Martin Williams, "The Problematic Mr. Shepp," *Saturday Review* 49 (November 12, 1966): 90; Ralph Berton, "Caught in the Act: The Jazz Composers Orchestra-New York Art Quintet," *Down Beat* 32 (September 9, 1965): 22. Tom Scanlon is quoted in "down beat in review: 1960–69," 21.

19. Nat Hentoff, "The New Jazz: Black, Angry, and Hard to Understand," *New York Times Magazine* (December 25, 1966): 37; David C. Hunt, "Coleman, Coltrane, and Shepp: The Need for an Educated Audience," *Jazz & Pop* 7 (October 1968): 19; Ira Gitler, "Archie Shepp: *Mama Too Tight*," *Down Beat* 34 (Novem-

ber 30, 1967): 30; Leonard Feather, "Jazz," *Cavalier* (December 1965): 16–17; Leonard Feather, "Hierarchy of the Jazz Anarchy," *Esquire* (September 1965): 123, 187.

20. "Chords and Discords," *Down Beat* 30 (October 24, 1963): 9.

21. Paul Friedlander, *Rock and Roll: A Social History* (Boulder, Colo.: Westview, 1996), 160–65; Ward, *Just My Soul Responding*, 183–84.

22. This definition of soul is quoted in Friedlander, *Rock and Roll*, 161. See also Craig Werner, *A Change Is Gonna Come: Music, Race & the Soul of America* (New York: Plume, 1998), 72–78; Ward, *Just My Soul Responding*, 30–34, 183, 281–82; Nelson George, *The Death of Rhythm and Blues* (New York: E. P. Dutton, 1988), 112.

23. Ward, *Just My Soul Responding*, 174–76, 218–25. See also Werner, *A Change Is Gonna Come*, 58.

24. William L. Van Deburg, *New Day in Babylon: The Black Power Movement and American Culture, 1965–1975* (Chicago: University of Chicago Press, 1992), 204–16; Friedlander, *Rock and Roll*, 171–72; Ward, *Just My Soul Responding*, 201–16, 289–93.

25. George, *The Death of Rhythm and Blues*, 106.

26. My discussion of rock music's maturation in this and succeeding paragraphs is informed by Friedlander, *Rock and Roll*, 77–157, 190–229. See also Ian Peel, *The Unknown Paul McCartney: McCartney and the Avant-Garde* (London: Reynolds and Hearn, 2002), 26–41.

27. Robert Shelton, *No Direction Home: The Life and Music of Bob Dylan* (New York: Da Capo, 1997), 91–100, 219–34, 209.

28. Friedlander, *Rock and Roll*, 214–15.

29. Quotation taken from Ralph J. Gleason, "Jazz-Rock Merger on Upswing" [September 12, 1967], Ralph J. Gleason file, Institute of Jazz Studies, Rutgers University, Newark, N.J. See also Nat Hentoff, "Will Rock 'n' Roll Take Over from Jazz?" *New York Times* (November 26, 1967) 13: 1, 5.

30. Quotation taken from Hentoff, "Will Rock 'n' Roll Take Over from Jazz?" 1. Scott Saul, *Freedom Is, Freedom Ain't: Jazz and the Making of the Sixties* (Cambridge, Mass.: Harvard University Press, 2003), 271–301.

31. Steve Chapple and Reebee Garofalo, *Rock 'N' Roll Is Here to Pay: The History and Politics of the Music Industry* (Chicago: Nelson Hall, 1977), 73–76, 107–11; Paul Friedlander, *Rock and Roll*, 198–201; Greil Marcus, *Mystery Train: Images of America in Rock 'n' Roll Music*, rev. ed. (New York: Plume, 1997), 69.

32. Chapple and Garofalo, *Rock 'N' Roll Is Here to Pay*, 143–47, 156–66; Scott Saul, *Freedom Is, Freedom Ain't*, 273. Quotation appears in Friedlander, *Rock and Roll*, 200.

33. Dan Morgenstern, interview with the author, August 10, 1995.

34. [Editorial] *Jazz & Pop* 6 (August 1967): 5; [Editorial] *Jazz & Pop* 6 (November 1967): 7.

35. Quoted in Rob Backus, *Fire Music: A Political History of Jazz* (Chicago: Vanguard, 1976), 67.

36. For more on Ornette Coleman, see John Litweiler, *Ornette Coleman: A Harmolodic Life* (New York: Da Capo, 1994), 106, 108–9. For more on musician-run record labels, see Brian Priestley, *Mingus: A Critical Biography* (New York: Quartet, 1982), 46–55, 81, 164, 176–77; Robert L. Campbell, "The Saturn Singles in Historical Perspective," liner notes for Sun Ra, *The Singles* (Evidence ECD 22164-2, 1996) [11–23]; Litweiler, *The Freedom Principle*, 139.

37. Barry Kernfeld, ed., *The New Grove Dictionary of Jazz* (London: Macmillan, 1988), 110; Brian Priestley, *Mingus*, 114–17; Rob Backus, *Fire Music*, 68.

38. John S. Wilson, "Dig That Free-Form Jazz," *New York Times* (January 24, 1965), Jazz Composers Guild file, Institute of Jazz Studies.

39. Bill Dixon, interview with the author, August 9, 1995.

40. Morgenstern and Williams, "The October Revolution," 15, 33; Pete Welding, "Bill Dixon-Archie Shepp," *Down Beat* 31 (October 8, 1964): 27–28; John S. Wilson, "Avant-Garde Jazz Series Offers Cecil Taylor and Dixon Quintet," [*New York Times*, December 29, 1964], John S. Wilson, "Concert Unveils Free-Form Jazz," [*New York Times*, December 30, 1964], Jazz Composers Guild file, Institute of Jazz Studies; Don Heckman, "Caught in the Act: The Jazz Composers Guild," *Down Beat* 32 (February 11, 1965): 37–38; A. B. Spellman, "Jazz at the Judson," *The Nation* (February 8, 1965): 149–51; Whitney Balliett, "Comes the Revolution," *New Yorker* 41 (February 27, 1965): 121–24.

41. Bill Dixon, interview with the author, August 9, 1995; Robert Levin, "The Jazz Composers Guild: An Assertion of Dignity," *Down Beat* 32 (May 6, 1965): 17–18; "Avant Garde: After the Revolution, Reaction Sets In," *Melody Maker* 40 (July 24, 1965): 6; Litweiler, *The Freedom Principle*, 139; Wilmer, *As Serious as Your Life*, 214–15.

42. "Avant Garde: After the Revolution," 6; Valerie Wilmer, *As Serious as Your Life*, 231–34. The ESP and Impulse! releases generated renewed critical examination of free improvisation, in particular the music of second wave performers. Thoughtful accounts include Robert Ostermann, "The Moody Men Who Play the New Music," *National Observer* (June 7, 1965): 22; Alan Beckett, "The New Wave in Jazz," *New Left Review* 34 (October 1965): 92–96. Hysterical accounts include Feather, "Hierarchy of the Jazz Anarchy," 123, 187; Feather, "Jazz," 16–17. *Down Beat* temporarily revived the double-review format to accommodate sharply polarized opinions. See Kenny Dorham and Bill Mathieu, "Two Views of Three Outer Views," *Down Beat* 32 (July 15, 1965): 29–31.

43. Barry McRae, "Archie Shepp," *Jazz Journal* 21 (January 1968): 34; Brett Primack, "Archie Shepp: Back to Schooldays," *Down Beat* 45 (December 21, 1978): 60; Wilmer, *As Serious as Your Life*, 232–35.

44. Morgenstern and Williams, "The October Revolution," 33.

45. Ronald M. Radano, "Jazzin' the Classics: The AACM's Challenge to Mainstream Aesthetics" *Black Music Research Journal* 12 (Spring 1992): 79.

46. Accounts of the AACM's history include Litweiler, *The Freedom Principle*, 172–99; Wilmer, *As Serious as Your Life*, 112–25; Ekkehard Jost, *Free Jazz* (Graz: Universal Edition, 1974), 163–79; Radano, "Jazzin' the Classics," 79–95.

47. Eric Porter, *What Is This Thing Called Jazz? African American Musicians as Artists, Critics, and Activists* (Berkeley: University of California Press), 209–10.

48. For background on the career of Muhal Richard Abrams, his role in the Experimental Band, and his leadership of the AACM, see John Litweiler, "Chicago's Richard Abrams: A Man With an Idea," *Down Beat* 34 (October 5, 1967): 23, 26, 41; Bob Blumenthal, "Blowing in the Windy City," *Boston Phoenix* [1976–79], Muhal Richard Abrams file, Institute of Jazz Studies; Barry McRae, "Muhal Richard Abrams," *Jazz Journal International* 33 (April 1980): 25–26; Peter Watrous, "A Jazz Fixture of No Fixed Style," *New York Times* [October 11, 1990], Muhal Richard Abrams file, Institute of Jazz Studies.

49. Flyers, programs, ticket stubs, and newsletters related to AACM activities are contained in the Jamil B. Figi Donation, Jazz Institute of Chicago Don DeMicheal Collection, Chicago Jazz Archive, University of Chicago Library.

50. Radano, *New Musical Figurations*, 77–92.

51. Abrams is quoted in "Jazz Musicians' Group in Chicago Is Growing,"

Down Beat 33 (July 28, 1966): 11. The AACM's benefit work is detailed in "Association for the Advancement of Creative Musicians" [unpublished history, 3], Record 4467, AACM file, Center for Black Music Research, Columbia College, Chicago.

52. The AACM school's mission statement is quoted in Backus, *Fire Music*, 75–76. For more on the school, see Bob Protzman, "Creative Musicians Get Walker Salute," *St. Paul Sunday Pioneer Press* (January 23, 1983) E: 4, 8; R. Bruce Dold, "School for Kids of Note," *Chicago Tribune* (March 25, 1983) 5: 1, 14; "Association for the Advancement of Creative Musicians" [2–3], AACM file, Center for Black Music Research.

53. Litweiler, *The Freedom Principle*, 183.

54. Radano, *New Musical Figurations*, 85; Wilmer, *As Serious as Your Life*, 119; Jost, *Free Jazz*, 163; Graham Lock, *Forces in Motion: The Music and Thought of Anthony Braxton* (New York: Da Capo, 1988), 49.

55. Ray Townley, "Muhal Richard Abrams," *Down Beat* 41 (August 14, 1974): 34; Radano, *New Musical Figurations*, 82.

56. "Phil Cohran-interviewed by J.B. Figi" (August 14, 1990), Jazz Institute of Chicago Don DeMicheal Collection, Chicago Jazz Archive, University of Chicago Library; Radano, *New Musical Figurations*, 86–87, 94.

57. For background on the Society for Contemporary Music, see untitled article by Jerry De Muth, *Chicago Sun-Times* (October 22, 1967), Chicago-Music-Jazz file, Chicago Historical Society. On the exodus of AACM members from Chicago, see Gary Giddins, "Inside Free Jazz: The AACM in New York," *Village Voice* (May 30, 1977): 46–48; Neil Tesser, "Chicago Jazz Blues," *Chicago* 28 (May 1979): 192–96, Chicago-Music-Jazz file, Chicago Historical Society; Litweiler, *The Freedom Principle*, 183–85, 193–97; Radano, *New Musical Figurations*, 140–48.

58. On the AACM's funding, see Bob Protzman, "Creative Musicians," 4, 8; R. Bruce Dold, "School for Kids of Note," 1, 14; "Press Release: 20th Anniversary Festival for Oldest U.S. Musicians Collective," AACM file, Center for Black Music Research; John Corbett, "The Music's Still Happenin'," *Down Beat* 57 (December 1990): 61, 66; Radano, "Jazzin' the Classics," 85; Backus, *Fire Music*, 76.

59. For more on African American urban communities since 1940, including growing economic and spatial polarization, see Michael C. Dawson, *Behind the Mule: Race and Class in African-American Politics* (Princeton, N.J.: Princeton University Press, 1994), 3–44; June Manning Thomas and Marsha Ritzdorf, eds., *Urban Planning and the African American Community: In the Shadows* (Thousand Oaks, Calif.: Sage, 1997); Lawrence B. De Graaf, "African American Suburbanization in California, 1960 Through 1990," in *Seeking El Dorado: African Americans in California*, ed. Lawrence B. De Graaf, Kevin Mulroy, and Quintard Taylor (Seattle: University of Washington Press, 2001), 405–49; Michael C. Dawson, "A Black Counterpublic? Economic Earthquakes, Racial Agenda(s), and Black Politics," *Public Culture* 7 (Fall 1994): 195–213.

60. Baraka is quoted in Lorenzo Thomas, "Ascension: Music and the Black Arts Movement," in *Jazz Among the Discourses*, ed. Krin Gabbard (Durham, N.C.: Duke University Press, 1995), 264.

61. Hsio Wen Shih, "Jazz In Print," *Jazz Review* (August 1960): 32–35. On the reception of free jazz in the black press, see, for example, Louise Davis Stone, "Ornette Coleman, The Sound and the Fury," *New York Citizen-Call* (June 18, 1960): 22; Louise D. Stone, "Another Look at the Controversial Ornette Coleman," *New York Citizen-Call* (July 2, 1960): 23. Of course, African American writ-

ers tapped into the Cold War discourse that cast jazz as "America's art form" on occasion. See, for example, the conclusion to Harold L. Keith, "Cecil Taylor and the 'Mad' Monk," *Pittsburgh Courier Magazine* (March 23, 1957): A7.

62. A. B. Spellman, *Four Lives in the Bebop Business* (New York: Pantheon, 1966); Lawrence P. Neal, "The Black Musician in White America," *Negro Digest* 16 (March 1967): 56–57.

63. LeRoi Jones [Amiri Baraka], liner notes for Archie Shepp, *Four for Trane* (Impulse A-71, 1964); "Archie Shepp: We Can't Let the Audience Escape," *Melody Maker* 40 (August 7, 1965): 6; Barry McRae, "Archie Shepp," 35; Rolland Snellings [Askia Touré], "Keep on Pushin': Rhythm and Blues as a Weapon," *Liberator* 5 (October 1966): 6–8; A. B. Spellman, "Not Just Whistling Dixie," in *Black Fire: An Anthology of African-American Writing*, ed. LeRoi Jones [Amiri Baraka] and Larry Neal (New York: William Morrow, 1968), 167; Baraka, *The Autobiography of LeRoi Jones*, 266–67.

64. LeRoi Jones [Amiri Baraka], "The Changing Same (R&B and New Black Music)," in *Black Music* (New York: William Morrow, 1967), 180, 187–89.

65. Jones [Baraka], "The Changing Same," 184–86, 192–96, 200–201, quotation 210–11.

66. Porter, *What Is This Thing Called Jazz?* 198.

67. Neal, "The Black Musician," 55–56.

68. Harold Cruse, *The Crisis of the Negro Intellectual* (New York: William Morrow, 1967), 454.

69. "Duke Says Jazz Means Fre[e]dom, Peace," *Louisville Defender* (September 17, 1959), Duke Ellington Collection, Series 8 (scrapbooks), microfilm reel 4, National Museum of American History, Washington, D.C.; "Jazzmobile," publicity brochure [n.d.], "Jazzmobile Workshop Orchestra," press release (March 13, 1973), Jazzmobile file, Institute of Jazz Studies.

70. Joe Goldberg, *Jazz Masters of the Fifties* (New York: Macmillan, 1965), 221.

71. James Lincoln Collier, *Jazz: The American Theme Song* (New York: Oxford University Press, 1993), 123–25; Donald Kagan, Steven E. Ozment, and Frank M. Turner, *The Western Heritage*, vol. 2, *Since 1648*, 6th ed. (Upper Saddle River, N.J.: Prentice-Hall, 1998), 705–11.

72. Hentoff, "The New Jazz," 36.

Chapter 5. Jazz Outside the Marketplace

1. Unless otherwise noted, all descriptions and quotations in the following paragraphs are taken from Howard Klein's report to the Rockefeller Foundation, "Antioch College Visit," January 18–20, 1969, 1–6, folder 2706, box 287, series 200R, Record Group (RG) 1.2, Rockefeller Foundation Archives, Rockefeller Archive Center, Sleepy Hollow, N.Y. (hereafter designated RAC).

2. A series of memos between Howard Klein and Norman Lloyd, Director of Arts Programs at the Rockefeller Foundation, dated between July 11, 1969, and April 2, 1970, confirm the series of events. Folder 2706, box 287, series 200R, RG 1.2, Rockefeller Foundation Archives, RAC.

3. Lawrence W. Levine, "Jazz and American Culture," *Journal of American Folklore* 102 (January–March 1989): 6–22; John Remo Gennari, "The Politics of Culture and Identity in American Jazz Criticism" (Ph.D. dissertation, University of Pennsylvania, 1993), 257–63.

4. Leonard Feather, "Hierarchy of the Jazz Anarchy," *Esquire* 57 (September

1965): 123, 187; "Readers' Poll," *Down Beat* 32 (December 30, 1965): 19–25; "Readers' Poll," *Down Beat* 33 (December 29, 1966): 16–22.

5. Scott DeVeaux, "Constructing the Jazz Tradition: Jazz Historiography," *Black American Literature Forum* 25 (Fall 1991): 549–50.

6. "Jazz Mailbox," *Jazz* 4 (November 1965): 6–10; Leonard Feather, "Blindfold Test: Tyree Glenn," *Down Beat* 27 (April 14, 1960): 39. See also Leonard Feather, "Blindfold Test: Miles Davis," *Down Beat* 31 (June 18, 1964): 31; Leonard Feather, "Blindfold Test: Miles Davis," *Down Beat* 35 (June 13, 1968): 34.

7. Rob Backus, *Fire Music: A Political History of Jazz* (Chicago: Vanguard, 1976), 84–85; Leo Smith, "Creative Music and the AACM," in *Keeping Time: Readings in Jazz History*, ed. Robert Walser (New York: Oxford University Press, 1999), 315–23.

8. "Popular Delusions and the Madness of Crowds: A Letter From George Russell," *Down Beat* 33 (April 7, 1966): 14; Archie Shepp, "An Artist Speaks Bluntly," *Down Beat* 32 (December 16, 1965): 11, 42.

9. LeRoi Jones [Amiri Baraka], "Apple Cores," *Down Beat* 31 (November 19, 1964): 14; Brooks Johnson, "Toms and Tomming: A Contemporary Report," *Down Beat* 33 (June 16, 1966): 24, 44; Brooks Johnson, "Racism in Jazz," *Down Beat* 33 (October 6, 1966): 15.

10. W. H. Cowley and Don Williams, *International and Historical Roots of American Higher Education* (New York: Garland, 1991), 188, 203; Martin A. Trow, "American Higher Education: Past, Present, and Future," in *The History of Higher Education*, 2nd ed., ed. Lester F. Goodchild and Harold S. Wechsler (Needham Heights, Mass.: Simon and Schuster, 1997), 571, 579; Richard M. Freeland, "The World Transformed: A Golden Age for American Universities, 1945–1970," in *The History of Higher Education*, 603.

11. David D. Henry, *Challenges Past, Challenges Present: An Analysis of American Higher Education Since 1930* (San Francisco: Jossey-Bass, 1975), 55–63, 100–103; Freeland, "The World Transformed," 588–90, 599–600.

12. Martin A. Trow, "American Higher Education," 572; Henry, *Challenges Past, Challenges Present*, 71–72, 117–33; Freeland, "The World Transformed," 590–91, 600–603; Cowley and Williams, *International and Historical Roots of American Higher Education*, 188–93, 197–99.

13. James W. Hall and Barbara L. Kevles, "Democratizing the Curriculum," *Change* 12 (January 1980): 39–40; Freeland, "The World Transformed," 592–93; Gerald Grant and David Riesman, *The Perpetual Dream: Reform and Experiment in the American College* (Chicago: University of Chicago Press, 1978), 21–24. For a virulent condemnation of postwar trends in access and curriculum reform, see Russell Kirk, *Decadence and Renewal in the Higher Learning: An Episodic History of American University and College Since 1953* (South Bend, Ind.: Gateway, 1978), x–xvi.

14. Charles Suber, "Jazz Education," in Leonard Feather and Ira Gitler, *The Encyclopedia of Jazz in the Seventies* (New York: Horizon, 1976), 368–70; Larry Austin, "Jazz in Higher Education," *Jazz: A Quarterly of American Music* 3 (Summer 1959): 244–53; Leonard Feather, "Sixty Years of Jazz: An Historical Survey, in *The Encyclopedia of Jazz* (New York: Da Capo, 1960), 50; Ron Riddle, "A Look Back at Lenox," *Jazz: A Quarterly of American Music* 1 (October 1958): 29–32.

15. Charles Suber, "Jazz Education," 369–72; Henry Pleasants, *Serious Music—and All That Jazz* (New York: Simon and Schuster, 1969), 123–27.

16. Dave Baker, "Jazz: The Academy's Neglected Stepchild," *Down Beat* 32 (September 23, 1965): 29–32. See also David Baker, "The Battle for Legitimacy: 'Jazz' Versus Academia," *Black World* 23 (November 1973): 20–27.

17. Alexander Astin et al., "Overview of the Unrest Era," in *The History of Higher Education*, 724–38; Hall and Kevles, "Democratizing the Curriculum," 39–40; Cowley and Williams, *International and Historical Roots of American Higher Education*, 196.

18. Sources on the establishment of Black Studies programs in higher education include Alphonso Pinckney, *Red, Black, and Green: Black Nationalism in the United States* (Cambridge: Cambridge University Press, 1976), 177–203; William L. Van Deburg, *New Day in Babylon: The Black Power Movement and American Culture, 1965–1975* (Chicago: University of Chicago Press, 1992), 65–75; Theodore Draper, *The Rediscovery of Black Nationalism* (New York: Viking, 1970), 148–66; Donald M. Henderson, "Black Student Protest in White Universities," in *Black America*, ed. John Szwed (New York: Basic, 1970), 256–70. Van Deburg reported a survey by the American Council on Education, which stated that 57 percent of all campus protests between 1968 and 1969 involved African American students, despite their accounting for less than 6 percent of the total college population (67).

19. Data on the proportion of colleges that offered courses in African American Studies in 1970 comes from Rhoda Goldstein et al., "The Status of Black Studies Programs at American Colleges and Universities," paper presented at the American Sociological Association, 1972, quoted in Pinckney, *Red, Black, and Green*, 186–87. On the increase in African American student enrollment, see Van Deburg, *New Day in Babylon*, 67; Nathan Hare, "Questions and Answers about Black Studies," in *Modern Black Nationalism: From Marcus Garvey to Louis Farrakhan*, ed. William L. Van Deburg (New York: New York University Press, 1997), 160–63.

20. LeRoi Jones [Amiri Baraka] and Larry Neal, eds., *Black Fire: An Anthology of Afro-American Writing* (New York: William Morrow, 1968). For an assessment of the critical importance of this text to Black Studies, see Norman Harris, "Larry Neal," in *Afro-American Writers After 1955: Dramatists and Prose Writers*, ed. Thadious M. Davis and Trudier Harris (Detroit: Gale, 1985), 227–28. Addison Gayle, Jr., ed., *The Black Aesthetic* (Garden City, N.Y.: Doubleday, 1971).

21. Bret Primack, "Archie Shepp: Back to Schooldays," *Down Beat* 45 (December 21, 1978): 60; Michael Patterson, "Archie Shepp," *Black World* 23 (November 1973): 58–61; David N. Baker, Lida M. Belt, and Herman C. Hudson, eds., *The Black Composer Speaks* (Metuchen, N.J.: Scarecrow, 1978), 290; John Runcie, "Max Roach: Militant Black Artist," *Jazz Journal International* 33 (May 1980): 20–21.

22. Primack, "Archie Shepp," 60; Roland Baggenaes, "Jackie McLean," *Coda* 11 (January 1974): 2–3; Herb Nolan, "Jackie McLean: The Connection Between Today and Yesterday," *Down Beat* 42 (April 1975): 11, 32; Richard Brown, "Ah! Unh! Mr. Funk!" *Down Beat* 46 (October 1979): 22–23; Marion Brown, *Recollections* (Frankfurt: Jürgen A. Schmitt, 1983), see introduction by Dr. Maceo Crenshaw Daley, Jr., 15–25.

23. Bill Dixon, "To Whom It May Concern," *Coda* 8 (October 1967): 2–10; Jack Anderson, "Judith Dunn and the Endless Quest," *Dance Magazine* 41 (November 1967): 48–51; Roger Riggins, "Professor Bill Dixon: Intents of an Innovator," *Down Beat* 47 (August 1980): 30–32.

24. On the circumstances surrounding Cecil Taylor's appointments at the University of Wisconsin-Madison and Antioch College, Ohio, see John Litweiler, "Needs and Acts: Cecil Taylor in Wisconsin," *Down Beat* 38 (October 1971): 16–17, 40. On the role of African American students in initiating the process that

brought Taylor to Antioch, see Lloyd to Klein, November 19, 1968, folder 2706, box 287, series 200R, RG 1.2, Rockefeller Foundation Archives, RAC. During the Spring 1971 semester, Sun Ra lectured for the Department of Afro-American Studies at the University of California-Berkeley and taught a Master's class at San Francisco State College. John F. Szwed, *Space Is the Place: The Lives and Times of Sun Ra* (New York: Pantheon, 1997), 294–95, 329.

25. Valerie Wilmer, *As Serious as Your Life: The Story of the New Jazz* (Westport, Conn.: Lawrence Hill, 1980), 241–43.

26. Jerry Coker, *Improvising Jazz* (New York: Simon and Schuster, 1964); Jamey Aebersold, *A New Approach to Jazz Improvisation*, multiple vols. (New Albany, Ind.: Jamey Aebersold, 1967–); David Baker, *Jazz Improvisation: A Comprehensive Method of Study for All Players* (Chicago: Maher, 1969); David Ake, *Jazz Cultures* (Berkeley: University of California Press, 2002), 112–45.

27. David N. Baker, *Jazz Pedagogy: A Comprehensive Method of Jazz Education for Teacher and Student*, 2nd ed. (Chicago: Maher, 1981), 19, 26, 52, 75, 84–92.

28. Paul J. DiMaggio, "The Nonprofit Instrument and the Influence of the Marketplace on Policies in the Arts," in *The Arts and Public Policy in the United States*, ed. American Assembly (Englewood Cliffs, N.J.: Prentice-Hall, 1984), 57–58. According to data gathered by Yale economist J. Michael Montias in the early 1970s, earned income represented 54 percent of all revenue for a sample of U.S. nonprofit performing arts agencies. The proportion of total revenues derived from earned income was much lower in most European countries, including Austria (23.2 percent), France (31.9 percent), Germany (17.8 percent), and Sweden (10.5 percent).

29. Paul J. DiMaggio, "Cultural Entrepreneurship in Nineteenth-Century Boston," in *Nonprofit Enterprise in the Arts: Studies in Mission and Constraint* (New York: Oxford University Press, 1986), 41–61; see also "Introduction," 12.

30. Milton C. Cummings, Jr., "To Change a Nation's Cultural Policy: The Kennedy Administration and the Arts in the United States, 1961–1963," in *America's Commitment to Culture: Government and the Arts*, ed. Margaret Jane Wyszomirski and Kevin V. Mulcahy (Boulder, Colo.: Westview, 1995), 95–120; Margaret Jane Wyszomirski, "The Politics of Arts Policy: Subgovernment to Issue Network," in *America's Commitment to Culture*, 50–51; Elaine A. King, "The National Endowment for the Arts: A Misunderstood Patron," in *Writings About Art*, ed. Carole Gold Calo (Englewood Cliffs, N.J.: Prentice-Hall, 1994), 361–62.

31. Margaret Jane Wyszomirski and Kevin V. Mulcahy, "The Organization of Public Support for the Arts," in *America's Commitment to Culture*, 122–23, 126, 132–34.

32. Wyszomirski, "The Politics of Arts Policy," 51–53.

33. David B. Pankratz and Carla Hanzal, "Leadership and the NEA: The Roles of the Chairperson and the National Council on the Arts," in *America's Commitment to Culture*, 152. See also Edward W. Arian, "The Unfulfilled Promise of Arts Subsidy in a Multicultural Society," in *Culture and Democracy: Social and Ethical Issues in Public Support for the Arts and Humanities*, ed. Andrew Buchwalter (Boulder: Westview, 1992), 65.

34. King, "The National Endowment for the Arts," 362; Wyszomirski, "The Politics of Arts Policy," 53–55; American Association of Fund-Raising Counsel, *Giving USA 1973*, 46; American Association of Fund-Raising Counsel, *Giving USA 1977* (New York: AAFC, 1977), 42.

35. Unless noted otherwise, the amounts and recipients of awards, panel memberships, and program and section budgets are taken from National

Endowment for the Arts and National Council on the Arts, annual reports, 1968–1980. The date of each report reflected appropriations and expenditures for that fiscal year.

36. National Endowment for the Arts and National Council on the Arts Annual Report 1970, 33–34.

37. Between 1970 and 1974 the NEA awarded individual fellowships to at least twenty-five musicians who used free improvisation regularly: Muhal Richard Abrams, Rashied Ali, Ed Blackwell, Carla Bley, Lester Bowie, Marion Brown, Dave Burrell, Kalaparusha Ahrah Difda (then Maurice McIntyre), Malachi Favors, Milford Graves, Charlie Haden, Joseph Jarman, Leroy Jenkins, Oliver Lake, Roscoe Mitchell, Grachan Moncur III, Don Moye, Claudine Myers, Dewey Redman, Sam Rivers, Roswell Rudd, Leo Smith, Henry Threadgill, Clifford Thornton, and Carlos Ward. The frequency of awards—and repeat awards—to free improvisers increased during the middle and late 1970s.

38. Information on funding for jazz projects outside the standard music section categories appears in a statement by former NEA Chairman Frank Hodsell in *New Perspectives on Jazz*, ed. David N. Baker (Washington, D.C.: Smithsonian Institution, 1990), xiv–xv. In order to circumvent the limited jazz budget during the early 1970s, Music Program Director Walter F. Anderson appropriated money from the Treasury Fund when he could find a matching donor. In order to sponsor Cecil Taylor's first-year residency at Antioch College, where Anderson still taught, he secured $49,000 from general music program monies after receiving pledges of matching funds from the Rockefeller Foundation and Antioch College. Anderson to Lloyd, April 3, 1970, folder 2706, box 287, series 200R, RG 1.2, Rockefeller Foundation Archives, RAC.

39. Arian, "The Unfulfilled Promise of Public Arts Subsidy," 65.

40. Ronald Berman, "Art Versus the Arts," in *Public Policy and the Aesthetic Interest*, ed. Ralph A. Smith and Ronald Berman (Urbana: University of Illinois Press, 1992), 105–8. Some creative artists continue to employ this rationale to support public funding for the arts. Presenting the Nancy Hanks Lecture on Art and Public Policy on March 20, 1990, Maya Angelou told an audience at the Washington, D.C., Departmental Auditorium: "We must infuse our lives with art. Our national leaders must be informed that we want them to use our taxes to support street theater in order to oppose street gangs. We should have a well-supported regional theater in order to oppose regionalism and differences which keep us apart." Maya Angelou, "Arts and Public Policy," in *Culture and Democracy*, ed. Buchwalter, 35.

41. Margaret J. Wyszomirski, "Controversies in Arts Policymaking," in *Public Policy and the Arts*, ed. Kevin V. Mulcahy and C. Richard Swaim (Boulder, Colo.: Westview, 1982), 13–14, 23–24.

42. Samuel Lipman, "The State of National Cultural Policy," in *Culture and Democracy*, 51–53; Berman, "Art Versus the Arts," 110; Kevin V. Mulcahy, "The Rationale for Public Culture," in *Public Policy and the Arts*, 48–53. Despite the NEA's considerable efforts to democratize the arts, Mulcahy found that throughout the 1970s audiences for the performing arts and museums remained more wealthy, educated, and professional than the population at large. He based this conclusion upon an independent evaluation commissioned by the Research Division of the NEA in 1978, which examined 270 audience studies (38–41).

43. National Endowment for the Arts and National Council on the Arts, Annual Report 1975, 5.

44. Carmen Subryan, "A. B. Spellman," in *Afro-American Poets Since 1955*, ed.

Trudier Harris and Thadious M. Davis (Detroit: Gale, 1985), 312. A detailed examination of the battle between cultural nationalists and established arts bodies in Washington, D.C. for control of public funds between 1968 and 1976, and the Commission's funding problems, appears in D.C. Commission on the Arts and Humanities, "Transitions Report II," January 23, 1979, i–xi, Larry Neal Papers, 1961–1985, box 29, file 6, Schomburg Center for Research in Black Culture, New York. For background on the political context of the Commission's work, see Ronald L. Sharps, "Arts Commission Faces Tough Review," *Artlink* (Spring 1979): 7, Larry Neal Papers, box 30, file 6.

45. National Endowment for the Arts and National Council on the Arts, Annual Report 1971, 57.

46. Margaret Jane Wyszomirski, "From Accord to Discord: Arts Policy During and After the Culture Wars," in *America's Commitment to Culture*, ed. Wyszomirski and Mulcahy, 26. See also Kevin V, Mulcahy, "Government and the Arts in the United States," in *Public Policy and the Aesthetic Interest*, ed. Smith and Berman, 16–17.

47. For more on the Orchestra's operation as a nonprofit entity, see "The Jazz Composer's Orchestra," *Jazz Monthly* (July 1968): 6–8; "Jazz Composer's Band to Issue Own Albums," *Down Beat* 35 (August 8, 1968): 11; Elisabeth van der Mei, "The Jazz Composers Orchestra," *Coda* 8 (November–December 1968): 2–11; "Service Set to Spur Avant-Garde Jazz," *Billboard* (July 1, 1972): 3. NEA Grants are listed in the NEA and NCA Annual Reports of 1970, 1971, 1972, 1975, and 1976.

48. For more on the origins and functions of Collective Black Artists, see Diane Weathers, "The CBA: A Grass Roots Movement," *Black Creation* (Fall 1973): 34; Diane Weathers, "The Collective Black Artists," *Black World* 23 (November 1973): 74–77. Details of grants made to the CBA appear in the Institute of Jazz Studies Manuscript Collection, Reggie Workman: Collective Black Artists, Box 1, and in the NEA and NCA Annual Report 1979, 59, 197.

49. Paul J. DiMaggio, "Support for the Arts From Independent Foundations," in *Nonprofit Enterprise in the Arts*, 136–37.

50. W. McNeil Lowry, "Introduction," in *The Arts and Public Policy*, 10–12, 16; American Association of Fund-Raising Counsel, *Giving USA 1968* (New York: AAFC, 1968), 52–53; Paul J. DiMaggio, "Support for the Arts From Independent Foundations," 114–18. The 1930 figure excludes donations from the Julliard Foundation to its own musical academy and the Rockefeller Foundation's support of "the industrial arts" through its General Education Board.

51. American Association of Fund-Raising Counsel, *Giving USA 1973* (New York: AAFC, 1973), 43.

52. "The New Jazz," *Newsweek* 68 (December 12, 1966): 104.

53. Ford Foundation Annual Report 1973, 46–48; Henry Pleasants, *Serious Music—And All That Jazz* (New York: Simon and Schuster, 1969), 129.

54. Andrew W. Mellon Foundation Annual Report 1973, 25.

55. For background on the rise of community foundations, see Peter Dobkin Hall, "The Community Foundation in America, 1914–1987," in *Philanthropic Giving: Studies in Varieties and Goals*, ed. Richard Magat (New York: Oxford University Press, 1989), 180–99. Amounts and recipients of grants taken from a search of the Foundation Center Database 1997. Further information available online at http://fdncenter.org/.

56. John Litweiler, *Ornette Coleman: A Harmolodic Life* (New York: Da Capo,

1992), 123–25; Wilmer, *As Serious as Your Life,* 247. List of Fellows in Music Composition provided by the John Simon Guggenheim Memorial Foundation.

57. Information on MacArthur Prize Fellows Program taken from the John D. and Catherine T. MacArthur Foundation, Report on Activities 1980 and 1981, and subsequent annual reports between 1982 and 1987. Supplementary information from Mitch Meyers, "Blindfold Test: Ken Vandermark," *Down Beat* 67 (April 2000): 86.

58. Freund to Kunst, December 2, 1963, folder entitled "Ja-Je to Ke," microfilm reel 19, series 200, RG 2, Rockefeller Foundation Archives, RAC; Klein to Lloyd, November 19, 1968, Howard Klein, "Antioch College Visit," January 18–20, 1969, 1, 5–6, folder 2706, box 287, series 200R, RG 1.2, Rockefeller Foundation Archives, RAC.

59. "Guggenheim to Mingus; Protest at Foundation," *Down Beat* 38 (May 27, 1971): 8; Robert Levin, "The Third World," *Jazz & Pop* (June 1971): 10–11; David N. Baker, Lida M. Belt, and Herman C. Hudson, eds., *The Black Composer Speaks* (Metuchen, N.J.: Scarecrow, 1978), 294–95.

60. Rockefeller officials worried constantly, however, that students affiliated with the Afro-American Studies Institute—which briefly won separatist status within the College—might "capture" the project and undermine interracial cooperation. Howard Klein, "Antioch College Visit," January 18–20, 1969, 4, Klein to Lloyd, July 11, 1969, Lloyd to Klein, March 11, 1970, Klein to Lloyd, April 2, 1970, folder 2706, box 287, series 200R, RG 1.2, Rockefeller Foundation Archives, RAC.

61. Jerome L. Himmelstein, *Looking Good and Doing Good: Corporate Philanthropy and Corporate Power* (Bloomington: Indiana University Press, 1997), 16–23; American Association of Fund-Raising Counsel, *Giving USA 1974* (New York: AAFC, 1974), 48–49.

62. On the motives and patterns of corporate philanthropy, see Michael Useem and Stephen I. Kutner, "Corporate Contributions to Culture and the Arts: The Organization of Giving and the Influence of the Chief Executive Officer and of Other Firms on Company Contributions in Massachusetts," in *Nonprofit Enterprise in the Arts,* 93–112; Peter Dobkin Hall, "Business Giving and Social Investment in the United States," in *Philanthropic Giving,* 221–45; Joseph Galaskiewicz, "Corporate Contributions to Charity: Nothing More than a Marketing Strategy?" in *Philanthropic Giving,* 246–60; Jerome L. Himmelstein, *Looking Good and Doing Good,* 3–6, 14–15, 24–32, 144–45.

63. Quoted in Ted Gioia, *The History of Jazz* (New York: Oxford University Press, 1997), 350.

64. Institute of Jazz Studies Manuscript Collection, Reggie Workman: Collective Black Artists, Box 1; Diane Weathers, "The CBA: A Grass Roots Movement," 34.

65. Krin Gabbard, "The Jazz Canon and Its Consequences," in *Jazz Among the Discourses* (Durham, N.C.: Duke University Press, 1995), 1.

66. Charles Suber, "Introduction," in David Baker, *Jazz Pedagogy,* vi–vii; J. F. Gould, "The Jazz History Course: An Update," *Jazz Educators Journal* (December 1981): 15, 61.

67. Horace M. Newcomb, "On the Dialogic Aspects of Mass Communication," Linda Steiner, "Oppositional Decoding as an Act of Resistance," and John Fiske, "Television: Polysemy and Popularity," in *Critical Perspectives on Media*

and Society, ed. Robert K. Avery and David Eason (New York: Guilford, 1991), 69–85, 329–43, 346–62.

Epilogue

1. Chords and Discords," *Down Beat* 29 (February 1, 1962): 9; "Chords and Discords," *Down Beat* 30 (November 21, 1963): 6.

2. Lewis Porter and Michael Ullman with Ed Hazell, *Jazz: From Its Origins to the Present* (Englewood Cliffs, N.J.: Prentice-Hall, 1991), 377–93. See also Gary Tomlinson's analysis of the critical reaction to Miles Davis's pioneer fusion albums *In a Silent Way* and *Bitches Brew,* in "Cultural Dialogics and Jazz: A White Historian Signifies," *Black Music Research Journal* 11 (Fall 1991): 249–53.

3. Francis Davis, "Struggling with Some Barbeque," *Village Voice* [July 21, 1987], Martin Williams file, Institute of Jazz Studies, Rutgers University, Newark, N.J. The Smithsonian Institution later issued other collections of "classic" jazz recordings, including sets dedicated to big bands, jazz singers, and Duke Ellington.

4. Paul Erickson, "Black and White, Black and Blue: The Controversy over the Jazz Series at Lincoln Center," *Jazz and American Culture* 2 (Summer 1997) [on-line journal, 1–5]; Grover Sales, *Jazz: America's Classical Music* (Englewood Cliffs, N.J.: Prentice-Hall, 1984); William "Billy" Taylor, "Jazz: America's Classical Music," in *Keeping Time: Readings in Jazz History,* ed. Robert Walser (New York: Oxford University Press, 1999), 327–32; David Hajdu, "Wynton's Blues," *Atlantic Monthly* 291 (March 2003): 54–55; Dan Ouellette, "Next Chapter," *Down Beat* 71 (April 2004): 38.

5. Walser, ed., *Keeping Time,* 327.

6. Scott DeVeaux, "Constructing the Jazz Tradition: Jazz Historiography," *Black American Literature Forum* 25 (Fall 1991): 549–51.

7. Frank Conroy, "Stop Nitpicking a Genius," *New York Times Magazine* (June 25, 1995): 30.

8. Martin Williams, *Smithsonian Collection of Classic Jazz,* rev. ed. [accompanying booklet] (Washington, D.C.: Smithsonian Institution, 1987), 26, 90; Martin Williams, "How Long Has This Been Going On?" in *Jazz in Its Time* (New York: Oxford University Press, 1989), 56.

9. Herman S. Gray, *Cultural Moves: African Americans and the Politics of Representation* (Berkeley: University of California Press, 2005), 32–51; Wynton Marsalis, "What Jazz Is—and Isn't," *New York Times* (July 31, 1988) Arts and Leisure: 21, 24; Ouellette, "Next Chapter," 38–40; Erickson, "Black and White" [5–6]. A series of promotional postcards circulated with a fundraising letter in 2005 by Jazz at Lincoln Center identified the music's characteristics as "swing," "groove," "blues form," and "improvisation," defining the latter as "making up music in the movement of performance by playing with the original theme of the song using an established set of chords in a progression." The confinement of improvisation to themes and chord progressions illustrates the neoclassicists' supplanting of the language of continuous innovation with an emphasis on discipline and rules. Wynton Marsalis fundraising letter, February 15, 2005, author's copy.

10. *Jazz,* dir. Ken Burns, Florentine Films, 2000, 10 DVDs; David Hajdu, "Not Quite All That Jazz," *New York Review of Books* (February 8, 2001): 31–33; Francis Davis, *Like Young: Jazz and Pop, Youth and Middle Age* (New York: Da Capo, 2001), 206–16; "Watching 'Jazz' for Its High Notes and Low," *New York Times* (January

7, 2001) Arts and Leisure: 33. Mark Gridley, Robert Maxham, and Robert Hoff offer these contrasting definitions of jazz in "Three Approaches to Defining Jazz," in *Jazz: A Century of Change*, ed. Lewis Porter (New York: Schirmer, 1997), 18–36.

11. Ronald M. Radano, *New Musical Figurations: Anthony Braxton's Cultural Critique* (Chicago: University of Chicago Press, 1993), 270–73.

12. Howard Mandel, "Ornette Coleman: Jazz Artist of the Year," *Down Beat* 65 (August 1998): 48; Ouellette, "Next Chapter," 38.

13. Taylor, "Jazz: America's Classical Music," in *Keeping Time*, 328–29.

14. H. Con. Res. 57, reproduced in *Keeping Time*, 332–33.

15. Thomas Sancton, "Horns of Plenty," *Time* 136 (October 22, 1990): 70; Eric Porter, *What Is This Thing Called Jazz? African American Musicians as Artists, Critics, and Activists* (Berkeley: University of California Press, 2002), 287–334; Gray, *Cultural Moves*, 33, 37. Sherrie Tucker's comments appear in "A Roundtable on Ken Burns's Jazz," moderated by Geoffrey Jacques, *Journal of Popular Music Studies* 13 (Fall 2001): 220–23.

16. William L. Van Deburg, *New Day in Babylon: The Black Power Movement and American Culture, 1965–1975* (Chicago: University of Chicago Press, 1992), 297–98.

17. Joanne Gabbin, "Askia Muhammad Touré (Rolland Snellings)," in *Afro-American Poets Since 1955*, ed. Trudier Harris and Thadious M. Davis (Detroit: Gale, 1985), 331.

18. Abraham Chapman, introduction to *New Black Voices: An Anthology of Afro-American Literature* (New York: Mentor, 1972), 30–31.

19. Van Deburg, *New Day in Babylon*, 301; Ameer [sic] Baraka, "Black Nationalism vs Pimp Art," *Rhythm* 1 (1970): 11. Baraka's voice is missing from Ken Burns's film.

20. Michael Eric Dyson, "Malcolm X and the Revival of Black Nationalism," in *The Politics of Race: African Americans and the Political System*, ed. Theodore Rueter (Armonk, N.Y.: M.E. Sharpe, 1995), 73; Erickson, "Black and White" [4, 6]; Gray, *Cultural Moves*, 37.

21. Whitney Balliett, "Wynton Looks Back," *New Yorker* (October 14, 1991): 100; John Ephland, "Jazz History Course," *Down Beat* 60 (November 1993): 6; Erickson, "Black and White" [6].

22. Erickson, "Black and White" [7–9].

Bibliography

Collections

Center for Black Music Research, Columbia College, Chicago.
Chicago Historical Society, General Collection.
Dorn Manuscript Collection, Lilly Library, Bloomington, Ind.
Duke Ellington Collection, National Museum of American History, Smithsonian Institution, Washington, D.C.
The Foundation Center Collection, Ruth Lilly Special Collections and Archives, University Library, Indiana University and Purdue University at Indianapolis.
Institute of Jazz Studies, Rutgers University, Newark, N.J.
Jazz Institute of Chicago Don DeMicheal Collection, Chicago Jazz Archive, University of Chicago Library.
Rockefeller Archive Center, Sleepy Hollow, N.Y.
Schomburg Center for Research in Black Culture, New York, N.Y.

Unpublished Interviews

Anderson, Iain. Interview with Bill Dixon, New York, August 9, 1995.
————. Interview with Dan Morgenstern, Newark, N.J., August 10, 1995.
Figi, J. B. Interview with Phil Cohran, August 14, 1990.
————. Interview with Donald Rafael Garrett, December 7, 1981.
————. Interview with Joe Segal, August 22, 1990.
Litweiler, John. Interview with Fred Anderson, August 7, 1990.
————. Interview with Joseph Jarman, November 4, 1981.

Liner Notes

Avakian, George. "1956–1996: A Fond Reminiscence." Liner notes for Gunther Schuller et al., *The Birth of the Third Stream*. Columbia/Legacy CK 64929, 1996.
Campbell, Robert L. "The Saturn Singles in Historical Perspective." Liner notes for Sun Ra, *The Singles*. Evidence ECD 22164–2, 1996.
Coleman, Ornette. Liner notes for *Change of the Century*. Atlantic 1327, 1959.
Hentoff, Nat. Liner notes for Ornette Coleman, *Something Else! The Music of Ornette Coleman*. Contemporary C-3531, 1958.
————. Liner notes for Ornette Coleman, *Tomorrow Is the Question!* Contemporary M-3569, 1959.
Stern, Chip. Liner notes for Dave Brubeck et al., *The Real Ambassadors*. Columbia/Legacy CK 64929, 1996.

Welding, Peter. Liner notes for Miles Davis, *Birth of the Cool.* Capitol D-154138, 1989.

Wild, David. Liner notes for John Coltrane Quartet, *The Complete Africa/Brass Sessions.* Impulse! IMPD-2–168, 1995.

Williams, Martin. Liner notes for Ornette Coleman, *The Shape of Jazz to Come.* Atlantic 1317, 1959.

———. Liner notes for Ornette Coleman Double Quartet, *Free Jazz.* Atlantic 1364, 1960.

Selected Sound Recordings (date of issue listed)

Abrams, Muhal Richard. *Levels and Degrees of Light.* Delmark 413, 1967.

Adderley, Nat. *Work Song.* Riverside 1167, 1960.

Art Ensemble of Chicago. *Certain Blacks.* Inner City 1004, 1970.

Ayler, Albert. *Bells.* ESP 1010, 1965.

———. *New York Ear and Eye Control.* ESP 1016, 1964.

———. *Spiritual Unity.* ESP 1002, 1964.

Braxton, Anthony. *For Alto Saxophone.* Delmark 420–421, 1968.

Brubeck, Dave. *Jazz at the College of the Pacific.* Fantasy 047, 1953.

———. *Time Out.* Columbia/Legacy CK 57663, 1992 [1959].

Brubeck, Dave et al. *The Real Ambassadors.* Columbia/Legacy CK 57663, 1994 [1962].

Charles, Teddy and Shorty Rogers. *Collaboration: West.* Prestige 7028, 1992 [1953].

Coleman, Ornette. *At the Golden Circle in Stockholm-Volume One.* Blue Note 84224, 1965.

———. *Dancing in Your Head.* A&M 0807, 1973.

———. *Free Jazz.* Atlantic 1364, 1960.

———. *Ornette on Tenor.* Atlantic 1394, 1962.

———. *The Shape of Jazz to Come.* Atlantic 1317, 1959.

———. *Something Else! The Music of Ornette Coleman.* Contemporary 3531, 1958.

———. *This Is Our Music.* Atlantic 1353, 1960.

Coltrane, John. *Ascension.* Impulse! AS-95, 1965.

———. *The Avant Garde.* Atlantic 90041, 1966.

———. *Blue Train.* Blue Note 46095, 1957.

———. *The Complete Africa/Brass Sessions.* Impulse! IMPD-2–168, 1995 [1961].

———. *Crescent.* Impulse! AS-66, 1964.

———. *Giant Steps.* Atlantic 1311, 1959.

———. *Live at the Village Vanguard.* Impulse! AS-10, 1961.

———. *A Love Supreme.* MCA 5660, 1986 [1964].

———. *Meditations.* Impulse! AS-9110, 1966.

———. *My Favorite Things.* Atlantic 1361, 1960.

Davis, Miles. *Birth of the Cool.* Capitol 154138, 1989 [1949].

———. *Bitches Brew.* Columbia 40577, 1969.

———. *Kind of Blue.* Columbia/Legacy CK 64935, 1997 [1959].

———. *Sketches of Spain.* Columbia 40578, 1960.

Dixon, Bill. *In Italy—Volume One.* Soul Note 121008, 1980.

Dolphy, Eric. *Out to Lunch.* Blue Note 46524, 1987 [1964].

———. *Outward Bound.* New Jazz 022, 1960.

Ellington, Duke. *Ellington at Newport.* Columbia 40587, 1956.

Gillespie, Dizzy. *Birks Works: The Verve Big-Band Sessions.* Verve 314527 900–2, 1995 [1956–1957].

Hancock, Herbie. *Headhunters.* Columbia 47478, 1973.

Jazz at the Philharmonic. *The First Concert.* Verve 314521 646-2, 1994 [1944].

Marsalis, Wynton. *Think of One.* Columbia 38641, 1983.

McLean, Jackie. *Destination Out.* Blue Note 4165, 1963.

———. *Let Freedom Ring.* Blue Note 46527, 1962.

Mingus, Charles. *The Black Saint and the Sinner Lady.* Impulse! IMPD-174, 1998 [1963].

———. *Mingus Ah Um.* Columbia 40648, 1959.

———. *Mingus at Antibes.* Atlantic 90532, 1960.

Mitchell, Roscoe. *Sound.* Delmark 408, 1966.

Modern Jazz Quartet. *Pyramid.* Atlantic 1325, 1960.

Mulligan, Gerry. *Gerry Mulligan Quartet/Chubby Jackson Big Band.* Fantasy 711–2, 1992 [1950–1953].

Roach, Max. *Freedom Now Suite.* Columbia 36390, 1960.

Rollins, Sonny. *Freedom Suite.* Riverside RLP 258, 1983 [1958].

———. *On the Outside.* Bluebird 2179–2, 1962.

———. *Saxophone Colossus.* Prestige 291–2, 1987 [1956].

Russell, George. *Ezz-thetics.* Riverside RLP 9375, 1992 [1962].

Schuller, Gunther, et al. *The Birth of the Third Stream.* Columbia/Legacy CK 64929, 1996 [1956–1957].

Shepp, Archie. *Four For Trane.* Impulse! 71, 1964.

———. *New Thing at Newport.* Impulse! 97, 1965.

———. *On This Night.* Impulse! GRD-125, 1993 [1966].

Smithsonian Collection of Classic Jazz. Volumes One to Five. Smithsonian Institution, RD 033–1 to 033–5, 1987.

Sun Ra. *The Futuristic Sounds of Sun Ra.* Savoy 0213, 1993 [1961].

———. *Holiday for Soul Dance.* Evidence 22011, 1969.

———. *Nothing Is.* ESP 1045–2, 1966.

———. *The Singles.* Evidence ECD 22164–2, 1996.

Taylor, Cecil. *Conquistador.* Blue Note 84260, 1989 [1966].

———. *Jazz Advance.* Blue Note 84462, 1991 [1956].

———. *Looking Ahead.* Contemporary 452, 1958.

———. *Three Phasis.* New World 303, 1978.

———. *Unit Structures.* Blue Note 84237, 1966.

Taylor, Cecil, and Buell Neidlinger. *New York City R&B.* Candid 79017, 1971.

Timmons, Bobby. *This Here Is Bobby Timmons.* Riverside VDJ-1529, 1985 [1960].

Weather Report. *Night Passage.* ARC/Columbia CK 36793, 1980.

Selected Secondary Bibliography

Ake, David. *Jazz Cultures.* Berkeley: University of California Press, 2002.

Austin, Larry. "Jazz in Higher Education." *Jazz: A Quarterly of American Music* 3 (Summer 1959): 243–53.

Avery, Robert K. and David Eason, eds. *Critical Perspectives on Media and Society.* New York: Guilford, 1991.

Backus, Rob. *Fire Music: A Political History of Jazz.* Chicago: Vanguard, 1976.

Baker, David N., ed. *New Perspectives on Jazz.* Washington, D.C.: Smithsonian Institution, 1990.

Balliett, Whitney. "Abstract." *New Yorker* 37 (October 21, 1961): 168–72.

———. "Abstract (Continued)." *New Yorker* 37 (October 28, 1961): 164–68.

———. *The Sound of Surprise: 46 Pieces on Jazz.* New York: Da Capo, 1978.

Baraka, Amiri. *The Autobiography of LeRoi Jones.* Rev. ed. Chicago: Lawrence Hill, 1997. [See also entries under Jones, LeRoi]

Barzun, Jacques. "America's Passion for Culture." *Harper's* 208 (March 1954): 40–47.

Bayles, Martha. *Hole in Our Soul: The Loss of Beauty and Meaning in American Popular Music.* New York: Free Press, 1994.

Belair, Felix. "United States Has Secret Sonic Weapon-Jazz." *New York Times* (November 6, 1955): 1, 42.

Belgrad, Daniel. *The Culture of Spontaneity: Improvisation and the Arts in Postwar America.* Chicago: University of Chicago Press, 1998.

Benston, Kimberly W. *Baraka: The Renegade and the Mask.* New Haven, Conn.: Yale University Press, 1976.

Bourdieu, Pierre. *Distinction: A Social Critique of the Judgement of Taste.* Trans. Richard Nice. Cambridge, Mass.: Harvard University Press, 1984.

Brands, H. W. *The Devil We Knew: Americans and the Cold War.* New York: Oxford University Press, 1993.

Brown, Lloyd W. *Amiri Baraka.* Boston: Twayne, 1980.

Brown, Marion. *Recollections.* Frankfurt: Jürgen A. Schmitt, 1983.

Buchwalter, Andrew, ed. *Culture and Democracy: Social and Ethical Issues in Public Support for the Arts and Humanities.* Boulder, Colo.: Westview, 1992.

Budds, Michael. *Jazz in the Sixties: The Expansion of Musical Resources and Techniques.* Iowa City: University of Iowa Press, 1990.

Bürger, Peter. *Theory of the Avant-Garde.* Trans. Michael Shaw. Minneapolis: University of Minnesota Press, 1984.

Cage, John. "The Future of Music: Credo." In *Silence: Lectures and Writings.* Cambridge, Mass.: MIT Press, 1961.

Calinescu, Matei. *Five Faces of Modernity: Modernism, Avant-Garde, Decadence, Kitsch, Postmodernism.* Rev. ed. Durham, N.C.: Duke University Press, 1987.

Carr, Ian. *Miles Davis: A Critical Biography.* New York: Quartet, 1982.

Carson, Clayborne. *In Struggle: SNCC and the Black Awakening of the 1960s.* Cambridge, Mass.: Harvard University Press, 1981.

Chapple, Steve, and Reebee Garofalo. *Rock 'N' Roll is Here to Pay: The History and Politics of the Music Industry.* Chicago: Nelson-Hall, 1997.

Collier, James Lincoln. *Jazz: The American Theme Song.* New York: Oxford University Press, 1993.

———. *The Reception of Jazz in America: A New View.* New York: Oxford University Press, 1987.

Cowley, W. C., and Don Williams. *International and Historical Roots of American Higher Education.* New York: Garland, 1991.

Cruse, Harold. "An Afro-American's Cultural Views." In *Rebellion or Revolution?* New York: William Morrow, 1968.

———. *The Crisis of the Negro Intellectual.* New York: William Morrow, 1967.

Dance, Stanley. *The World of Duke Ellington.* New York: Da Capo, 1970.

Dates, Janette L. and William Barlow, eds. *Split Image: African-Americans in the Mass Media.* Washington, D.C: Howard University Press, 1990.

Dawson, Michael C. *Behind the Mule: Race and Class in African-American Politics.* Princeton, N.J.: Princeton University Press, 1994.

———. "A Black Counterpublic? Economic Earthquakes, Racial Agenda(s), and Black Politics." *Public Culture* 7 (Fall 1994): 195–213.

DeMicheal, Don. "Jazz in Government [part I]." *Down Beat* 30 (January 17, 1963): 15–17, 45.

———. "Jazz in Government, part II." *Down Beat* 30 (January 31, 1963): 19–20.

———. "John Coltrane and Eric Dolphy Answer the Jazz Critics." *Down Beat* 29 (April 12, 1962): 20–23.

———. "On the Problem of Fork-Moving." *Down Beat* 28 (May 11, 1961): 13–14.

DeVeaux, Scott. *The Birth of Bebop: A Social and Musical History.* Berkeley: University of California Press, 1997.

———. "Constructing the Jazz Tradition: Jazz Historiography." *Black American Literature Forum* 25 (Fall 1991): 525–60.

———. *Jazz in America: Who's Listening?* Carson, Calif.: National Endowment for the Arts/Seven Locks Press, 1995.

Diggins, John P. *The Proud Decades: America in War and Peace.* New York: W.W. Norton, 1988.

DiLugoff, Art. "'Experimentation' in Public: The Clubowner's Point of View." *Down Beat* 32 (April 8, 1965): 14–15.

DiMaggio, Paul J., ed. *Nonprofit Enterprise in the Arts: Studies in Mission and Constraint.* New York: Oxford University Press, 1986.

———. "The Nonprofit Instrument and the Influence of the Marketplace on Policies in the Arts." In *The Arts and Public Policy in the United States,* ed. American Assembly. Englewood Cliffs, N.J.: Prentice-Hall, 1984.

Dizard, Wilson. *The Strategy of Truth: The Story of the United States Information Service.* Washington, D.C.: Public Affairs Press, 1963.

Draper, Theodore. *The Rediscovery of Black Nationalism.* New York: Viking, 1970.

Dudziak, Mary L. "Desegregation as a Cold War Imperative." *Stanford Law Review* 41 (November 1988): 61–120.

Ellison, Ralph. *Shadow and Act.* New York: Random House, 1964.

Erickson, Paul. "Black and White, Black and Blue: The Controversy over the Jazz Series at Lincoln Center." *Jazz and American Culture* 2 (Summer 1997). On-line journal.

Esman, Aaron. "Jazz—A Study in Cultural Conflict." *American Imago* 8 (June 1951): 219–26.

Feather, Leonard. "Hierarchy of the Jazz Anarchy." *Esquire* (September 1965): 123–25, 187.

———. "Jazz Millionaire." *Esquire* 47 (January 1957): 99–114.

———. "A Plea for Less Critical Infighting, More Attention to the Music Itself." *Down Beat* 32 (December 16, 1965): 13.

Floyd, Samuel A., Jr. *The Power of Black Music: Interpreting Its History From Africa to the United States.* New York: Oxford University Press, 1995.

Foner, Eric. *The Story of American Freedom.* New York: W. W. Norton, 1998.

Fraim, John. *Spirit Catcher: The Life and Art of John Coltrane.* West Liberty, Ohio: Great House, 1996.

Frazier, George. "Blue Notes and Blue Stockings: Impresario Wein and the Newport Jazz Festival." *Esquire* 44 (August 1955): 55–58.

Freeland, Richard M. "The World Transformed: A Golden Age for American Universities, 1945–1970." In *The History of Higher Education Second Edition,* ed. Lester F. Goodchild and Harold S. Wechsler. Needham Heights, Mass.: Simon and Schuster, 1997.

Friedlander, Paul. *Rock and Roll: A Social History.* Boulder, Colo.: Westview, 1996.

Gabbard, Krin. *Jammin' at the Margins: Jazz and American Cinema.* Chicago: University of Chicago Press, 1996.

———. "The Jazz Canon and Its Consequences." In *Jazz Among the Discourses.* Durham, N.C.: Duke University Press, 1995.

Gans, Herbert J. "American Popular Culture and High Culture in a Changing Class Structure." In *Public Policy and the Aesthetic Interest: Critical Essays on Defining Culture and Educational Relations,* ed. Ralph A. Smith and Ronald Berman. Urbana: University of Illinois Press, 1992.

Gayle, Addison, Jr., ed. *The Black Aesthetic.* Garden City, N.Y.: Doubleday, 1971.

Gennari, John. "Jazz Criticism: Its Development and Ideologies." *Black American Literature Forum* 25 (Fall 1991): 449–523.

———. "The Politics of Culture and Identity in American Jazz Criticism." Ph.D. dissertation, University of Pennsylvania, 1993.

George, Nelson. *The Death of Rhythm and Blues.* New York: E.P. Dutton, 1988.

Gerard, Charley. *Jazz in Black and White: Race, Culture, and Identity in the Jazz Community.* Westport, Conn.: Praeger, 1998.

Giddins, Gary. *Satchmo.* New York: Doubleday, 1988.

Gillespie, Dizzy, with Al Fraser. *To Be or Not . . . to Bop.* Garden City, N.Y.: Doubleday, 1979.

Gillespie, Dizzy, with Ralph Ginzburg. "Jazz Is Too Good for Americans." *Esquire* 47 (June 1957): 55, 140–43.

Gioia, Ted. *The Imperfect Art: Reflections on Jazz and Modern Culture.* New York: Oxford University Press, 1988.

———. *West Coast Jazz: Modern Jazz in California, 1945–1960.* New York: Oxford University Press, 1992.

Gleason, Philip. "World War II and the Development of American Studies." *American Quarterly* 36 (September 1984): 341–58.

Goldberg, Joe. *Jazz Masters of the Fifties.* New York: Macmillan, 1965.

Gordon, Robert. *Jazz West Coast: The Los Angeles Jazz Scene of the 1950s.* London: Quartet, 1986.

Gorman, Paul R. *Left Intellectuals and Popular Culture in Twentieth Century America.* Chapel Hill: University of North Carolina Press, 1996.

Gray, Herman S. *Cultural Moves: African Americans and the Politics of Representation.* Berkeley: University of California Press, 2005.

Gray, John, comp. *Fire Music: A Bibliography of the New Jazz, 1959–1990.* Westport, Conn.: Greenwood, 1991.

Guilbaut, Serge. *How New York Stole the Idea of Modern Art: Abstract Expressionism, Freedom, and the Cold War.* Trans. Arthur Goldhammer. Chicago: University of Chicago Press, 1983.

Hall, Fred. *It's About Time: The Dave Brubeck Story.* Fayetteville: University of Arkansas Press, 1996.

Hall, James C. *Mercy, Mercy Me: African-American Culture and the American Sixties.* New York: Oxford University Press, 2001.

Hall, James W. and Barbara L. Kevles. "Democratizing the Curriculum." *Change* 12 (January 1980): 39–43.

Halle, David. *Inside Culture: Art and Class in the American Home.* Chicago: University of Chicago Press, 1993.

Hammond, Thomas T., ed. *Witnesses to the Origins of the Cold War.* Seattle: University of Washington Press, 1982.

Harrison, Max. "Coleman and the Consequences." *Jazz Monthly* 12 (June 1966): 10–15.

Hasse, John Edward. *Beyond Category: The Life and Genius of Duke Ellington.* New York: Simon and Schuster, 1993.

Henderson, Donald M. "Black Student Protest in White Universities." In *Black America*, ed. John Szwed. New York: Basic, 1970.

Hentoff, Nat. "Jazz in Mid-Passage." *High Fidelity* 4 (September 1954): 44–46, 118.

———. *The Jazz Life*. New York: Dial, 1961.

———. "The New Jazz-Black, Angry, and Hard to Understand." *New York Times Magazine* (December 26, 1966): 10, 36–39.

———. "The New York Jazz Scene: The Establishment, The Clubs, and Those Who Wait." *New York Herald Tribune Sunday Magazine* (April 7, 1963): 9, 16, 26.

———. "The Truth Is Marching In: An Interview with Albert and Don Ayler." *Down Beat* 33 (November 17, 1966): 16–18, 40.

Himmelstein, Jerome L. *Looking Good and Doing Good: Corporate Philanthropy and Corporate Power*. Bloomington: Indiana University Press, 1997.

Hobbs, Stuart. *The End of the American Avant-Garde*. New York: New York University Press, 1997.

Hollinger, David. *In the American Province: Studies in the Historiography of Ideas*. Baltimore: Johns Hopkins University Press, 1985.

Holmes, John Clellon. "The Golden Age of Jazz: Time Present." *Esquire* 51 (January 1959): 98–106.

Hughes, Allen. "The Voice of America." *Musical America* 80 (April 1960): 9–10, 46.

Johnson, Brooks. "Toms and Tomming: A Contemporary Report." *Down Beat* 33 (June 16, 1966): 24, 44.

Jones, LeRoi [Amiri Baraka]. *Black Music*. New York: William Morrow, 1967.

———. *Blues People: Negro Music in White America*. New York: William Morrow, 1963.

———. *Home: Social Essays*. New York: William Morrow, 1966.

———. "Voice from the Avant Garde: Archie Shepp." *Down Beat* 32 (January 14, 1965): 18–20, 36.

[See also entries under Amiri Baraka.]

Jones, LeRoi [Amiri Baraka], and Larry Neal, eds. *Black Fire: An Anthology of Afro-American Writing*. New York: William Morrow, 1968.

Jost, Eckhart. *Free Jazz*. Graz: Universal, 1974.

Karolyi, Otto. *Modern American Music: From Charles Ives to the Minimalists*. London: Cygnus Arts, 1996.

Kerber, Linda. "Diversity and the Transformation of American Studies." *American Quarterly* 46 (September 1989): 415–31.

Key, Susan and Larry Rothe, eds. *American Mavericks*. Berkeley: University of California Press, 2001.

Kofsky, Frank. *Black Nationalism and the Revolution in Music*. New York: Pathfinder, 1970.

Kouwenhoven, John. *Made in America: The Arts in Modern Civilization*. Garden City, N.Y.: Doubleday, 1948.

———. "What's 'American' About America." *Harper's* 213 (July 1956): 25–33.

Kuspit, Donald. *The Cult of the Avant-Garde Artist*. New York: Cambridge University Press, 1993.

Larkin, Philip. *All What Jazz: A Record Diary, 1961–1971*. New York: Farar-Straus-Giroux, 1985.

Lees, Gene. *The Leader of the Band: The Life of Woody Herman*. New York: Oxford University Press, 1995.

Levine, Lawrence W. *Highbrow/Lowbrow: The Emergence of Cultural Hierarchy in America*. Cambridge, Mass.: Harvard University Press, 1988.

————. "Jazz and American Culture." *Journal of American Folklore* 102 (Jan-Mar 1989): 6–22.

————. *The Opening of the American Mind: Canons, Culture, and History.* Boston: Beacon Press, 1996.

Lhamon, W. T., Jr. *Deliberate Speed: The Origins of a Cultural Style in the American 1950s.* Washington, D.C.: Smithsonian Institution, 1990.

Litweiler, John. *The Freedom Principle: Jazz After 1958.* New York: William Morrow, 1984.

————. "Needs and Acts: Cecil Taylor in Wisconsin." *Down Beat* 38 (October 1971): 16–17, 40.

————. *Ornette Coleman: A Harmolodic Life.* New York: Da Capo, 1992.

Lock, Graham. *Forces in Motion: The Music and Thought of Anthony Braxton.* New York: Da Capo, 1988.

Lockwood, Bert B. "The United Nations Charter and the United States Civil Rights Litigation: 1946–1955." *Iowa Law Review* 69 (July 1984): 901–49.

Loeb, Peter. "Jazz and the White Middle Class." *Jazz* 4 (August 1965): 23.

————. "The Man on Cloud No. 7." *Time* 64 (November 1954): 67–76.

Lopes, Paul. *The Rise of a Jazz Art World.* Cambridge: Cambridge University Press, 2002.

Margolis, Norman M. "A Theory on the Psychology of Jazz." *American Imago* 11 (Fall 1954): 263–91.

McRae, Barry. *Ornette Coleman.* London: Apollo, 1988.

Matthews, Jane De Hart. "Art and Politics in Cold War America." *American Historical Review* 81 (October 1976): 762–87.

Matusow, Allen. *The Unravelling of America: A History of Liberalism in the 1960s.* New York: Harper and Row, 1984.

Miller, Marc H., ed. *Louis Armstrong: A Cultural Legacy.* Seattle: University of Washington Press, 1994.

Millstein, Gilbert. "Jazz Makes It Up the River." *New York Times Magazine* (August 24, 1958): 14, 50–54.

Monson, Ingrid. "The Problem with White Hipness: Race, Gender, and Cultural Conceptions in Jazz Historical Discourse." *Journal of the American Musicological Society* 48 (Fall 1995): 396–422.

————. *Saying Something: Jazz Improvisation and Interaction.* Chicago: University of Chicago Press, 1996.

Morgenstern, Dan, and Martin Williams. "The October Revolution: Two Views of the Avant Garde in Action." *Down Beat* 31 (November 19, 1964): 15, 33.

Morris, Aldon D. *The Origins of the Civil Rights Movement: Black Communities Organizing for Change.* New York: Free Press, 1984.

Neal, Lawrence P. "The Black Musician in White America." *Negro Digest* 16 (March 1967): 53–57.

————. "The Social Background of the Black Arts Movement." *Black Scholar* 18 (January 1987): 11–22.

————. *Visions of a Liberated Future: Black Arts Movement Writings.* Ed. Michael Schwartz, with commentary by Amiri Baraka, Stanley Crouch, Charles Fuller, and Jayne Cortez. New York: Thunder's Mouth, 1989.

Neal, Mark Anthony. *What the Music Said: Black Popular Music and Black Public Culture.* New York: Routledge, 1999.

"The Need for Racial Unity in Jazz: A Panel Discussion." *Down Beat* 30 (April 11, 1963): 16–21.

"The New Jazz." *Newsweek* 68 (December 12, 1966): 101–8.

Nisenson, Eric. *Ascension: John Coltrane and his Quest.* New York: Da Capo, 1995.

Ostermann, Robert. "The Moody Men Who Play the New Music." *National Observer* (June 7, 1965): 22.

Panish, Jon. *The Color of Jazz: Race and Representation in Postwar American Culture.* Jackson: University Press of Mississippi, 1997.

Parks, J. D. *Culture, Conflict, and Coexistence: American-Soviet Cultural Relations, 1917–1958.* Jefferson, N.C.: McFarland, 1983.

Pinckney, Alphonso. *Red, Black, and Green: Black Nationalism in the United States.* Cambridge: Cambridge University Press, 1976.

Pleasants, Henry. *Serious Music—And All That Jazz.* New York: Simon and Schuster, 1969.

Porter, Eric. *What Is This Thing Called Jazz? African American Musicians as Artists, Critics, and Activists.* Berkeley: University of California Press, 2002.

Porter, Lewis. *John Coltrane: His Life and Music.* Ann Arbor: University of Michigan Press, 1998.

Porter, Lewis and Michael Ullman, with Ed Hazell. *Jazz: From Its Origins to the Present.* Englewood Cliffs, N.J.: Prentice-Hall, 1993.

Priestley, Brian. *Mingus: A Critical Biography.* New York: Quartet, 1982.

Primack, Bret. "Archie Shepp: Back to Schooldays." *Down Beat* 45 (December 21, 1978): 27–28, 59–61.

"Racial Prejudice in Jazz, part I." *Down Beat* 29 (March 15, 1962): 20–26.

"Racial Prejudice in Jazz, part II." *Down Beat* 29 (March 29, 1962): 22–25.

Radano, Ronald M. "Jazzin' the Classics: The AACM's Challenge to Mainstream Aesthetics." *Black Music Research Journal* 12 (Spring 1992): 79–95.

———. *New Musical Figurations: Anthony Braxton's Cultural Critique.* Chicago: University of Chicago Press, 1993.

Randal, Edward L. "The Voice of American Jazz." *High Fidelity* 8 (August 1958): 30–31, 86–88.

Riggins, Roger. "Professor Bill Dixon: Intents of an Innovator." *Down Beat* 47 (August 1980): 30–32.

Ross, Andrew. *No Respect: Intellectuals and Popular Culture.* New York: Routledge, 1989.

Ross, Lillian. "You Dig It, Sir?" *New Yorker* 30 (August 14, 1954): 31–47.

Rubin, Joan Shelley. *The Making of Middlebrow Culture.* Chapel Hill: University of North Carolina Press, 1992.

Sanjek, Russell, and David Sanjek. *Pennies from Heaven: The American Popular Music Business in the Twentieth Century.* New York: Da Capo, 1996.

Saul, Scott. *Freedom Is, Freedom Ain't: Jazz and the Making of the Sixties.* Cambridge, Mass.: Harvard University Press, 2003.

Saunders, Frances Stoner. *The Cultural Cold War: The CIA and the World of Arts and Letters.* New York: New Press, 1999.

Schipper, Henry. *Broken Record: The Inside Story of the Grammy Awards.* New York: Birch, 1992.

Schoenfeld, Herm. "Jazz Mugged By 'New Thing': Latest Idiom Poison at B.O." *Variety* (April 14, 1965): 49.

Schuller, Gunther. "Jazz and Classical Music." In Leonard Feather, *The Encyclopedia of Jazz.* New York: Horizon, 1960.

Shaw, Arnold. "The Dilemma of Jazz." *Jazz* 4 (April 1965): 8–11.

Shepp, Archie. "An Artist Speaks Bluntly." *Down Beat* 32 (December 16, 1965): 11, 42.

Sidran, Ben. *Black Talk.* New York: Holt, Rinehart, Winston, 1971.

Simpkins, Cuthbert Ormond. *Coltrane: A Biography.* New York: Herndon, 1975.

Smith, Russell. "The New Music." *Harper's* 218 (April 1959): 37–44.

Sollors, Werner. *Amiri Baraka/LeRoi Jones: The Quest for a "Populist Modernism."* New York: Columbia University Press, 1978.

Spellman, A. B. *Four Lives in the Bebop Business.* New York: Pantheon, 1966.

———. "Revolution in Sound: Black Genius Creates a New Music in Western World." *Ebony* (August 1969): 84–89.

Spigel, Lynn. "High Art in Low Places: Television and Modern Art, 1950–1970." In *Disciplinarity and Dissent in American Cultural Studies,* ed. Cary Nelson and Dilip Parameshwar Gaonkar. New York: Routledge, 1996.

Starr, S. Frederick. *Red and Hot: The Fate of Jazz in the Soviet Union, 1917–1980.* New York: Oxford University Press, 1983.

Stearns, Marshall W. "Is Jazz Good Propaganda?" *Saturday Review* 39 (July 14, 1956): 28–31.

———. *The Story of Jazz.* New York: Oxford University Press, 1956.

Suber, Charles. "Jazz Education." In Leonard Feather and Ira Gitler, *The Encyclopedia of Jazz in the Seventies.* New York: Horizon, 1976.

Szwed, John F. *Space Is the Place: The Lives and Times of Sun Ra.* New York: Pantheon, 1997.

Taylor, Arthur. *Notes and Tones: Musician-to-Musician Interviews.* New York: Coward, McCann & Geoghegan, 1982.

"This Trumpet Madness." *Newsweek* 46 (December 19, 1955): 48.

Thomas, Lorenzo. "Ascension: Music and the Black Arts Movement." In *Jazz Among the Discourses,* edited by Krin Gabbard. Durham, N.C.: Duke University Press, 1995.

Thomson, Charles A., and Walter H. C. Laves. *Cultural Relations and U.S. Foreign Policy.* Bloomington: Indiana University Press, 1963.

Tischler, Barbara L. *An American Music: The Search for an American Musical Identity.* New York: Oxford University Press, 1986.

Trow, Martin A. "American Higher Education: Past, Present, and Future." In *The History of Higher Education Second Edition,* ed. Lester F. Goodchild and Harold S. Wechsler. Needham Heights, Mass.: Simon and Schuster, 1997.

Turner, Sherry. "An Overview of the New Black Arts." *Freedomways* 9 (Spring 1969): 156–63.

Tynan, John. "Take Five." *Down Beat* 28 (November 23, 1961): 40.

Tyson, Timothy B. *Radio Free Dixie: Robert F. Williams and the Roots of Black Power.* Chapel Hill: University of North Carolina Press, 1999.

Van Deburg, William L. *New Day in Babylon: The Black Power Movement in American Culture, 1965–1975.* Chicago: University of Chicago Press, 1992.

Vihlen, Elizabeth. "Jammin' on the Champs-Elysées: Jazz, France, and the 1950s." In *"Here, There, and Everywhere": The Foreign Politics of American Popular Culture,* ed. Reinhold Wagnleitner and Elaine Tyler May. Hanover, N.H.: University Press of New England, 2000.

Von Eschen, Penny M. *Race Against Empire: Black Americans and Anticolonialism, 1937–1957.* Ithaca, N.Y.: Cornell University Press, 1997.

———. *Satchmo Blows Up the World: Jazz Ambassadors Play the Cold War.* Cambridge, Mass.: Harvard University Press, 2004.

Wagnleitner, Reinhold. *Coca-Colonization and the Cold War: The Cultural Mission of the United States in Austria After the Second World War.* Trans. Diana M. Wolf. Chapel Hill: University of North Carolina Press, 1994.

Ward, Brian. *Just My Soul Responding: Rhythm and Blues, Black Consciousness, and Race Relations.* Berkeley: University of California Press, 1998.

Watts, Jerry Gafio. *Amiri Baraka: The Politics and Art of a Black Intellectual.* New York: New York University Press, 2001.

Welding, Peter. "Review: This Is Our Music." *HiFi/Stereo Review* 7 (July 1961): 78.

Werner, Craig. *A Change Is Gonna Come: Music, Race & the Soul of America.* New York: Plume, 1998.

Whitfield, Stephen J. *The Culture of the Cold War.* 2nd ed. Baltimore: Johns Hopkins University Press, 1996.

Williams, Martin. *Jazz Masters in Transition, 1957–69.* New York: Macmillan, 1980.

———. *The Jazz Tradition.* New York: Oxford University Press, 1993.

———. " 'The New Thing' in Jazz." *Harper's* (October 1961): 69–75.

Wilmer, Valerie. *As Serious as Your Life: The Story of the New Jazz.* Westport, Conn.: Lawrence Hill, 1980.

Wilson, John S. *Jazz: The Transition Years, 1940–1960.* New York: Appleton-Century-Crofts, 1966.

Woodard, Komozi. *A Nation Within a Nation: Amiri Baraka (LeRoi Jones) and Black Power Politics.* Chapel Hill: University of North Carolina Press, 1999.

Wyszomirski, Margaret J. "Controversies in Arts Policymaking." In *Public Policy and the Arts,* edited by Kevin V. Mulcahy and C. Richard Swaim. Boulder, Colo.: Westview, 1982.

Wyszomirski, Margaret Jane, and Kevin V. Mulcahy, eds. *America's Commitment to Culture: Government and the Arts.* Boulder, Colo.: Westview, 1995.

Index

Acknowledgments

During the course of this project I have drawn upon the advice, support, criticism, counsel, and good humor of many individuals. I benefited most from professors and mentors at Indiana University with a diverse array of strengths. Casey Blake supervised my research and, in a broader sense, my intellectual development. His teaching, scholarship, and dedication gave me a model of excellence to aspire to and reinforced my belief that issues of cultural and intellectual history matter because they reveal something important about America and its people. David Baker provided a living link to the jazz tradition, and brought to our one-on-one tutorials an international reputation for achievement in music and education. His unflagging encouragement and belief in the value of my work gave me the confidence to explore and develop my own interpretations of African American music and American culture. Michael McGerr taught one of my first graduate school classes, and his high standards and interest in this topic inspired me to think through the implications of my writing. Claude Clegg's input proved invaluable at critical junctures.

For their constructive suggestions on early papers and manuscript drafts I owe a debt also to Penny Von Eschen, John Szwed, Lawrence Levine, and Daniel Borus. I am fortunate to have found colleagues in academia whose friendship and encouragement made the process enjoyable and rewarding, including Marion Boulby, Stewart Brewer, Tom Buchanan, Patrick Ettinger, Daniel Gahan, Scott Hermanson, Dave Spaeder, and Willard Sunderland. My editor at Penn, Bob Lockhart, has been supportive, incisive, professional, and above all patient as I learned what it takes to write a book.

I am grateful to Bill Dixon and Dan Morgenstern for consenting to lengthy interviews that enhanced my understanding of the music business during the 1960s. Mr. Morgenstern and his colleagues ably facilitated my search for materials at the Institute of Jazz Studies at Rutgers University, Newark. Victor Cardell proved equally helpful, directing me to unpublished interviews and other useful sources in the Chicago Jazz Archive at the University of Chicago Library. For similar assistance I thank the staffs of the Center for Black Music Research at Columbia College, Chicago, the Chicago Historical Society, the Lilly Library in Bloomington, Indiana, the Duke Ellington Collection at the National Museum of American History in Washington, D.C., the Ruth Lilly Special Collections and Archives at Indiana University and Purdue University at Indianapolis, the Rockefeller Archive Center in Sleepy Hollow, New York, and the Schomburg Center for Research in Black Culture, New York.

I received valuable financial support, and equally valuable teaching release time, from the Leitha K. and Willard A. Richardson Professorship in Liberal Arts at Dana College. I have taken advantage of generous assistance from the Charles and Mary Caldwell Martin Fund, administered by the Department of History at the University of Nebraska at Omaha, and Indiana University's Department of History, College of Arts and Sciences, and Office of Research and the University Graduate School. The support of my parents Rosemarie and Roy, and my sister Fiona, has always meant an enormous amount to me. Finally, Caroline has shown me what academic integrity and dedication should look like, kept me honest, split the housework, and shared my life. I hope she still remembers what Duke Ellington used to say.

Excerpts from *The Real Ambassadors* by Dave and Iola Brubeck, copyright © 1962, 1963 (renewed) Derry Music Company, all rights reserved, used by permission.

Four lines of "Beautiful Black Men" from Nikki Giovanni, *Black Feeling, Black Talk, Black Judgement.* Copyright © 1968, 1970 Nikki Giovanni. Reprinted by permission of HarperCollins Publishers.

Excerpt from A. B. Spellman, "Did John's Music Kill Him?" reprinted by permission of the author.

An earlier version of Chapter 5 appeared as "Jazz Outside the Marketplace: Free Improvisation and Nonprofit Sponsorship of the Arts, 1965–1980," *American Music* 20 (Summer 2002): 131–67. Copyright 2002 Board of Trustees of the University of Illinois, used by permission of University of Illinois Press.